IT TAKES A HERO

To Bill

one of my heroes —

Perry

IT TAKES A HERO

THE GRASSROOTS BATTLE AGAINST ENVIRONMENTAL OPPRESSION

A Project of
Mountain States Legal Foundation

William Perry Pendley

THE FREE ENTERPRISE PRESS
BELLEVUE, WASHINGTON

IT TAKES A HERO

First Edition
Published by the Free Enterprise Press

Typeset in Stone Serif on DTK computers by the Free Enterprise Press,
Bellevue, Washington. Cover design by Northwoods Studio.

The Free Enterprise Press is a division of the Center for the Defense of
Free Enterprise, 12500 N.E. 10th Place, Bellevue, Washington 98005.
Telephone 206-455-5038. Fax 206-451-3959.

This book distributed by Merril Press, P.O. Box 1682, Bellevue, Washington 98009. Additional copies of this quality paperback book may
be ordered from Merril Press at $14.95 each. Telephone 206-454-7009.

LIBRARY OF CONGRESS CATALOGING-IN-PUBLICATION DATA

Pendley, William Perry, 1945-
    It takes a hero : the grassroots battle against environmental
oppression / William Perry Pendley. — 1st ed.
        p.   cm.
    "A project of Mountain States Legal Foundation."
    Includes index.
    ISBN 0-939571-16-1 (pbk.) : $14.95
    1. Environmentalists—United States—Biography. 2. Environmental
responsibility-United States.   I. Mountain States Legal
Foundation. II. Title.
GE55.P46 1994
363.7'00973—dc20   94-5517
                                                        CIP

PRINTED IN THE UNITED STATES OF AMERICA

CONTENTS

CREDO

W
ho are the men and women of these pages? We are the true environmentalists. We are the stewards of the Earth. We're the farmers and ranchers, the hunters and trappers, the fishermen and watermen—people who've cared for the land and the waters for generations. We're the men and women who have clothed and fed the nation and the world.

We're the miners and the loggers and the energy producers who have provided this nation with the building blocks of a modern civilization. We're the workers, the builders, the doers. Together, we hard-working Americans built this country, made it strong and prosperous, delivering to generation after generation not just a better and more abundant life, but also the hope for such a life.

We're the land owners, the home owners, the holders of a piece of the American Dream, secure that it belongs to us and to our children and that we have the right to use that land—prudently and properly—as we wish. We know that it is this one right, to own and use property, that has provided the incentive for generation after generation to dream, to strive, to build and to prosper.

We're the consumers of the products of a technological society. We know that all of our material needs are met, first and foremost, by natural resources that would remain unavailable to mankind but for the greatest resource of all: human creativity. We know that it is technology, developed by the indomitable human spirit, unfettered by the yoke of oppression, that made this nation so richly blessed. We know as well that our ability to use the out of doors for recreation and revitalization is sustained by those few who work and live in the nature we only visit.

We believe in clean air, clean water and safe lands. We believe in being good stewards, in taking care of the land and waters of the world around us. We believe that mankind and nature can live together in productive harmony. That is what we and our forefathers have done for generation after generation. We believe in people, our sanctity, our ability to overcome all obstacles. We believe in our need, not just for a better, more abundant life, not just to be secure in our homes and our property, but also to be assured the freedoms for which so many have given so much. Most of all we believe in the American Dream—the dream of our Founding Fathers, who were farmers themselves, committed to eternal opposition to the forces of tyranny.

Today the tyranny that our Founding Fathers feared threatens the American Dream and the Constitutional liberties that assure the future of that dream. Jefferson feared the tyranny of those "who fear and distrust the people, and wish to draw all power from them into the hands of the higher classes." Madison feared the tyranny of the majority and the "abridgment of the freedom of the people by gradual and silent encroachments of those in power." John Adams feared "all men," recognizing that "the only maxim of a free government ought to be to trust no man living with power to endanger the public liberty."

Today, those who "fear and distrust the people" have acquired, by "gradual and silent encroachments" the "power to endanger the public liberty." From their glass towers in New York City and San Francisco, and from their grand offices along the corridors of power in Washington, D.C., environmental elitists have seized upon the people's wish to ensure the quality of the human environment to declare war upon millions of Americans. Using lawsuits, lobbyists and sky-is-falling language and literature, and working in concert with their allies in Congress and in an ever-growing federal bureaucracy, environmental extremists have destroyed jobs, businesses, homes and even entire communities. With their purist ideology and their insatiable demands for power and control, they threaten not just the lives of the men and women engaged in economic pursuits to which they object, not just communities that depend upon wise use of the Earth, not just the strength and vitality of the nation's economy, but also the ability of the American people to live free.

We, the nation's true environmentalists, want a safe and healthy environment just as much as we want jobs and opportunity and progress. We know that the battle being fought today is not about safety or survivability or sustainability. It is about the future of America's precious freedoms and with them the American Dream. Once, in reply to the question of whether the Founders had given the people a republic or a monarchy, Ben Franklin replied, "A republic, if you can keep it." We the people of these pages, the real environmentalists, the men and women who trace our lineage to the first nationally known conservationist, Teddy Roosevelt, intend to keep it.

Edmund Burke once declared, "The only thing necessary for the triumph of evil is for good men to do nothing." We intend to do something. As Winston Churchill once noted, "We have not journeyed all this way across the centuries, across the oceans, across the mountains, across the prairies, because we are made of sugar candy."

INTRODUCTION
by
U.S. Senator Larry R. Craig
Republican of Idaho

Americans' love of individual liberty is the cornerstone of our Republic. Our rights to own private property and live free from the intrusion of an oppressive government are fundamental to our great success as a nation and the very essence of the heritage we seek to pass on to our children.

Thankfully, from the nation's beginning, Americans with vision and courage have been willing to risk their lives and fortunes defending liberty from those who would compromise it or take it away.

This collection of stories about current day defenders of principle is a sobering reminder that today is no different.

INTRODUCTION

by
U.S. Congressman W. J. (Billy) Tauzin
Democrat of Louisiana

All Americans owe a debt of gratitude to the environmental movement of old, the movement that grew out of conservationism and the desire, not only to be good stewards, but to ensure the quality of the human environment. Americans are proud of the progress that has been made over the last 25 years in ensuring a healthy environment.

However, somewhere along the line we lost track of the fact that people are part of the environment and that our goal should be to preserve a healthy environment while promoting a vibrant, growing economy. As the experience in Eastern Europe demonstrates, we cannot have a quality environment without a strong economy.

Today farmers and ranchers, timber workers, fishermen and women, energy developers, and property owners feel besieged by environmental laws and regulations that have lost all touch with reason and reality. For example, "wetlands" and endangered species policies are damaging the economy while threatening liberties guaranteed under our Constitution.

We must return reason and the original sense of mission to environmentalism. It is refreshing and encouraging to learn that such an effort is now underway, led by the men and women of these pages. However, it is not surprising. America's great strength has always been its people, their good sense, their courage and their personal heroism.

Author's Preface

I t takes a hero. It takes a hero to battle the environmental juggernaut—the most powerful political force in America today. It takes a hero to fight back against organizations with hundreds of millions of dollars, millions of members, and thousands of friends in the nation's media.

It takes a hero to oppose the United States Government, to stand fast against its tens of thousands of bureaucrats, its thousands of lawyers, and its ability to demonize those who deign to challenge its authority or rectitude.

It takes a hero to challenge conventional wisdom, to dispute what is politically correct, to stand fast against "the slings and arrows of outrageous fortune," not to mention the distortion and deceit, visited upon those labeled "anti-environment."

It takes a hero to start with nothing but a belief in the Constitution, in principle, in fundamental truths, and build a body of resistance—inspiring others to action while instilling in them a belief in the future and in themselves.

It takes a hero to set aside personal wants and desires, to lay aside plans, to forego time with family and friends, to keep one's head when all about are losing theirs, to maintain an equilibrium, a sense of humor, a belief in mankind, and the courage to carry on when others have given up.

The men and women of whom I have written are such heroes. They are heroes to me for their personal courage, for what they have accomplished, and for the inspiration they have provided to millions of others.

These heroes are a most disparate assemblage of people from all parts of the country. They do not all belong to any one organization, entity, religion or political orientation. They do not agree on all things. In fact, sometimes they disagree on goals, methods, tactics, style, and even rhetoric. However, they do have one thing in common, in addition to their personal heroism: they have concluded that environmental extremists and their allies in the U.S. Government are good neither for people nor for the environment.

While I have worked with many of these people and others like them, some for many years, I only recently came to understand that behind each one of them is a most compelling personal drama. While I knew what my friends and colleagues were doing, I didn't know how or why they came to be where I had found them.

In the Spring of 1992, at the urging of a mutual friend, I first met Kathleen Marquardt of Putting People First. During a lunch in Washington, D.C., she told me the amazing story of why she formed her phenomenally successful organization. Later, on my return flight to Denver, I put what she had told me into an essay. Subsequently, I published it as one of my monthly columns. The more I thought about what had happened to Kathleen Marquardt, the more convinced I became that there were other equally compelling stories to tell.

Since I had shared many a podium with my good friend, Bruce Vincent, and had heard Bruce's personal testimony of his metamorphosis from local logger to national leader, I wrote next about Bruce. By the time I finished writing Bruce's essay, I had decided to gather together fifty such narratives and publish them as a book of heroes. When I told Bruce of my idea, he was euphoric: "You'll put a human face on our movement."

That, reduced to its bare essence, is what the people of whom I have written are all about: people who care about people. They are people who believe that, in the mad rush to "save the planet," the environmental movement and the U.S. Government have forgotten the people—people created in the image of God— who live upon the planet. One common thread that runs through these essays is that, in case after case, some powerful group of elitists deemed people to be "irrelevant." What all of these heroes have sought to do is to put people back into the environmental equation.

It is vital that the American people learn about these heroes and understand what moved them to action. While the American people have heard often, but not often enough, about the human impact of so-called "environmental policy," most of the time what they have heard are dry, impersonal statistics. They have not heard of the personal tragedies produced by environmental policy. This is unfortunate because the American people are not moved by statistics on mining or forestry or agriculture or property rights or jobs. Instead, they are moved by the extraordinary experiences of real people. People care about people. People become emotionally involved and intellectually interested when the drama is a human one. What better people to care about than the remarkable men and women—many of whom have been hurt personally by environmental policy—who have moved to the forefront of controversy in order to influence the resolution of public policy.

It is important to tell these tales, not just to put a face on who we are, not just to establish as heroes the unselfish men and women who have made a difference, but to give others the courage to do likewise. There are many among us who still believe that one person cannot make a difference, or who believe that they do not have what it takes to become involved. Without diminishing the incredible accomplishments of those of whom I have written, if their stories prove one thing, they prove that one person can make a difference and that anyone can get the job done. In fact, these men and women do not see themselves as heroes, but simply as people who saw a job that had to be done and did it.

The men and women about whom I have written are my selections. Although I asked many people for their suggestions, in the final analysis, I chose the fifty-three who are profiled in these pages. Frankly, I could have written a thousand such tales, as the directory at the back of this book attests. Although I sought to identify the fifty or so most outstanding individuals, I also endeavored, to the maximum extent practicable, to ensure some geographic and issue distribution.

Environmental issues have long ceased being primarily "western" or "federal lands" issues. The response to environmental policy gone wild is not simply another Sagebrush Rebellion against yet another War on the West, but rather a nationwide Second American Revolution. Today, almost any use of any land, public or private, fee or federal, anywhere in the country, is controversial and hence subject to challenge through a variety of federal statutes. Furthermore, the covetousness of federal bureaucrats and their desire to bring more and more land under their control are of great concern to people throughout the country. As a result, it was vital that these heroes be selected from throughout the country, whether considered part of the property rights movement, the pro-growth-and-jobs movement, or the public-lands-multiple-use movement.

A note as to methodology: I contacted each one of the individuals of whom I have written, or in some cases, I contacted someone familiar with the work of that individual and asked for background material, primarily public documents and news reports. Based upon those materials, and sometimes based upon conversations with the individual, I wrote a draft of the essay. I then asked each individual with whom I had spoken to review the material for substantive accuracy, but did not relinquish editorial control. The content of each profile was entirely my decision. I am indebted to the individuals who gave so freely of their time to help me complete this work. Any virtues this book may possess belong to those who helped. Any errors of fact or judgment are my responsibility alone.

Several notes of thanks. I am most thankful to Ron Arnold for his faith in this project, for his willingness to do whatever was necessary to ensure that I was able to press on to completion and for his helpful role as editor. I am particularly thankful to Ron in his role as editor for his careful attention to detail and for his sensitivity to the fact that I tend to be a tad touchy about my writing. While in the final analysis every word is mine, Ron patiently prodded me to ensure that the words selected and the way they were put together made sense.

I am appreciative of my wife, Lis, and my sons, Perry and Luke, for their willingness to hear these essays over and over again, to put up with me camped out at the computer for weeks on end and to disregard the mess I made of our office while I was doing all of this. I also greatly appreciate Lis' willingness to proofread these works more than once.

Finally, I am thankful that I met the men and women who make up the pages of this book. They are an outstanding group of people and I feel privileged and honored to know them and to have had the opportunity to work with them.

William Perry Pendley
Denver, Colorado
February 1994

DEDICATION

To my heroes:

my mother,
who told me tales of heroism and taught me
anything was possible;

my father,
who showed me anything could be endured
with grace and character;

my wife, Lis,
who lives a daily life of heroism, as wife, mother,
daughter, friend, lawyer, editor, chauffeur, cook, and
"other duties as assigned;"

and my sons, Perry and Luke,
whose heroes are not the fictional characters of
celluloid, but, like me, the real people of these pages.

IN MEMORIAM

Warren Brookes
Hero of Journalism

Prof. Aaron Wildavsky
Hero of Science

Dr. Petr Beckmann
Hero of Activism

Man will not merely endure: he will prevail . . .
because he has a soul, a spirit capable of
compassion and sacrifice and endurance.

—William Faulkner, Nobel Prize
acceptance speech, 1950

THE PROFILES

KATHLEEN MARQUARDT
Washington, D.C.

A storm was about to break loose at the home of Kathleen Marquardt. Yet the storm had a most unlikely and tranquil origin: along the quiet sunny tree-lined street, children were coming home from school. Among them were Kathleen Marquardt's daughters, Shane and Montana. Montana was particularly anxious to get home to tell her mother the astonishing lessons she had learned in school. "Mommy," Montana cried out as she threw open the door, "we're murderers."

For three days representatives of People for the Ethical Treatment of Animals (PeTA, as the group prefers to be abbreviated) had held forth in Montana's classroom. Using photographs and games and stories, they told Montana and her classmates that they were no better than rats and chickens and pigs and dogs. They told them that it is not just human life that is sacred but *all* life. They told them that anyone who hunted or fished, who wore clothing made from the fur or skin of animals, who ate fish or fowl or feral creatures, who condoned animal research—even to find cures for cancer, AIDS, and sudden infant death syndrome—was a murderer.

For Kathleen Marquardt, who grew up in western Montana hunting and fishing, wearing leather and fur, eating beef and chicken and lamb, and believing that mankind was both created in the image of God and blessed with dominion over the earth and all of its creatures, such teachings were an abomination. She couldn't believe there were people who thought such things, let alone taught them in her children's classrooms. The realization that there were and that they were filling the minds of her daughters and their classmates with nonsense evoked a very visceral reaction: "I got mad."

Yet Kathleen Marquardt didn't just become angry, she became active. She immersed herself in a study of PeTA and its ilk. She read their books and studied their literature. The more she learned, the more upset she became, and the more commit-

1

ted. Someone had to do something! She learned something else—little was being done to combat the great evil she saw spreading across the country.

She realized that if anything was going to be done, she was going to have to do it. She knew what she was up against. She had read of the terrorist response of some animal rights advocates to their opponents: the break-ins, the destruction of facilities, the trashing of reputations and careers. None of this dissuaded Kathleen Marquardt.

What would have terrified her, had she known it, was that to do what she wanted to do she would be required to stand in front of hundreds, even thousands, of strangers and speak. For the quiet, almost hermit-like recluse who wanted nothing more than to sit in her home listening to classical music and being the fabric designer she had trained to be, the rough and tumble public policy arena was a foreign and horrifying place. Yet as great as was her fear of public appearances, speaking, and confrontation, her fear of what would happen if she did nothing was much greater. She pressed on.

Kathleen Marquardt's remarkable transformation from recluse to activist was completed by a close brush with death. Returning from a trip abroad, she was stricken with a painful and debilitating illness, an illness all the more terrifying because doctors could not isolate the cause. For eight months she suffered mind-numbing headaches, cramping and nausea, and sensory loss that rendered all food tastelessly inedible.

After months in which doctors administered a pharmacy of drugs, the doctors determined that she was infected with a parasite, a parasite whose insidious and pernicious work the doctors could see—it was eating away her liver—but which itself could neither be seen nor destroyed. Kathleen feared she would die.

Late one night, in the grip of the pain that would not let her sleep, she remembered a doctor in nearby suburban Maryland, who for years had labored in seclusion to discover the secret and deadly dangers of parasites like the one that was eating away her insides. Just as quickly as she remembered the doctor and his work, her thoughts of hope turned to despair when she remembered that his laboratory and years of painstaking research had been destroyed by an invasion of animal rights advocates.

Eventually Kathleen Marquardt's doctors—aided by years of medical research that coincidentally involved the use of animals—discovered that she was infected by both an amoeba and a protozoan and prescribed a course of therapy that ensured her recovery. Her determination bolstered rather than weakened by the long and painful recovery process, she continued to build her grassroots opposition to the animal rights advocates.

Today, a few short years after she began, Kathleen Marquardt has turned her third child—Putting People First, the organization that she bore so painfully—into a national grassroots force, some 40,000 strong, and growing. She has testified before state legislatures, appeared on national television, spearheaded opposition to legislative initiatives, become involved in lawsuits and spoken to thousands all across the country. She writes a monthly nationally syndicated column, has developed a "facts and fiction" counter to the information dispensed by the other side and has written materials for distribution in schools. She set down her experiences recently in an excellent book, *AnimalScam: The Beastly Abuse of Human Rights*, published by Regnery Gateway.

Much more lies ahead. "We're just getting started," she says.

Most remember the line of anger and frustration from Paddy Chayefsky's movie *Network*, the line spoken by the late Academy Award-winning actor Peter Finch: "I'm as mad as hell and I'm not going to take it anymore." Forgotten, but just as meaningful were the sentences that preceded the cry, which became a national expression of defiance: "I'm a human being, God damn it. My life has value."

Kathleen Marquardt understands the value of human life, understands that human beings are innately more valuable than other living things. Like millions of Americans, Kathleen cried out, "I'm mad as hell and I'm not going to take it anymore." But she didn't just say it. She did something about it. Would that there were more like her.

BRUCE VINCENT
Libby, Montana

Through the thin walls of the trailer that was his family's home, Bruce Vincent could hear his mother and father talking. He was listening because earlier in the day his parents had been summoned to Bruce's elementary school to meet with the principal. As everyone knows, when the principal tells your parents to come to school, life as you know it is about to come to an end.

Bruce Vincent is a grown man now with children of his own, but he remembers the words he heard that night as if he heard them yesterday. The principal told his father and mother that Bruce, like all of his classmates, had taken a scholastic aptitude test. However, that was where the common ground ended, for unlike everyone else in the class, Bruce scored extremely high on the test. In the principal's words, "Bruce has exceptional academic ability."

Then the principal told Bruce's parents that there was another reason for summoning them to his office. "With Bruce's aptitude," he said, "it would be a terrible waste if he were not able to stay in school and to go to college. Whatever you do," he concluded, "don't let Bruce be a timberman like his father. He has too much ability to spend the rest of his life cutting trees."

Bruce Vincent did stay in school and he did go to college where he earned two degrees. But each summer he returned home to the forests of northwestern Montana, where, alongside his father and brothers, he shouldered a chain saw and an axe and drove deep into the woods to harvest the timber that fed the mills of the tiny community of Libby.

Bruce Vincent studied with the professors of academia. He read their books and took their tests. He dueled intellectually with the bright young men and women who populated his classes. He did better than survive. He did well. Yet with each day he spent in the woods with his father and brothers, with each day he stood shoulder to shoulder with them swinging an axe, manhandling a chain saw, or operating equipment, he realized he was the dumbest member of the family.

5

It wasn't just his father's knowledge of the woods that he held in awe. It was the way his father picked a path through decades of fallen and decaying timber, the way he recognized immediately in which direction a tree would fall, or which one would yield a deadly snag ("a widow-maker"), his ability to track and to hunt, the acuteness of his senses, attuned to the nuances of the forests and the mountains, his mastery at making almost anything work somehow, and his ability, even in the toughest of times, to find a way for his family.

For as demanding as were the battles of academia—the volumes to read and to digest, the compositions to write and reports to deliver, the dialectic and polemic challenges of colleagues and erudite professors—they were nothing compared to the battles for survival in which his father and brothers engaged on a daily basis.

The challenges of academia were theoretical, hypothetical, with little more riding on them than status, the respect of peers, or, at best, a grade. While his professors and classmates were skilled in the rarefied air of academia, many were out of their element when faced with real world challenges. The very traits which ensured their success in the scholastic world—the endless search for additional data, the constant questioning of assumptions, the demand for exhaustive inquiry—often rendered them incapable of responding to the crises of the real world.

It was the real world that Bruce Vincent wanted: the smell and look of the wooded hills that surrounded tiny Libby, the sound of the creek that babbled past his home, the noises of the animals in the forest, the openness of his neighbors and the sense of accomplishment that came from a hard day felling trees and bucking them into logs. So after years of study Bruce Vincent returned with the California girl he had met and married at college to the woods of Libby, Montana, to join with his father and brothers to build the business that was all his father ever knew and that Bruce had chosen for his life's work.

Then one day the federal bureaucrats came to town. They had decided, the bureaucrats told everyone, to create a grizzly bear habitat out of the woods in which the people of Libby lived, worked and played. While the people knew they shared the woods with this majestic but ferocious beast—which can stand as high as 8 feet and weigh as much as 1000 pounds—the bureaucrats had something more in mind than an occasional grizzly bear.

From their offices in Washington, D.C. and far off modern Missoula (population 25,000), the bureaucrats had decided that northwestern Montana—site of Libby (population 2,800), Eureka (population 1,150) and Troy (population 900), not to mention other even smaller communities—would become a "Grizzly Bear Habitat One" area. In plain English that meant that some 120 grizzly bears would be relocated to their neighborhood.

"What does that mean for us?" asked someone.

"Minor behavioral changes," said the bureaucrats. "You'll have to do what the natives on Alaska's Kodiak Island do: their children wear bells to ward off the grizzly bears. Of course, if we ever hear of a 'bad' bear, we'll come and remove it."

Today Bruce Vincent jokes that a "bad" bear is distinguishable only by the presence of bells in its "poop." But back on that grim day neither Bruce Vincent nor his neighbors were laughing, for the bureaucrats had other even more grandiose plans. They intended, for example, to engage in "cross-fostering"—the planting of grizzly bear embryos in the wombs of brown bears, a rather challenging notion since the two bear types are hardly what one would call on friendly terms. The townspeople realized that the bureaucrats had gone from the sublime to the ridiculous.

They realized something else. The bureaucrats had not come to town to get their permission. They had come to town to tell them the way things were going to be. It was that realization that at once ignited and enervated the community. "What can we do?" some asked. No one really knew, but they were going to do everything possible to stop this insane experimentation with their lives.

Meetings were held, telephone calls were made, letters were written, petitions were drawn up and circulated. Bruce Vincent, the man who had gone away to college, the natural leader and gifted speaker, the man who had returned home for the peace and tranquillity of his mountain community, was drawn into the fray. The people needed someone to lead them, someone to give them hope, someone to inspire them to rise above themselves, someone to help them to believe they could make a difference. He did and they did. In the end, they stopped the grizzly bear plan.

Unfortunately, it was only the beginning. After the ill-fated grizzly bear plan came challenges by environmental groups to every U.S. Forest Service plan to harvest timber in the forest, which makes up nearly 80% of the land of Lincoln County, Montana. Then came proposals to turn much of the area into wilderness in which no timber harvesting or off-highway recreation would be allowed. Then, in response to environmental challenges, came decisions by the Forest Service to drastically lower planned timber harvests.

But by now the people were ready. They fought back. In battle after battle, challenge after challenge, the people of northwestern Montana refused to yield to the attempts by those who live far, far away to turn their home into a mythic and distant wilderness playground. They refused to be treated as if their needs and their lives were irrelevant, were—in the grander scheme of things—unimportant when compared with grizzly bears or endless wilderness or "nature's way."

In the lead through all of it was Bruce Vincent. Comforted by his faith, supported by his family and firm in the conviction that people are part of the environment, Bruce Vincent battled on. Soon the voice that had stirred the people of his community was called upon to stir those similarly afflicted throughout the country, and stir them he did.

Derided by environmentalists as the "Oliver North of the timber industry" for his compelling advocacy, his boyish charm and his disarming, likable manner, Bruce wins grudging admiration even from his worst critics. When he isn't home helping to run the business or organizing the fight against the latest challenge to the survival of his community, he can be found before some distant group that wants and needs to hear his message.

With his youthful good looks, a body hardened by years in the woods, a voice as soft and smooth as the summer air of the forests near his home, he is every woman's model son, every man's best friend. When he is finished more are believers, and those who aren't have a new understanding of the word "environmentalist."

Bruce Vincent, who returned home for peace and tranquillity, has little of that now. His time is not his own. He belongs to the cause, to the movement of which he is a part. What keeps him going?

"The memory of the night I found out that someone thought that my father's life was worthless because he was a timberman," says Bruce Vincent. "That's what lets them think they can do this to us—turn our homes into their playgrounds, destroy the economy of our communities, wipe out our families—because we're worthless, because, in their eyes what we do and how we live has no value. But we're not disposable. We're not some inconvenience that society can brush aside like a piece of lint simply because of where we live or what we do for a living.

"Sometimes when I don't think I can get on another plane or drive to another town or make another phone call or write another letter, I remember how I felt that night in the trailer. Then I try to think how my dad must have felt. I hold that feeling deep inside me and I tell myself that's the pain that millions of Americans feel and I know that I have to try to make it stop."

Someday, he will.

Dr. Elizabeth M. Whelan
New York, New York

On October 18, 1969, when the U.S. Government banned cyclamates, an artificial sweetener, Elizabeth Whelan was working toward her Doctor of Science degree at the Harvard School of Public Health. Long intrigued with the cause and prevention of premature death, she had chosen the study of epidemiology, public health, demography and biostatistics as her life's work. She had already obtained a Masters of Public Health degree from Yale and a Masters of Science degree from the Harvard School of Public Health. As someone knowledgeable in the field, she was shocked by the Government's ban of a soda pop sweetener because rats that were virtually swimming in it had developed tumors.

Elizabeth Whelan promised herself that one day she would get to the bottom of the cyclamate controversy, since it reminded her of yet another similar episode: the "cranberry scare" of 1959. Coming as it did just before Thanksgiving, it devastated hundreds of cranberry growers in New England.

She was appalled by what seemed to be a pattern: the Government's irrational approach to food safety and its illogical pursuit of non-risks. She immersed herself in a study of the Delaney Clause, which bans the tiniest presence of anything alleged to cause tumors in laboratory animals. Her research culminated in "How Sweet It Isn't," an article published by William F. Buckley, Jr. in the *National Review*.

The article was so well received and such an authoritative rebuttal to the life-causes-cancer crowd, that Elizabeth decided to turn the article into a book. The result was *Panic in the Pantry: Food Facts, Fads and Fallacies,* co-authored with Fredrick J. Stare, M.D. of the Harvard School of Public Health. *Panic,* published in 1975, was the first serious look at the fallacious assumption that artificial is bad and natural is good.

During the same period, Elizabeth Whelan and her attorney husband began to discuss whether or not to have a child. (Christine is now 16 years old.) Frustrated by the absence of any

11

book on the important decision they were about to make, Elizabeth wrote her own. *A Baby? . . . Maybe: A Guide To Making the Most Fateful Decision of Your Life,* became an instant hit and her only million-seller among the 23 books she has authored and co-authored.

The release during 1975 of *Panic* and *A Baby?* by two different publishing houses put Elizabeth on a virtually simultaneous tour for both books. "I learned very quickly what it means to be a media darling as well as a media goat."

While *A Baby?* drew praise and warm feelings, *Panic* brought only censure and icy hostility. Dr. Elizabeth Whelan of the Harvard School of Public Health, author of *Panic in the Pantry*, was condemned as a "paid liar." For fear that her appearances for *Panic* would adversely affect sales of *A Baby?*, she began to disguise herself between talk shows.

"I was so incredibly naïve. I hadn't received a penny from industry to write my book. Why, I didn't even know the name of a chemical company. I wrote it because I believe our food supply is safe. Apparently that's not enough."

A turning point came for Elizabeth Whelan late one night when she received a telephone call from the *Today* show. She had been scheduled to appear early the next morning for an interview with Barbara Walters. The caller told her that the interview would not take place. Barbara Walters had determined that Dr. Whelan was little more than a "paid liar," and not fit to appear on morning television.

By this time Elizabeth Whelan had written yet another book: *Preventing Cancer: What You Can Do To Reduce Your Risks By Up To 50%* setting forth what was known and what was only hypothetical regarding cancer. Once again, the dominant liberal media gave Dr. Whelan's book short shrift. She now knew two things: there was a serious problem out there and she couldn't tackle it alone.

Dr. Whelan decided to form the American Council on Science and Health to provide consumers with up-to-date scientifically sound information on the relationship between human health and chemicals, foods, nutrition, lifestyle and the environment. She called the nation's most prominent scientists to ask them to join with her. None refused. Most echoed the response of Nobel Laureate Dr. Norman Borlaug, "Yes! I wanted to do this for years but I never had the time!"

Elizabeth Whelan had only one condition regarding the creation of ACSH. She would not accept any money from industry. She did not fear that the money would corrupt her scientific integrity, only that it would expose her to the same sort of attack she had endured for *Panic*. Instead, she obtained funding from two conservative private foundations.

ACSH's first major project culminated in a press conference at which its study "New Jersey: Garden State Or Cancer Alley?" was released to the public. Research conducted by ACSH scientists had found no unusual incidence of cancer deaths in New Jersey, as compared, for example, to any other urban area in the United States. However, not surprisingly, the first question at the press conference did not relate to statistics or epidemiology, but to money. "Where," asked the reporter, "do you get your funding?" Dr. Whelan was proud to disclose that ACSH was supported solely by two independent foundations.

The next day the *Newark Star Ledger* ran the headline: "Industry Front Group Says No Cancer Threat." Furious, Dr. Whelan called the reporter demanding an explanation. Responded the reporter: since one of the foundations owned stock in an oil company, ACSH could be described as an "industry front group."

Suddenly Dr. Whelan realized that it was not her funding that the media found objectionable, but her point of view. She concluded that ACSH's work product would be attacked as biased regardless of ACSH's source of funding. As a result she decided that so long as she maintained her scientific integrity, it didn't matter who contributed to ACSH. "After all, in one way or another, all money comes from industry."

Today, Elizabeth Whelan's ACSH serves as a consumer education consortium to bring reason, balance and common sense to public debates about food, nutrition, chemicals, pharmaceuticals, lifestyle, the environment, and health. ACSH's nucleus is a board of 200 physicians, scientists, and policy advisors—experts in a variety of fields—who review the Council's reports and participate in ACSH's seminars, press conferences, media communications, and other educational activities.

In addition to authoring a plethora of articles (more than 500) and books (including her 1985 classic *Toxic Terror*, released as a new book in 1993), Dr. Whelan guides ACSH's numerous publications: peer-reviewed reports on health and environmental issues; the quarterly magazine *PRIORITIES: For Long Life and*

Good Health; and a quarterly newsletter. Recently, ACSH released its first documentary film, "Big Fears, Little Risks," narrated by Walter Cronkite.

Elizabeth Whelan's ACSH insists upon mainstream, peer-reviewed (not shortcut or pseudo) science. ACSH's voice is unique, one that, backed by scientific evidence, defends the achievements and benefits of responsible technology within America's free enterprise system.

It was Elizabeth Whelan and ACSH that revealed what the 1989 Alar/apple scare was—a hoax. It is Dr. Whelan and ACSH that daily note that cigarette smoking is the leading cause of premature disease and death. "We know the difference between a health elephant (cigarettes) and a health ant (pesticide residues). We help Americans sort the real health risks from the myriad of hypothetical ones in the media daily."

Elizabeth Whelan's chief concern is the "specter of fear and antipathy toward science and technology, and the resulting attempt to purge our land of hypothetical risks at any costs. If we succumb to exaggeration about alleged risks posed by our technologically advanced civilization, we will jeopardize our chance for better health by dismantling the very system that brought us to our present state of well-being."

For Dr. Whelan, what she does is nothing less than a crusade. "America has the best standard of living and is the most sought-after country to live in, yet these toxic terrorists are dismantling our standard of living. I am not just upset, I am furious, when I see the manner in which these terrorists take on and destroy the people who are feeding this country. It's a crime.

"Our nation is founded on the principle that people will be rewarded for their achievement. When we punish people for no reason, we set back the nation's ability to make progress. That is what the terrorists are doing, stopping technology in the name of fear."

The most frustrating challenge for Elizabeth Whelan, the scientist, is dealing with the media. For the media, by its very nature, is incapable of addressing scientific issues and by its philosophical predisposition is uninterested in the story that science has to tell. Yet she keeps trying.

Almost 25 years to the day from the moment the Government banned cyclamates, Elizabeth Whelan declined to appear on Larry King Live. Larry King had ruled that she could appear only if ACSH were described as being funded by industry.

Dr. Whelan responded that she would agree to such a statement if anyone appearing opposite her were similarly described and if Larry King also added, "and I, Larry King, receive all of my money from industry."

Elizabeth Whelan, who has a million things to do to focus the nation on real threats and real dangers to human health, isn't holding her breath waiting for Larry King to call back.

CLARK L. COLLINS
Pocatello, Idaho

Clark Collins is a working man and a union man, the son of a working man and a union man. Born in Boise, Idaho, he grew up in Pocatello where he graduated from Pocatello High in 1960. In 1961 he joined the United States Navy, where he served for four years. For nearly thirty years he has been a member of the International Brotherhood of Electrical Workers (IBEW), Local #449 in Pocatello. He has children, and now grandchildren. He is proud of all that.

Clark Collins is proud of something else. He is proud of the fact that he rides motorcycles, snowmobiles, all terrain vehicles (ATV), and other recreational machines. He is proud of the men and women—the families—with whom he has associated over the years. He is proud of their appreciation for the out-of-doors, their interest in gathering together to enjoy a sport they love, and their commitment to good clean fun.

Clark Collins is also good at it. In 1972 he was the Eastern Idaho Motorcycle Association overall points leader and the 100cc champion. In 1986 he was named "Trailbike Rider of the Year" by the Idaho Trail Machine Association.

As a union man, Clark realizes the value of people banding together for a common purpose. In 1970 he helped found the Eastern Idaho Motorcycle Association (EIMA) to control off-highway motorcycle racing in southeast Idaho. In 1973 he joined a family-oriented recreational organization, the Pocatello Trail Machine Association. Over the years, he has served as its president several times. He has also served as the vice president and president of the Idaho Trail Machine Association.

In 1983 something changed. For the first time Clark saw that many of the proposals for wilderness designation in Idaho were directed at him and his friends—the off-highway recreational community. Idaho already had more than four million acres of designated Wilderness. As a result, many miles of trails previously used by OHV recreationists had been lost to Wilderness. However, in the early 1980s the land lockup being pushed

17

by environmental elitists focused on many more popular backcountry recreation areas.

In 1985 Clark Collins met with Idaho Governor John Evans to ask for help in opposing wilderness designation that would cut back on motorized recreation. Evans replied that Clark and his friends were "politically insignificant."

Clark intended to prove that the Governor was wrong. He began to work with local snowmobilers and four-wheelers on public land use issues. He encouraged Idaho recreationists to become more politically involved. In the end, he succeeded in blocking several wilderness proposals that included recreational areas important to the off-highway vehicle community.

As a result of that success, in 1987 Clark Collins helped form the Idaho Public Land Users Association. For the first time, membership included motorized recreational organizations as well as other multiple use groups. That same year Clark incorporated the Blue Ribbon Coalition. He recognized that motorcyclists, snowmobilers, ATVers, four-wheelers, hunters, and even mountain bicyclers and horse-back riders had many common interests regarding public lands. Today the Blue Ribbon Coalition represents several hundred member organizations nationwide and more than half a million recreationists and resource users.

The Blue Ribbon Coalition works with land managers to provide recreation opportunities, to preserve resources, and to promote cooperation with other public lands users. The Blue Ribbon Coalition publishes a monthly professionally produced newsletter, *Blue Ribbon*. Across its masthead reads the Blue Ribbon motto: "Preserving our natural resources FOR the public instead of FROM the public."

In 1991 Clark achieved his greatest success to date: the signing by President George Bush of legislation that was the culmination of several years of networking and grassroots-building. Modeled after a number of very successful state laws, the Symms Recreational Trails Fund Act sets aside a portion of federal gas tax receipts for trails and facilities used by all recreationists in all 50 states. While former U.S. Senator Steven B. Symms was the legislation's chief sponsor, Clark Collins was the man responsible for its final passage.

According to one publication, "Environmentalists are still trying to figure out how they got KOed on the Trails Act, but they admit it wasn't a lucky punch." One environmental leader, commenting on Clark Collins, concluded, "The guy is good. . . . [H]e is one hell of a tactician."

Clark prevailed against overwhelming odds. Every major environmental organization in the country opposed the Symms bill. The National Wildlife Federation, the Sierra Club, the Wilderness Society, and others pulled out all the stops to kill it. Clark believes that by opposing responsible legislation to provide for the nation's outdoor recreational needs these groups "exposed their true agenda. It is not 'green' that drives them, it is greed. They don't want reasonable use, they want non-use."

The incredible success of Clark Collins in getting Congress to vote for multiple use and against the mainline environmental groups has made him one of the primary focuses of an unprecedented and unparalleled attack. That assault does not surprise writer Candice Crandall of the Science and Environmental Policy Project: "If this [onslaught] sounds as though environmentalists are falling victim to unbridled hysteria, it is perhaps understandable. . . . There is a pressing need to stifle the growing chorus of dissent among scientists, business leaders and members of the public if environmental pressure groups hope to maintain their clout on Capitol Hill."

Clark Collins is proud of who he is and what he has accomplished. As someone more familiar with the off-highway trails of eastern Idaho than the corridors of Congress, Clark Collins has shown he can maneuver both with ease, skill, and more than a little bit of daring.

ANN CORCORAN
Sharpsburg, Maryland

Ann G. Corcoran's most vivid childhood memory is that of awakening in the middle of the night, amidst the green hills of Ireland—her father's ancestral homeland—to watch a calf being born. She was only six years old, but from that day, she never wanted to be anything but a farmer. Her father—who knew first-hand of the often heartbreaking work of farming—wanted more for her: a life in America, college, and a career as a professional.

But Ann Corcoran wanted to be a farmer. As a high school student, her English teacher's instruction to read *The New York Times* each day sent her to the library, not to study the news of the day or to revel in reviews of books and plays, but to pore over advertisements of farms for sale. In the sanitary solitude of the library she dreamed about those farms and what it would be like to own them and the beautiful lands surrounding them.

At college the dream faded as the reality of life intervened. "Where would I ever get a farm?" she asked herself. Ann Corcoran changed her major from animal science to wildlife biology thinking that would at least allow her a job in the countryside she loved. However, after obtaining her master's degree at Yale she found herself in Washington, D.C., where, following a short stint with The Nature Conservancy, she hired on as a lobbyist for the National Audubon Society.

A few years later she learned the answer to the question she gave up asking as an undergraduate: the family of the man with whom she fell in love owned a farm. In time that farm was sold, and with their share of the proceeds, Ann Corcoran and her husband set out in search of a farm of their own.

In the rolling piedmont of western Maryland they found it. However, it was hardly her vision in the library of long ago: the buildings were dilapidated, the house unlivable, the fences falling down, the weeds chest-high. Yet it was a farm they could afford and it was next to a unit of the national park system—the Antietam National Battlefield. How wonderful, thought Ann Corcoran and her husband, to live next to a park.

21

After some research they learned that their farm played a part in the bloody battle of Antietam: their house had been a hospital, the cannons had fired from near their barn, and 20,000 men had camped in their fields in preparation for the battle that left 23,110 soldiers dead—the bloodiest one-day battle of the Civil War.

One night as Ann and her husband sat together discussing "their" farm they realized they had first seen it on September 17th—the anniversary of that long-ago battle. It was more than a good omen. It was an irresistible force. Ann Corcoran and her husband bought the farm and threw themselves into the demanding but fulfilling work of putting the farm back into business, to raise cattle, to grow hay and wheat and to be home for their two young boys. Fifteen years after she had abandoned her dream, it became a reality.

Then the dream became a nightmare. Ann Corcoran and her husband read stories in the local newspaper that their neighbor—the Antietam National Battlefield—was threatened by development and that the county needed to adopt restrictive zoning to protect the parklands. Then the bombshell hit. Ann Corcoran discovered that the National Park Service had initiated a "planning process" to expand the park and to eventually buy out all private landowners within the newly expanded park boundary. Their idyllic and benevolent neighbor had become an ugly and avaricious monster that coveted their land.

One cold January night in 1989, local farmers—recognizing a threat to the future of farming in the valley and aware too that agriculture was still the number one industry in the county—gathered at the Antietam Battlefield Visitor's Center along with National Park Service officials to discuss how they could keep farming as a part of the community. After all, they reasoned, since Antietam was farmland in 1862, and since it was the 1862 scene that the National Park Service wanted to preserve, everyone had the same goal.

At the visitor's center that night, Ann Corcoran met a colleague from her days in Washington. She was surprised to see an environmental lobbyist so far from the halls of Congress. Upon seeing her and sensing a friendly and sympathetic ear, he confided, "We've got big plans for your county." Who was "we?" asked Ann. "We" was the Conservation Fund—bankrolled by the Mellons, one of America's wealthiest families—the National

Park Service, the Governor of Maryland, and a handful of local politicians.

Ann Corcoran wanted to know more, and arranged a luncheon some weeks later. Her friend brought along colleagues from the American Farmland Trust. Together they unveiled plans to "greenline" Ann Corcoran's county. "Greenline" was what they said. "Control" was what they meant. From Washington, D.C. and Pittsburgh, "they" had decided that Ann Corcoran's county should become a tourism mecca with Antietam Battlefield its core attraction. People would come from all over to see the battlefield, to marvel at the "living landscape," to drive past the working farms and to stay in the bed and breakfast inns into which the locals would have converted their homes.

What of the farmers? asked Ann Corcoran. Oh, they could stay as long as they practiced approved, "low impact" agriculture. Ann Corcoran suddenly realized that "they" had been involved behind-the-scenes from the beginning. Now everything that had been happening made sense.

Ann Corcoran soon learned that the Conservation Fund had been quietly buying up farms surrounding the Antietam Battlefield Park pursuant to an agreement with the National Park Service. Although the National Park Service had no authority to buy more land or to expand the boundary of the park without the express approval of Congress, it planned to present the lands owned by the Conservation Fund as a wonderful opportunity Congress could not forego. Once Congress authorized boundary expansion for Antietam Battlefield Park, the National Park Service would acquire the land from the Conservation Fund.

The farmers were not to know of these plans since they might demand a high price as their constitutionally required "just compensation" for the conversion of their land to such a "public use," or, even more unthinkable, demand to keep what was rightfully theirs. Ann Corcoran and her neighbors may have been farmers, but they weren't the stupid yokels the outsiders must have thought. They decided to find out what was happening to them.

Using the Freedom of Information Act on both federal and state government officials, the grand strategy was brought slowly to light. Ann Corcoran and her neighbors worked hard to learn what was happening to them and why. But it wasn't just hard work. They enjoyed what some—but not Ann Corcoran—called good luck.

For example, one night a neighbor called to report the National Park Service was spying on them from a satellite! Ann Corcoran, dressed for bed in pajamas and curlers, stood by the kitchen telephone, stunned and incredulous. The neighbor might just as well have reported that an alien spaceship had beamed him up for a "Vulcan mind meld." Her husband was less dubious. "Let's check it out," he said.

Down the road they found the incredible: a satellite monitoring station. Said the operator: "The park service just wants to see what they should buy next." Soon neighbors were calling from all over the southern end of the county. One farmer found government monitoring equipment well inside his property, past the gate with the "No Trespassing" sign.

An investigation by the local newspaper discovered that the National Park Service was mapping 2,400 square miles by satellite, well beyond the boundaries of the county or even the State of Maryland. This disclosure forced the National Park Service to abandon its egregious plans. Yet the National Park Service has not abandoned other plans for the county. The farmers fight on.

Often Ann Corcoran and other leaders found themselves the victims of scurrilous attacks in the local newspaper: Those who were once respected as guardians of Antietam's farming tradition were suddenly "greedy" landowners bent upon "avaricious" development of their property. One three-letter attack was so mean-spirited that Ann Corcoran wondered—through the hurt and humiliation—how anyone could be so spiteful. When she attempted to speak with the author she found he wasn't listed in the county phone book. Later the newspaper discovered the attacks were the work of a National Park Service employee writing under an assumed name.

There was a silver lining to the dark cloud that, for more than 3 years, had hung over the farm that Ann Corcoran dreamed of since that faraway night in Ireland. The publicity surrounding her battle for freedom put her name before hundreds of thousands of Americans, many of whom call to learn more of her fight, to tell her of their fight, and to draw comfort from the fact that there are others like them. Says Ann Corcoran of the demands on her time: "The good news is, you are not alone. The bad news is, you are not alone."

Early in the morning before the boys wake up and the cattle and horses need to be fed, before the phone starts ringing and before she starts work on *Land Rights Letter*—the popular newsletter she founded—Ann Corcoran sits at the kitchen table and recalls her years in Washington, D.C. as an "environmental lobbyist." She tries to remember a clue that the "us" of which she was once so much a part would one day become the "they" who would try to take her home away.

"I don't remember anyone I went to school with or anyone I worked with in those early days in the environmental movement believing that he or she wanted power over other peoples' lives and homes and farms. They truly believed that they were working to make a better world. Looking back I realize I was there at the end of the old conservation movement—a movement that espoused the wise use of resources and a balance between the needs of man and nature."

"It's a war," Ann Corcoran says looking out across the fields that once flowed red with the blood of men fighting so that all might be free. "It's a war for freedom just as surely as the war that was fought here. It's a war the extreme environmentalists and the government think we'll be too busy to fight. They couldn't be more wrong."

WAYNE HAGE
Tonopah, Nevada

Country western singer and songwriter Tom T. Hall once sang of a cowboy built "like a whip." He might have been thinking of Wayne Hage of Nye County, Nevada.

Wayne Hage is tall and lean, all sharp angles and no fat. He sits tall and erect in the saddle, and at nearly sixty still does all his own roping and branding, setting a pace that would do men young enough to be his grandchildren proud.

Wayne Hage is also no nonsense. As a man who knows there's only so much sunlight in the day, he's careful with his time, doesn't waste it and doesn't abide those who try to waste it for him. He's courteous and mannerly in the way that most westerners, and especially western cowboys, are, but he's not outgoing.

Wayne Hage conserves more than just his time. As someone who has spent his whole life close to the land, he is a careful steward of the range. Living out where less than ten inches of rainfall come each year, he knows he has to take care of more than just his cattle, he has to take care of the land on which they graze. Like most western cowboys, he prides himself on his ability to make something out of nothing, to understand a part of the world others might call a "wilderness," to be able to "read" a herd of cattle or a stretch of prairie or the afternoon sky.

Wayne Hage can read more than nature. With a master's degree in biological science from the University of Nevada at Reno and as past chairman of numerous range policy boards and committees, Wayne can talk animal husbandry with the best veterinarians, range management with the nation's top range managers.

Yet like most westerners, Wayne likes to listen. Apparently he listens well, for he remembers the tales his father, grandfather and great grandfather told him about the old days. He remembers the stories of why Nevada, as its flag says, was "Battle Born" and what the price was to be for coming into the Union. He remembers the stories of the adoption of the Taylor Grazing

27

Act in 1934, and the promise Secretary Harold L. Ickes, FDR's close friend, made to the western ranchers that their private rights in federal lands would be honored.

Thus it was that when Wayne began to have trouble, as even the best western ranchers do, with the bureaucrats who act as if the land they manage is their own, he remembered the stories and wondered. A lot of western ranchers wonder and a lot of them talk it out. Wayne Hage did something else.

Wayne Hage began to study. At the time his daughter Ramona was in Washington, D.C. He asked her to spend some spare time in the Library of Congress and in the National Archives.

The research grew out of Wayne's concern "with the incessant attack on the western range livestock industry." For, as he saw it, "the assault begun by the conservation movement in the 1890s continues today under key environmental leaders and the government agencies they politically control."

As Wayne investigated the "endless barrage of anti-grazing rhetoric," he "discovered that the attack on western livestock interests was not a mindless manifestation of urban ignorance but rather a well-planned, superbly orchestrated attempt to destroy the property rights of western interests."

Wayne Hage reached another conclusion: "The question never was one of preservation of natural resources as opposed to development of those resources. The basic question is, 'Who is going to develop those resources.'"

In 1989 his years of research and study led to the publication of *Storm Over Rangelands*, in which Wayne Hage maintained, with fastidious documentation, that major federal range management agencies were submitting to pressure from environmental groups to deny the property rights of ranchers.

Wayne documented government abuses of private property rights. He detailed the long chain of private property rights in federal range lands: the water, the roads, the fences, the stock watering ponds, and other improvements whose value far exceeds any value attributable to the grass the rancher's stock consumed. He delineated the history of wildlife populations on the range and how the rancher, through predator control, good stewardship and the availability of private water greatly enhanced those populations.

Wayne Hage and his book were suddenly much in demand. Western cattlemen wanted to know more about the facts Wayne had discovered and the details behind his novel legal theories. Yet in the end, the U.S. Government appears to have exacted its revenge. Accusing Wayne Hage's cattle of being in trespass, U.S. Forest Service officials asked him to ride down to round up his herd. When Wayne arrived he was met by an army of federal agents armed with automatic weapons.

In the end the U.S. Forest Service confiscated his cattle, sold them at auction, destroyed the value of the Hage ranch and devastated the family's finances. He filed a lawsuit in the U.S. Court of Claims asserting an unconstitutional "taking" of his private property for public use, without "just compensation." The legal issues in Wayne's case will take years to resolve. Even then they will be the subject of endless debate by legal scholars.

However, one thing is no longer the subject of serious debate: the attack on western ranchers is not about protecting the environment. According to a nationally syndicated and highly regarded columnist, the attack is "simply a smoke screen for three hidden agendas ruthlessly pursued by Interior Secretary Bruce Babbitt:" (1) to replace ranchers with 40-acre ranchettes, condos and hotels; (2) to seize Western water and destroy Western water law; and (3) to abolish local control of grazing advisory boards. It was Wayne's book that raised American awareness to the point that such a column could be written.

Wayne Hage of Nye County Nevada, who already looks mighty tall in the saddle, is casting a very long shadow these days.

Sister Thomas More Bertels
Manitowoc, Wisconsin

One newspaper reporter said it this way: "Put Erma Bombeck in a black-and-white habit, add a Ph.D. in history and a knack for political stumping, and you've got Sister Thomas More Bertels—better known as agriculture's hell-raising nun."

Born in Ironwood, Michigan, Sister Thomas More's father was a first generation Belgian immigrant who worked in the iron mines. Her mother was the daughter of French Canadian immigrants who pioneered in the Upper Peninsula. Of her parents she writes that they possessed the "personal characteristics that would make possible the fulfillment of God's plan for me. My Mother loved people; my Father loved books."

In 1940 she joined the Franciscan Sisters of Christian Charity at Holy Family College (later named Silver Lake College). There the curriculum was "the very embodiment of . . . a solid values-oriented education built on the liberal arts." In the early 1960s she completed her formal education by obtaining a doctorate from The Catholic University of America in Washington, D.C., where she studied under "professors who were grounded in the value system in which I had been reared."

It was at Catholic University that her eyes were opened to what she refers to as her life's work, a "research and lecturing apostolate to North American farmers and ranchers." Yet it was the words of Mother Agna Beller, daughter of Czechoslovakian peasant parents, who lit the fire: "If you can use the education given you by this religious congregation to help farmers in any way, never say 'No.'" Sister Thomas More never said "No."

For nearly thirty years Sister Thomas More has traveled throughout the United States and Canada lecturing in every state and province in North America. Her mission: empower and energize farmers and ranchers.

"I tried love for 20 years and nothing happened, so I

31

got out of that racket," Sister Thomas More says with a laugh. "I'm into power now. What the world needs now is not love, sweet love, but power; that is, simply, the ability to get things done."

From her podium as a history professor at Silver Lake College in Manitowoc, Wisconsin, and from the "bully pulpit" of her public appearances throughout the country, Sister Thomas More is an unabashed advocate of farmers and ranchers. One of the reasons: "Farmers and ranchers are more devoted to the free-enterprise system than are any other businessmen in this country."

In 1988 she wrote and self-published *In Pursuit of Agri-Power: The One Thing North American Farmers and Ranchers Can't Produce.* She is a prolific writer and a frequent contributor to many national and regional publications.

Sister Thomas More is not afraid to cross swords or go toe-to-toe with the Church hierarchy: "My graduate studies were completed before the bureaucracy in American mainline churches threw out Thomas Aquinas and the *Book of Common Prayer*, replacing both with Karl Marx and *Das Kapital.*

"The greatest threat I see today are those who would serve as coercive utopians. Most utopians have not one smidgen of respect for miners, loggers, farmers, ranchers, oil drillers, tourist-facility providers; that is, anyone involved on the ground floor in any of the extractive industries—those who make available the natural resources needed to protect and sustain human life. They are the guts of any economy."

Environmentalists are particularly suspect and part of what Sister Thomas More calls "one-issue dogmatists." Worse yet, "they build on two emotions, fear and guilt. It's the Chicken Little syndrome."

Her concern regarding farmers and ranchers is national in scope, including the ongoing battle in the American West where "radical eco-activists are challenging the use of federal range land by ranchers."

The solution? Obtain and use power. "Your sin is not the abuse of power. It's non-use," she tells her audiences. "You have to face the fact that you can't accomplish anything alone."

Sister Thomas More faults "clergymen, moral philosophers and ethicists" for their failure to "take on the coercive utopians in the so-called environmental movement who are the professed enemies of American farmers and ranchers.

"Who are the foes of American agriculture? The coercive utopians who are drawn from the media, church and academia under the umbrella concept of environmental policy as well as the authorities in the church, media and academia who support them by their silence."

That's one thing Sister Thomas More will never be: silent.

DANIEL MAKUAKANE
Pahoa, Hawaii

Environmental elitists continue to assert that they are not against everything, that they are not really advocating what has become known as a "BANANA"—a Ban Against Nearly Anything Nearly Anywhere. Instead, they assert, they oppose only those endeavors that are, in the words of Vice President Gore, "environmentally inappropriate."

Yet, as almost anyone who has had experience with these powerful organizations knows, quite the opposite is true. It should come as no surprise, therefore, that despite the interminable advocacy by environmentalists of alternative forms of energy, several environmental groups have sued to stop geothermal power development on Hawaii's Big Island.

The Big Island—which has depended for its electric power upon the burning of foreign oil—possesses enormous geothermal energy potential, a resource the island's residents are eager to develop. Hawaiians are disgruntled by power shortages yielding rolling blackouts and brownouts throughout the Big Island and by the continued dependence upon foreign oil. Broad public support for geothermal energy has been generated by its clean operation and the local jobs, taxes and revenues it will bring.

Unfortunately, the lawsuit by environmental organizations threatens to end geothermal development in the foreseeable future, if not forever. If the environmental lawsuit is successful, a 25-megawatt geothermal plant now nearing completion will likely be abandoned. Instead, demands for electric power will be met by the use of oil from Indonesia or coal from Australia. Ironically, when one considers environmental group rhetoric in favor of alternative energy sources, the 25-megawatt geothermal power plant would reduce the amount of oil brought through Big Island coastal waters by 450,000 barrels of oil a year. Geothermal energy is hardly an untested resource. It is already an important power source in Idaho, Nevada, California, Italy and Iceland.

Environmentalists opposing the geothermal project have not confined themselves to activities in the courtroom. They have taken out advertisements in major newspapers throughout the mainland, decrying the imminent demise of America's only rain forest, the loss of ground sacred to native Hawaiians and the eradication of a variety of threatened and endangered species. These advertisements have not only raised opposition to the project but have also been a very successful fundraising tool for opponents of geothermal power.

Protesters have been flown in, since relatively few locals oppose the project, to protest at various locations and to engage in acts of civil disobedience for which they have been arrested, requiring a return trip from the mainland for legal proceedings. As always, the opponents appear to have mastered the local media, since the newspapers frequently carry headlines proclaiming the latest allegation of impending doom.

Of course, the charges are without substance. The lands in question are not threatened rain forests. In fact, the State of Hawaii, in cooperation with officials of the National Park Service (involved due to the proximity of Hawaii Volcanoes National Park), selected the current geothermal drilling site due to the absence of any impact upon the forest. No endangered species are at risk. As for allegations that the property is sacred ground or contains medicinal plants, neither is true.

While the geothermal companies and the State of Hawaii battled back in court, local residents who favor geothermal power realized that they were losing the battle of public opinion. They decided to get organized and to demonstrate that the majority of local residents want geothermal power on the Big Island.

The result was the formation of the Hawaii Island Geothermal Alliance (HIGA) to speak with one voice in favor of geothermal energy as a means of supplying much needed local power. Made up of a diverse and unusual mixture of organizations and entities from business groups to trade unions, one thing united them: the desire to develop geothermal energy.

While a number of individuals were responsible for the formation of HIGA and its continued vitality, one leader was key, given the sensitivity of the issues he addressed. Daniel

Makuakane is not only an outspoken advocate of geothermal power. He is also a native Hawaiian, familiar with and respectful of the traditions of Hawaii. When any question was raised regarding religion, medicinal plants or sacred lands, it was Daniel Makuakane (in his words "a real Hawaiian who will write, speak his mind and not be intimidated") who stepped forward with an always-robust rebuttal.

Daniel Makuakane supports geothermal power for the jobs and opportunities it provides to his friends and neighbors. "One can't help but focus on the variety of work being completed or that will be accomplished, and the amount of workers employed, due to the prosperity of geothermal development. These workers are people trying to earn a decent living or lifestyle for their families and themselves, by doing the work they are trained and hired to do. The time cannot be any sooner than now, for all who are employed, directly or indirectly because of geothermal, to join together and resist against this vocal and unconcerned group opposing geothermal development."

Daniel Makuakane was outspoken in his recognition of those who opposed geothermal power. "This opposition has always been against any and all development here in the islands. The majority of the protesters are outsiders and new people, with no real purpose or interest, other than their own, and trying to create an impression that they are protecting our environment and concerned about the Hawaiian lifestyle and livelihood."

When geothermal opponents raised concerns about the potential presence near the geothermal site of sulfur dioxide, Daniel Makuakane responded: "Volcano, the source of our origin, left a concentration of sulfur dioxide so prevalent that life of any kind should never have survived if we believe those against geothermal development. Yet my people grew in numbers, large in stature, strong and healthy. Cook counted nearly a half-million. The cause of the Hawaiian race to diminish was disease and the lifestyle introduced by the Western world. Sulfur and the smell was accepted from ancient times for its medicinal value. Our kahunas had a saying for it: ha'nu ola— the breath of life."

Daniel Makuakane on endangered species and medicinal plants: "I am having a hard time believing some of the stories about this area: the habitats of rare animals, plants of medicinal value found nowhere else and a Hawaiian shrine being disturbed or destroyed. I have hunted and picked *maile* and know that this area harbors little or none of the above. I challenge the claim that the geothermal development site is a medicinal chest and the best of our medicinal plants are being destroyed."

Daniel Makuakane was particularly contemptuous of those who asserted that geothermal development threatened traditional religious freedoms. "Who are these Hawaiians and religious practitioners? Where are they from and how did they attain their Kahuna (Pule) status? Where are the shrines located and who are the ones caring for them? Do they agree to human sacrifice as was practiced with the traditional belief? I am a native (75%) Hawaiian, the product of two (Chinese/Hawaiian) cultures and do not understand how our lifestyle and livelihood are being undermined, including customs, beliefs and practice. This is absurd, and I find no valid truth in such a perception."

Daniel Makuakane also challenged the concept of the fire-goddess Pele as imagined by one of the environmental organizations, the Pele Defense Fund. "This misguided notion about Pele and the Ancient Religion has never been a household word in my and my parents' time. If your belief is that Pele is a God (goddess) 'a deity with greater powers than man' then why must she be defended or provided monetary help? Is this a plot to feather someone's nest?"

In Daniel Makuakane's view, geothermal power is a resource to be used, used wisely, but used nonetheless. "I am a Hawaiian who enjoys everything past and present and like the idea of being self-sufficient. And this includes Pele's gift for geothermal development."

Daniel Makuakane and other HIGA leaders slowly began to change the public perception that most were opposed to the geothermal project. Daniel Makuakane was particularly prolific in his letters to the editor and especially energetic, despite his 70-plus years, in his attendance at public meetings and other gatherings regarding geothermal power.

In March 1992 HIGA sponsored a rally at the Edith Kanakaole Stadium in Hilo. More than 7,000 attended, a powerful contrast to the 150 protesters, many of whom were paid to be there, some months earlier at the geothermal site.

The people of HIGA and the Big Island have not as yet emerged victorious. If past litigation on geothermal development in Hawaii is any indication, they have a way to go. However, they have shown other communities that local involvement and activism are essential. If there is any hope of preventing environmental elitists from stopping everything, everywhere, it is in the efforts of local grassroots groups like HIGA and in leaders like Daniel Makuakane. As he wrote recently, "E maka'ala ena poe Hawaii. Awaken and be aware, my Hawaiian people. Pa'a ka waha, hana ka lima. Your voice may be silent but the action is with the hands."

Marilyn Parkes
East Liverpool, Ohio

When President-elect Bill Clinton and Vice President-elect Al Gore emerged from the Library of Congress on December 8, 1992, hundreds of people were lined up waiting to catch a glimpse of the newly-elected boy wonders. Secret Service agents and Capitol Hill Police had roped off a broad pathway down which the smiling men were proceeding slowly, shaking hands with well-wishers.

Bill Clinton could not help but notice the attractive woman who, despite the bitter cold, had just removed her scarf to reveal a head of luxuriant blonde hair. In a crowd of enthusiastic supporters she was positively euphoric, screaming, waving her arms and jumping excitedly up and down. Clinton moved right for her with Al Gore in tow.

When Clinton grasped her outstretched hand, she gripped his tightly and pulled him toward her. "Thank you very much sir, but he's the one I want." Perplexed, Clinton looked over his shoulder as the woman pointed at Gore. She pulled a letter from her pocket. "Here," she said, thrusting it at Gore. Momentarily stunned, Gore took the letter. "You're wrong about WTI," she said with Clinton still in her grip. "Please read my letter. Don't kill my town."

Governor Clinton, Senator Gore, meet Marilyn Parkes of East Liverpool, Ohio.

East Liverpool is a town trying to come back from economic disaster. The trip has not been easy. East Liverpool was once a bustling industrial city, thriving on the 200 potteries that lined the Ohio River. Then in 1981 Crucible Steel Works in nearby Midland, Pennsylvania, closed down. Soon plants were closing up and down the valley, and the jobs that once sustained a population of nearly 30,000 barely supported a community of 13,000. In the end only 3 potteries remained, buildings were boarded up, shops and businesses were closed, families moved away, and property values plummeted. Bruce Springsteen's *My Hometown*, with its poignant evocation of a

41

dying industrial town, could have been written with East
Liverpool in mind.

If there's anyone for whom Bruce Springsteen's touch-
ing song has special meaning, it is Marilyn's husband, Mike.
Mike was born and raised in East Liverpool. He has been a
junior high school teacher, vice president of the local savings
and loan, vice president of the city's bank, and has headed up
United Way, the Chamber of Commerce, the planning for an
all-school reunion that brought 6,000 people back to East
Liverpool for a week, and serves on the East Liverpool Hospital Board. The only occasion when Mike, the quintessential
"East Liverpudlian," was ever away for any length of time was
when he attended Kent State University.

It was at Kent State University that Mike met Marilyn.
Marilyn was born and raised in Cincinnati where her father
was a chemical engineer and her mother a librarian. In the
fall of 1970, a few short months after the campus protest that
left four students dead, Marilyn went off to college. While
her parents had their misgivings, she was under scholarship
and, after all, Kent State had an excellent fine arts and per-
forming arts department. Despite her liberal arts training and
her early interest in the arts, today her greatest interest, as a
fourth grade school teacher, is in the teaching of science.

Marilyn Parkes attributes her fascination with science
to her father and the matter-of-fact way in which scientific
issues were discussed around the dinner table. She was also
naturally inquisitive. "I was always asking, 'why' and my father was only too glad to tell me." It was her father who
taught her the importance of what scientists call proof and
what lawyers call evidence. It was the teaching of science and
Marilyn's demand for proof and evidence that eventually
brought her to Washington, D.C., and her meeting with
Clinton and Gore.

With the closing of the potteries, East Liverpool had
embarked upon a world-wide search for new industry. Eventually that search focused upon Waste Technologies Industries (WTI) and its plans to dispose of hazardous waste by burning it at extremely high temperatures. Yet waste incineration
was something new and there were doubts. A task force was
established to study the proposal and any possible environmental consequences.

Marilyn Parkes, wife, mother, teacher and neighbor, read the Task Force Report. "I didn't understand all of it but I understood enough. Then I asked my father, 'Dad, you have a daughter, a son-in-law and two grandchildren living here, what do you say?' He said, 'Are you kidding, it's the cleanest thing you've ever had in town.' Then I did some reading on my own as to why people thought this was a bad thing. I looked at dump sites and thought this was better. I made up my mind that it was a good thing, and then I went on with my life."

While Marilyn was sitting on the sidelines, things began to get a little crazy in Mike Parkes' home town. As Marilyn says, "Soon, we were a national issue and people from all over the country began coming to town to tell us what we should do. Every time WTI got a new permit, there would be another lawsuit. After Greenpeace came to town, you couldn't learn anything at the public hearings because the opponents would cause a fuss and shut things down. People who supported the project openly were harassed and threatened. A good friend of mine is in therapy because of the threats, the intimidation, and the stalking."

Shortly after Mike Parkes, as President of the East Liverpool Chamber of Commerce, announced that WTI had donated money for a concert series in the park and a photograph to that effect appeared in the paper, Mike and Marilyn began to get nasty, sometimes threatening telephone calls. One night when Mike was preparing to take a proposal to the City Council to refurbish the downtown district, he told Marilyn to stay home. He feared violence and he didn't think she would handle it well. He thought she would start fighting back. Sure enough, Mike was restrained by WTI opponents. Says Marilyn, "I'm glad I wasn't there. I probably would have slugged someone.

"About that time I was teaching a unit on environmental science. I told my students to walk around their neighborhoods and make a list of any pollution they saw and to write down whether it was water, air or land pollution. I didn't care what kind of pollution it was, but the students had to be specific, and they had to identify it."

When one little boy reported that WTI, which had not yet begun operations, was polluting the land, Marilyn Parkes asked why. "I asked how WTI would be polluting the land

and he kept saying, because it was burning things. I would ask how that was land pollution. It kept going around and around. Finally, another child said it was land pollution because, even after the burn, a very small amount of material would be left and would have to be buried. That's the answer I wanted."

She was unprepared for the hate campaign that was launched against her for that rather harmless Socratic exchange. The child's mother was an opponent of WTI. When she related the classroom exchange to one of the leaders of the opposition, she was told this was an outrageous assault upon her child. This was an opportunity she was told, to discredit Mike and Marilyn Parkes, and by inference, WTI. At the very next meeting of the local school board, the irate mother excoriated Marilyn Parkes, who was not present to rebut the accusations. The next day the local paper ran the front page headline: "Parent: Son Being Harassed By Teacher." No teacher was named. People quickly figured out that the "teacher" was Marilyn Parkes.

"I called the publisher and let him have it. I told him to print my name, at least then I would be able to defend myself publicly. They had already accused me of the worst thing that a teacher can be charged with. I also called the superintendent to urge him to make a public statement that the accusations were unfounded. He never did."

Within days, Marilyn Parkes was exonerated. The truth came out and everyone acknowledged what had really happened. In the process there were hugs all around from upset children a little older than the hug stage, flowers and a *mea culpa* from the mother who had make the accusations and apologies from the newspaper. Yet the experience had awakened Marilyn Parkes. She realized that she could no longer sit on the sidelines. Like it or not she would have to become involved.

Marilyn took a tour of the WTI facility, spent two hours with the manager asking questions and studied everything she could to be able to speak out publicly. In June 1991 an Ohio State Senator introduced legislation to outlaw, retroactively, the WTI facility. Marilyn drove to Columbus to speak against the bill.

She told the committee about growing up in Cincinnati, about how the Cuyahoga River began to burn while she was at Kent State, about how her father had been the superintendent of a paper mill when the smoke stack broke down and how he had struggled to get the plant back on line and the people to work. Marilyn said she remembered those days and knew that Ohio had cleaned up. In the process, plants had closed and jobs had been lost, especially in East Liverpool. "But now East Liverpool has a chance to come back. Please don't stop us," she pleaded.

Marilyn Parkes said something else that the committee remembered. "Science, technology, and the industry that goes with it brought us our standard of living. They brought us a longer life span, an improved quality of life, and better medical care. We can't go back to a subsistence standard of living. We can't go back to living hand to mouth, to eating only what we can grow or kill, to living in only what we can build ourselves. That is what the Khmer Rouge did to the people of Cambodia. Don't let it happen here."

The chairman of the committee summed it up: "Ms. Parkes, you have done your profession very proud today." The Ohio legislature tabled the bill.

Marilyn became more active locally. She went from merchant to merchant to collect enough money to take out advertisements in the local paper. She wanted to rally the locals who supported the WTI project and to get some national media attention. She knew most of those opposing the project were not from East Liverpool. She often points out that at a Greenpeace protest demonstration against WTI only five of the 75 people arrested were from East Liverpool.

Marilyn Parkes called her organization the Coalition for Progress. She took out a large advertisement based upon the groundbreaking research done by *Forbes* magazine regarding Greenpeace. Headlined Marilyn's advertisement, "Greenpeace Lies." Demanded the advertisement, "Investigate Greenpeace."

Her next advertisement used as its source an article in the *New York Times Magazine* regarding the relationship between Governor Clinton and U.S. Senator Gore. The article discussed an early meeting between Clinton and Gore at which Gore practiced his answers to the media on being chosen as Clinton's vice president. In response to one answer, Clinton cautioned Gore, "We don't want to look like Greenpeace warriors." Gore replied, "What you mean *'we,'* kemosabe?" Marilyn Parkes' full pager headlined, "Save Us From The Greenpeace Warriors—Come To The Meeting."

Marilyn gave speeches, wrote letters, made telephone calls and did everything she could to stem the tide, to help rally the locals and to inform the media that the way it was portraying the WTI battle was wrong. Marilyn, who remembers from her vantage point at Kent State how and why the Vietnam War came to an end, knew that the fact that WTI had obtained every permit and won every lawsuit wasn't enough. WTI and the people of East Liverpool had to win the public relations battle being conducted in the media.

Not surprisingly, the biggest rally in East Liverpool took place after newly elected Vice President Al Gore announced that he would personally stop the WTI project. Following a Thursday press conference at City Hall, Marilyn Parkes and others gathered to present their local version of a Christmas classic: "How Al Gore (Not The Grinch) Stole Christmas." According to the Pittsburgh newspapers 1,000 people were there. The people signed Christmas cards to Gore and sang carols.

Marilyn says it was a beautiful snowy day, standing there overlooking the Ohio River, the Christmas lights sparkling on the trees and houses, big fat wet flakes falling upon the frozen ground. Near the end of the rally she stood up and addressed the crowd. She found it difficult to control her emotions. She thanked everyone for coming and for their efforts. For several long moments she was close to tears, greatly moved by the scene and the people around her. Then she became angry. She decided to end her remarks with a shout, "Greenpeace! Go home!" Her shout did not end the speech and the rally. Instead it became a chant that reverberated through the crowd. Soon the thousand men, women and children at the rally were shouting at the top of their voices, their fists in the air, "Greenpeace! Go home!"

Later Marilyn wrote a letter to Senator Gore. She wanted him to know what he was doing to her town and to its people. Mailing the letter wasn't enough. She traveled to Washington to ask her Congressman to make sure Gore received the letter.

When she met with her Congressman, he asked her to

read the letter. She didn't make it all the way through. When she got to the part about how only 4 of her 33 students paid for their own lunch, about how she buys the school supplies for 15% of her class, about how her church group provides the coats and gloves and shoes for most of her students, she broke down and wept. The Congressman finished the letter for her, "and now you want to close the first industry that has been interested in us in years."

The Congressman had a copy of her letter sent by courier to Senator Gore's office along with an angry letter from the Congressman asking why he had not been consulted before Gore announced his plan to kill a project that was providing 160 jobs, had significantly enhanced the assessed land value of East Liverpool, had spent $165 million to get started and would pay $2 million a year in taxes.

When Marilyn Parkes and her friends emerged from the Longworth House Office Building and saw the crowd gathered before the Library of Congress, she knew immediately that Clinton and Gore were inside. "I think I'll deliver this personally," she told her friends. "Marilyn," one responded, "that only happens in the movies."

Marilyn was not to be denied. She stepped through the metal detectors, and stood waiting for Clinton and Gore. As they began to move down the stairs, she wondered, "how, out of all of these people am I going to get them to pay attention to me?

"Then I thought, they're both married to blondes. So I pulled off my scarf, tousled my hair and began to jump up and down. I was going crazy. If anyone who knew me had seen me they would have thought me a fool."

Her meeting with Clinton and Gore on the steps of the Library of Congress, within sight of the Capitol and the Supreme Court, reveals the combination of planning, courage, and serendipity that has characterized her short term as an activist. That moment, frozen in time, with Marilyn Parkes, school teacher, grasping the hand of the man who would be president while handing her letter to his vice president, is one that would have made America's Founding Fathers very proud.

Marilyn Parkes a fool? Not likely. The only fool on the steps of the Library of Congress that day was Bill Clinton's Greenpeace Warrior who heard from the people.

DR. PETER STRITTMATTER
Tucson, Arizona

"**S**pace—the final frontier . . . These are the voyages of the starship *Enterprise.* Its five-year mission: to explore strange new worlds, to seek out new life and new civilizations, to boldly go where no man has gone before."

The opening lines of television's *Star Trek™* are known to millions, as are the perpetual reruns of the popular but short lived television series of the 1960s. Millions more who never saw Captain Kirk and Spock when they were a little less long in the tooth have seen the motion picture versions of the *Star Trek* adventures. Today, millions of "Trekkies" celebrate the excitement, the vision and the dream of exploring that final frontier.

Yet as real as Hollywood can make the *Star Trek* adventures and as genuine as is the delight of the "Trekkies," they are still just the stuff of fiction. For Dr. Peter Strittmatter exploring the final frontier is real life.

Dr. Strittmatter was born and raised in Bexleyheath, Kent, England, receiving his B.A., M.A. and Ph.D. from St. John's College at Cambridge. In 1970 he came to the United States, first to the University of California at San Diego, then to the University of Arizona where he has been since 1971. In 1975 he became Director of the Steward Observatory at the University of Arizona— one of the world's most prestigious and highly regarded astronomical institutes.

The world of astronomy has undergone a complete revolution in the past several decades. Until 1945 mankind's acquisition of electromagnetic radiation, which is the source of almost all astronomical information, came almost entirely from observations in optical light. However, since the end of World War II, technology has increased accessible wavelength range by more than a trillion: from radio waves to infrared, to ultraviolet, to X-ray radiation, and gamma rays. As a result, astronomers have discovered quasars, pulsars, stars in the process of forming and black holes.

Dr. Peter Strittmatter has been a part of that quiet revolution as a result of his work in the development of better telescopes. In the past the construction of larger telescopes to achieve higher sensitivity was thought impossible or at least prohibitively expensive. Since 1980 the University of Arizona, together with the Smithsonian Institution and other organizations, has been developing technological breakthroughs to permit construction of telescopes in the 8 to 12 meter class, increasing sensitivity by a factor of 4 to 100 over existing telescopes. This new generation of telescopes will allow mankind to look back over more than 90% of the age of the universe, to explore the early universe, to study the process of galaxy and chemical element formation as well as star and planet formation.

However, the ability of Dr. Strittmatter and his colleagues to reach further into that final frontier is hampered by the opacity of the Earth's atmosphere and the fact that all wavelengths shorter than that of visible light are absorbed by the Earth's atmosphere. While the best location from which to observe space would be the Earth's Moon or an orbital platform such as the trouble-plagued Hubble telescope, such locations are extremely expensive. The second best site is anywhere on Earth with clear dry skies and relatively high mountains that rise above most of the dust, aerosols and water vapor.

Archimedes once proclaimed, "Give me a place to stand on, and I will move the Earth." Since Dr. Peter Strittmatter and his colleagues now had the telescope technology in hand, all they required was the place to stand. Following a nation-wide search initiated in 1980, they chose Mount Graham in the Coronado National Forest in Southeastern Arizona. At 10,717 feet, Mount Graham had all they wanted: clear skies, low water vapor, little artificial light sources and low wind speeds.

While some excellent U.S. sites had to be eliminated due to their earlier designation as federal wilderness areas or as a result of the lack of access, Mount Graham had been accessible by roads for decades. A paved two-lane highway went to 8,770 feet and all but one of several peaks above 9,700 feet were accessible by dirt roads. Dr. Peter Strittmatter and his colleagues were enthusiastic about Mount Graham. "By some incredible miracle, Mount Graham was not only the best possible site in the continental United States from an astronomical standpoint, it also entailed the least cost from an economic and an environmental standpoint. Let's face it, Mount Graham had been used intensively since the late 1800s. Even our most ambitious plan would have required the use of less than 60 acres compared to the 5,000 to 10,000 acres that had previously been logged."

Yet just as Archimedes failed to mention the need for a fulcrum, so Dr. Peter Strittmatter forgot to consider the *Star Trek* generation and its demands for environmental purity. One other factor he overlooked was that any relationship between the science practiced by the U.S. Fish and Wildlife Service and the science with which Dr. Peter Strittmatter was familiar was purely coincidental.

By 1988 the University of Arizona's 1984 proposal to the U.S. Forest Service to establish an international observatory on Mount Graham had led to two federal environmental impact studies. However, in 1987 the U.S. Fish and Wildlife Service had listed the red squirrel, which was found on Mount Graham, as endangered. Despite two Fish and Wildlife Service biological opinions and four public hearings, no significant adverse impact by the observatory upon the red squirrel was ever discovered.

Although the University of Arizona accepted the conditions demanded by the U.S. Fish and Wildlife Service (but not the science underlying those demands), Dr. Strittmatter and his colleagues were dismayed to learn that it would be another four years before construction could begin. Such a delay would have killed the major international scientific projects planning to locate on Mount Graham.

As a result, the Arizona Congressional delegation moved the Arizona-Idaho Conservation Act through Congress to establish a scientific research site of 150 acres on Mount Graham's Emerald Peak. Congress authorized the Forest Service to proceed with the first three telescopes, limiting the ultimate size of the observatory to 24 acres—instead of the 60 acres desired— and 7 telescopes. In the process, Congress adopted the Fish and Wildlife Service's biological opinion, an opinion that has been discredited by some of the nation's top small animal biologists.

The irony of all this did not escape Dr. Peter Strittmatter and his colleague, Dr. Conrad Istock, a noted biologist. "The red squirrel is neither threatened nor endangered in the United States. In fact, the red squirrel is widely distributed throughout North America in a wide range of habitats, including Douglas fir,

Corkbark fir, Engelmann spruce, Ponderosa pine, and a number of other coniferous and hardwood tree species. Yet because the Fish and Wildlife Service asserts that the red squirrel is a putative subspecies, it comes under the Endangered Species Act."

A further irony is the failure of the Fish and Wildlife Service to recognize the true source of any survival difficulties faced by the red squirrel. Not surprisingly for anyone familiar with the work of the Fish and Wildlife Service, the Service concluded that the red squirrel was in trouble because of mankind—that is, the presence near Mount Graham of roads, summer homes, and a Bible camp. In all of those places, red squirrels were in abundance. Barely mentioned by the Fish and Wildlife Service, but recognized by every other scientist who has researched the issue, is the role of the Abert's or tassel-eared squirrel.

Mankind may be somewhat responsible for the difficulty the tassel-eared squirrel poses for the red squirrel since the former was introduced into the area by mankind in the early 1940s. However, that is where the responsibility ends. Currently the tassel-eared squirrel is in avaricious competition for the same food eaten by the red squirrel. "Incredibly," notes Dr. Peter Strittmatter, "the Fish and Wildlife Service ignored that fact as well as the fact that the tassel-eared squirrel now dominates much of the former range of the red squirrel."

Instead the Fish and Wildlife Service focused upon how it could get mankind off Mount Graham. "Not only did the Fish and Wildlife Service fail to adopt a strategy for dealing with the tassel-eared squirrel, but it never provided any explanation for its failure to do so. As the price for allowing the telescopes on Mount Graham, the Fish and Wildlife Service demanded the closure of summer homes, the Bible camp and a wide variety of roads used for recreation.

"It is hard to believe that the main purpose of the Fish and Wildlife Service was to help the red squirrel. The more likely goal seems to have been that of stopping or delaying the observatory. It is indeed remarkable that the Fish and Wildlife Service is so concerned about occasional use by humans and so silent on the potential solutions to the far more serious biological problems such as that posed by the Abert's squirrel. After all, the Abert's squirrel competes all the time for the red squirrel's food. The hikers, campers, and Bible students don't."

Not surprisingly, neither the willingness of Dr. Peter Strittmatter and the University of Arizona to do everything demanded by the Fish and Wildlife Service, nor the adoption by Congress of legislation to permit the observatory to go forward was enough. In 1989 the Sierra Club Legal Defense Fund, acting on behalf of a number of environmental organizations, sued to stop the observatory. For several years, the litigation dragged on at a cost to the University of almost $1,000 a day. Finally, in 1993, the lawsuit was over. The University won.

The legal challenge by environmental radicals was not the only public issue for Dr. Peter Strittmatter and his colleagues. The environmental terrorist group, Earth First!, and other environmental organizations assaulted the University of Arizona in the local and national media. Allegations of harm to a unique forest, a rare and unusual mammal (the red squirrel), and the sacred lands of native Americans were made almost constantly. With such charges came campus disruptions and protests. Furthermore, environmental radicals attempted to undermine the financial support for the observatory among the various members of the consortium. Nonetheless, polls conducted by the University of Arizona showed that more than 70% of Arizonans supported the observatory.

Support was also very strong from the communities near Mount Graham. Graham County and the communities of Safford and Thatcher, as well as Cochise County, supported the $200 million observatory. In addition, the town of Safford planned a $10 million Museum of Science and Discovery. One reason why the locals opposed the Fish and Wildlife Service was that the roads targeted for closure had been used for recreation by the people of the valley for generations.

Of course, the greatest hurdle was technological. Doing what Dr. Peter Strittmatter and the University of Arizona were doing had never been done before, and certainly not at an elevation approaching Mount Graham's Emerald Peak. Working in such often extreme conditions, and under the nonsensical demands of the Fish and Wildlife Service, even a seemingly simple task became challenging. Yet Dr. Strittmatter and his colleagues prevailed. "We tried to be guided by the facts and felt that what we were doing is important to an understanding of our world, our universe. Of course, that didn't make the task any easier."

Dr. Strittmatter believes that one benefit of his experience is that others will come to understand that the environmental battle is not about the environment and it is certainly not about science. "If they had really been interested in helping the red squirrel, we could have done something to help. But that wasn't their objective. They wanted to kill the observatory.

"I hope these extremist groups will be recognized for what they are—anti-human anti-technology Luddites for whom the natural human concern for the world around us is turned into a weapon to stop progress, science and the achievement of a better life for all of us. It is ironic that in so doing they actually hinder the improvement of the environment about which they claim such concern."

There is one sidelight to the long battle over the Mount Graham observatory, a sidelight that demonstrates not only the true objective of those opposing the observatory but the total absence of any real science to support their position. That sidelight became known to the University's lawyers as a result of a General Accounting Office investigation and during depositions of the Fish and Wildlife Service "expert" in charge of the Mount Graham project. According to her notes, the long list of demands she made of the University of Arizona, allegedly to protect the red squirrel, were labeled "poison pills," designed not to benefit the squirrel but to make the project too burdensome for the U.S. Forest Service and the University. In her testimony she admitted that she opposed the project and, by her demands, sought to kill it.

As Spock would have said, "Fascinating."

BARBARA KEATING-EDH
Modesto, California

In her best selling book, *Trashing the Planet*, Dr. Dixy Lee Ray asked the question, "Who speaks for Science? Or, to put it another way: On whom does the press rely to speak for science?" Dr. Ray concluded that all too often the press turns to the sky-is-falling, mankind-is-a-cancer-on-the-planet crowd for their prophecies of gloom.

One might ask a similar question regarding consumers. Who speaks for consumers? On whom does the press rely to speak for the American consumer? For years, the answer was the same as discerned by Dr. Ray regarding science, that is, the gloom-and-doom merchants, those who rail against the free enterprise system, against commerce and technology.

Unlike so many scientists who have yet to find their voice, consumers who understand that they benefit when businesses flourish have had a voice since 1977. That was the year when Barbara Keating-Edh helped to found Consumer Alert.

Consumer Alert is an organization that recognizes the truth of William Jennings Bryan's warning that, "The more do-gooders profess their selflessness and good intentions toward others, the faster we should count the silverware." For more than 15 years Barbara Keating-Edh's Consumer Alert has served as a research and education foundation that monitors and promotes competitive enterprise, supports the development of safe technology through science and encourages the dissemination of accurate information regarding risk to enable consumers to make informed decisions.

What Barbara Keating-Edh has done has not been easy—not when one takes on, in her words, "the no-growthers who are funding public policy careers for themselves, fueled by scare tactics, enhanced by exaggerations carried forth enthusiastically by the media and promulgated by ignorant and opportunistic lawmakers." Almost anyone else would have wilted under the relentless assault visited upon her by the Naderites. Yet Barbara Keating-Edh is made of sterner stuff.

In 1968, as a 29-year-old mother of five small children ranging in age from two to seven, she was notified that her husband, Major Daniel J. Keating, Jr., USMC, had been killed in action in Vietnam. Already politically involved, she increased her tours of college campuses in support of those serving their country in Vietnam. In the process she found herself debating the likes of Bella Abzug, William Kunstler, Ramsey Clark and members of the Black Panthers.

Barbara Keating-Edh founded a group called Honor America and joined the New York State Conservative Party. In 1974, with William F. Buckley, Jr. as her Honorary Chairman, she ran for the U.S. Senate seat held by Senator Jacob Javits, garnering nearly a million votes on her first run for political office.

Barbara Keating-Edh went on to become a key aide to then-U.S. Senator—now federal appeals court judge—James L. Buckley and appeared regularly as a conservative on *Good Morning America*'s Face-off Debates. Her creation of Consumer Alert led, following the election of Ronald Reagan as President, to an invitation to head his transition team at the U.S. Consumer Products Safety Commission.

Over the past 15 years Barbara Keating-Edh has led the fight for a reasonable view of risk, technology, the free enterprise system, and government regulation. In her view, any attempt to placate what she calls "the coercive utopians" simply doesn't work. "First of all because they will never be sated and secondly because they have goals that are unreasonable and at odds with the free enterprise system."

As a consumer advocate, Barbara Keating-Edh is most outraged by the cost imposed, unnecessarily, upon the American consumer as a result of the demands of environmental extremists. The great irony she says, quoting U.S. Geological Survey scientist Malcolm Ross, is that "we now live in a country with the highest standard of living, and the greatest technology, but we are well on our way to becoming the most frightened nation on earth."

The reason: "the environmental movement in the U.S. today, in the extreme, exaggerates in order to alarm, mocks science, chases zero risk, despises people and opposes developing technology, the ownership of private property and the profit motive." Barbara Keating-Edh believes that the ulterior motives of the nation's environmental leaders, if known, "would shock and repel the general public and today constitute the most serious threat to our liberties, lifestyles and economic well being."

Yet Barbara Keating-Edh is confident about the future. "We are growing every day. Consumer Alert is but one of hundreds of organizations similarly committed. We have an effective network in place. We are drawing able economists, authors, journalists, scientists, legislators, spokesmen, attorneys, financial supporters and a whole range of activists to our team. Together we will build the counter force of a stature and might necessary to defeat the environmental extremists."

Thanks to Barbara Keating-Edh many consumers now have a voice.

DAVID HOWARD
Bleecker, New York

In 1981 David Howard, seeking roots and a place to call home, abandoned his life as a manager and corporate trouble shooter for a Fortune 100 company. He moved to Bleecker, New York, where he established Thetford Hill Joinery and engaged in the architectural design and building of one-of-a-kind homes and the reproduction of architectural detailing.

David Howard was born in New York City and raised in Vermont, where his family's roots predate the French and Indian War. (The ancestral Howards founded Norwich, Connecticut.) When he was a teenager, his family moved to Jonesville, some 30 miles north of Albany, New York.

After a decade of traveling, and moving almost annually, David returned to upstate New York to settle into a Civil War-era home which he and his wife, Bonnie, set to restoring on 120 wooded acres just inside the southern boundary of Adirondack Park. The Town of Bleecker, population 512, is the kind of small community that takes reluctantly to strangers. That was just fine with David Howard, who jealously guarded his privacy. He didn't even want a phone. Life was good.

On a spring afternoon in 1990 David stopped in the Town Clerk's office and was handed a beautifully printed volume titled "The Governor's Commission Report on the Adirondacks in the 21st Century." Filled with artful photographs and possessed of a noble purpose, the report contained some 245 proposals to "Save the Adirondacks." That was 2:00 p.m. on a Saturday. By 3:00 a.m. the next morning David, sitting alone in his home office, had reached the conclusion that anyone who owned property within the "Blueline" (the boundary of the Adirondack Park) was in jeopardy of losing all control over his or her land. As he stared into the darkness beyond his window, he yearned for daybreak that he might either confirm or contradict his fears.

The next morning, shortly after church, David Howard spoke to a lawyer friend. "Yes. Yes," said his friend, "we could all be in serious trouble." David's fear turned to anger and then

59

to action. He drafted a warning letter to his fellow residents and, with the help of a neighbor, photocopied and distributed it, urging everyone to come to a meeting at the Town Hall.

That next evening, nearly half of the town's residents filled to overflowing the former one room school house that is the Town Hall. As a result of that meeting, the Adirondack Blue Line Confederation was formed. David Howard, the "newcomer," was elected Chairman for the first two years.

Soon David learned that the Town of Bleecker and its neighbor communities were not alone in their outrage and their organization. Some half dozen other groups had been formed and were active throughout the Adirondacks. Together they realized that the first order of business was the defeat of New York's Environmental Quality Bond Act—a law that proposed making $800 million available for land purchases by the State of New York throughout the Adirondacks.

Come November the fledgling groups had their first victory: the bond act was defeated. Within the boundary of the Adirondack Park, 90% of those voting said "No!" Never before had the 130,000 diverse and diffident people within the Blue Line reacted with such unity and vigor.

Soon David Howard's Blue Line Confederation was networking, not only with their counterparts in the Adirondacks, but also throughout New England. New Englanders, who pride themselves on the fact that most of their land is privately owned and therefore not subject to the whims and fancies of faraway federal bureaucrats, were shocked to learn of environmentalist-spawned plans for federal takeover throughout New England.

If it is this bad here in the East, thought David, how bad must it be in the West? There federal lands predominate and environmentalists' power to influence the federal government must be at its peak. Says David, "I wanted to know just how widespread this whole nightmare had become."

In July 1991 David Howard learned of something called the Fly-In for Freedom scheduled for September in Washington, D.C. "I thought this would be the vehicle to pull east and west together. For the next three days we called every contact we had in New England and urged them to send someone to the Fly-In to join with our new friends from the Pacific Northwest. I'm thankful we did. The camaraderie was unbelievable. Here were people from 3,000 miles away who understood our fears."

One of his new friends was Tom Hirons, a logger from Oregon. Tom suggested that a way should be found to continue working together. David was asked to serve as Chairman of a Steering Committee to create such an organization.

Less than two months later, 118 people from 24 states gathered in St. Louis, Missouri, to return common sense to regulatory decision making and to preserve and protect Constitutional rights. "It was the most uplifting, heart wrenching and powerful experience I have ever had. Two days after we arrived we—all of us—had created an organization which the Sierra Club would soon call 'the fiercest political action organization, ever.'"

David Howard, who a year and a half earlier had stared into the darkness of an Adirondack night, saw the breaking of a new dawn through the St. Louis Arch. At last defenders of freedom from coast to coast would have the information exchange network David had only dreamed about from his office in Bleecker.

David Howard, the midwife at the birth of this new powerful coalition, remembers its first moments. "We were told, in selecting a name, to avoid use of the word 'America' since that would make us look overly nationalistic. We choose Alliance for America, because we remember why, and by whom, this country was founded and we're proud of that for which it has always stood—freedom and liberty. We were also told to avoid any reference to God since that would be seen as taking a stand on matters of faith. We chose to open our meetings with a prayer asking for His guidance in our deliberations and His strength in our endeavors."

David, not surprisingly, was selected as the first president of Alliance for America. Today, with Alliance for America embracing 512 groups from 50 states, he is Vice President for Property Rights and President of The Lands Rights Foundation, which publishes the *Land Rights Letter,* a newsletter started by Ann Corcoran of Maryland. Land Rights Foundation is also involved in the creation and expansion of a property rights information archive, an information collection and distribution network available to all who are fighting regulatory excess anywhere in the country.

"The bottom line in the war in which we find ourselves engaged is people: the men, women and children who live, work and play in the rural places these environmental extremists covet so much—areas and communities that in many cases have existed for hundreds of years. It is the little people who are the casualties in these battles.

"Thousands of families are being terrorized each day by the Green Machine, never knowing if the homes that have been in their families, sometimes for four or five generations, are safe from condemnation forced on them by the alleged need to preserve their backyards for someone else's 'wilderness' experience.

"Our foes are not the well-meaning members of environmental organizations who truly believe they are helping. Our foes are the multi-million-dollar megabucks businesses that are the huge environmental organizations and their hierarchy whose commitment to the Big Lie, the Media Blitz and the Secret Self-Aggrandizing Agenda have bought us to where the nation finds itself today.

"Our goal is to bring balance back to environmental policy and rediscover the original goal of environmental protection while recommitting ourselves to the Constitution's guarantee of life, liberty and the pursuit of happiness. In so doing, we must never forget that private property is what made this country great and what sets it apart from the rest of the world.

"One of the goals of the Alliance is to remove the political safety of the so-called 'free environmental vote.' No longer can a Senator in Vermont vote to lock up land in Nebraska without paying a political price at home. No longer can a Senator in Georgia do the bidding of powerful environmental lobbyists and in the process destroy jobs in Oregon without paying a political price come Election Day.

"We will return common sense to environmental policy. We will win the battles and then the war and at that point all of us, the reluctant warriors, will go back home. None of us will ever be the same, but we will never forget those who have become our friends, and yes, our family, with whom we have stood shoulder to shoulder and risked it all for nothing more, but certainly nothing less, than principle."

David Howard, who in 1981 sought roots in upstate New York, has found them, but not where he was looking. He found them, not within the "Blue Line" of the Adirondack Park, but all across the nation. He found them everywhere from Portland, Oregon, to Portland, Maine and from the Davis Mountains of Texas to the White Mountains of New Hampshire and the Rocky

Mountains of Montana. He found them in that part of America where, in his words, "the flame burns yet today for all the world to see."

JUNE CHRISTLE
Hoonah, Alaska

When June Christle and her husband sat down to Thanksgiving dinner on Sunday, November 28, 1993, (they celebrated on Sunday since they worked Thanksgiving Day), they had much for which to be thankful. While the fire that had swept through their tiny Alaska village the previous week had destroyed 3 homes, the school, 2 bunk houses, half of June Christle's office and a third of Whitestone Logging Company's main office, no lives had been lost.

That everyone was safe was no small miracle. For when the school became a conflagration—ignited by flaming metal spewed by an exploding boiler—the children stood frozen in terror, screaming. With the men off logging in the woods—not a single man was in camp—June Christle and the other women rushed into the burning school and pulled, dragged, and carried the children to safety.

Notwithstanding the destruction, it could have been much worse. Everyone knew they had come very close, not just to the loss of lives, but also to the loss of the entire village. Hours from the rest of the civilized world—hours when the temperature can drop tens of degrees below zero—if their village went up in flames, the people of Hoonah might have perished before help could have arrived. While it could have been much worse, it was bad enough for three families. The day after the fire, they packed up their belongings and boarded the ferry for a one way trip back to less harsh surroundings.

Not June Christle. Despite her upbringing in the urbane environs of San Francisco, June Christle, the daughter of an attorney, grew up firm and resolute. It's a good thing. She would come to need that natural born toughness.

Growing up in northern California did one thing for June Christle. It gave her a fascination with the faults and fissures of the hills of San Francisco. As a result, at the University of San Francisco she studied geology. Not surprisingly, given her father's influence, she continued her education at the University of San

Francisco School of Law. Despite her preparation for a career in law, she returned to college once more to study Greek and to obtain her masters degree in geochemistry. At last in 1973 she had completed college.

Free of the ivory towers of academia, June Christle wanted to apply her knowledge in the real world. She did geologic field mapping in Canada, throughout much of British Columbia, and in Chiquiamata, Chile, site of what would become the world's largest copper mine.

Not much later June Christle first began to see the effects of the incessant attack by radical environmentalists upon the petroleum and mining industries. As a result of regulatory costs and resultant cutbacks, layoffs in her field were common. What work was done was performed by contract. Nonetheless, June pressed on.

June Christle did more than simply press on. She developed a highly technical process to be used for heap leach mining—a process that permitted the maximum recovery of the ore. Although her process was 99% clean, it drew the withering fire of environmental opponents of mining. Not surprisingly, jobs became harder to come by. June stopped doing geology.

For the next several years, June Christle became a field engineer for cable television, working in such cities as Boston, Massachusetts, Columbus, Ohio, and Taos, New Mexico. She did the field mapping and designing, addressing such matters as: the placement of boosters, how to get electricity to the system, whether to use microwave, how many homes would be served from each tap, and the computer designs accompanying each installation. When she was done her work was sold to one of the major cable companies to perform the installation. It was in the midst of one such project that she met the man who would become her husband.

In 1989 they moved to Hoonah, Alaska, a native village near Glacier Bay, 60 miles west of Juneau on Chichagof Island in the northernmost part of the Tongass National Forest. Despite its isolation, June Christle eagerly anticipated life in her new home, far from the world in which she had done so well. She wanted to get away from it all, to disappear into the peace, beauty, tranquillity and serenity of rural Alaska. It was not to be.

June Christle's husband, Fred, is a logger with Whitestone Southeast Logging, harvesting the plentiful natural resources in

the nation's largest and most sparsely populated state. Her husband and his colleagues knew all too well the view held of them
by folks in what was sometimes derisively called the Lower 48.
Nine years before, the U.S. Congress, ignoring the pleas of the
then bipartisan Alaska Congressional delegation and responding only to the demands of radical environmentalists, imposed
massive land lockup legislation on Alaska.

For a state possessing vast natural resources—in timber,
strategic and critical minerals, oil and gas, and fisheries—the
legislation was devastating. Vast areas were designated as parks,
preserves and wilderness areas, others were set aside as wild and
scenic rivers. Lands that had been used for generations for hunting or fishing, for timber harvesting, lands that held great potential for the discovery of world-class mineral or oil and gas
deposits, were placed off limits to everything but short visits in
float planes and helicopters by the most hardy and wealthy of
the nation's elite. Although Alaskans were told that their needs
for subsistence living as well as their needs to make use of natural resources to survive economically were assured, they had their
doubts.

The misgivings of Alaskans were well founded. The vast
500-mile-long Tongass National Forest, which for generations
has provided timber resources for hundreds of Alaskans, including Alaskan natives, had seen much of its resources locked into
the vast Admiralty Island National Monument and Wilderness,
South Prince of Wales Wilderness and the Misty Fiords National
Monument and Wilderness. However, even that was not enough.
The ink was not yet dry on the Alaska National Interest Lands
Conservation Act (ANILCA) before national environmental
groups began to attack the very legislation they had helped to
author. Much of the attack focused upon the timber harvesting
in the Tongass.

Year after year, environmentalists harassed and hampered
the U.S. Forest Service in its efforts to develop the statutorily-
required Tongass Land Management Plan ("Tee-LUMP"). By 1991
the TLMP was in the midst of its fifth revision. Not surprisingly,
as loggers anxiously awaited news as to what areas would be
available for harvesting, the administrative delays continued.

Even while environmentalists were fighting the regulatory battle within the Executive Branch, they were waging an
even more audacious assault before the Legislative Branch. The
goal: repeal legislation that guaranteed 50-year timber harvest-

ing contracts established by Congress in the early 1950s and cut back even further on areas available for timber harvesting. Only ten percent of the Tongass had ever been available for timber harvesting, but environmentalists thought that was too much. In 1991 they succeeded when Congress reneged on the deal it had struck only 11 years earlier. Once again the cries of Alaskans were ignored.

The entire Alaska Congressional delegation—by now all Republicans—appealed to President Bush to veto the Tongass bill. There was ample precedent for such an appeal and for responsive presidential action. In 1988 President Reagan, responding to the calls of the people of Montana, had vetoed wilderness legislation for Big Sky Country. His veto led to the defeat at the polls of U.S. Senator John Melcher, the author of the unpopular bill.

Yet, as he often liked to say, President Bush was not Ronald Reagan. As he had done to the people of Nevada, and their pleas to veto wilderness legislation, as he had done to the people of rural Nebraska, and their pleas to veto wild and scenic river designation, President Bush ignored the pleas of Alaskans. He signed the Tongass Reform Act.

Shortly after arriving in Alaska, June Christle got a job driving the "crummy," the logging crew bus that transported some 60 men from Hoonah to the logging camp where they joined the other 140 men who comprised the logging camp crew. It was while driving the bus that she learned of an injunction on logging obtained by the Sierra Club Legal Defense Fund on behalf of itself, the Audubon Society, the Wilderness Society and Alaska Legal Services. The claim was relatively simple: logging in the area threatened the subsistence lifestyle of two Alaska natives.

June Christle was incredulous. First, she was shocked that the lives of 200 men and their families and this valuable and most useful economic activity could be sacrificed simply because of an alleged decrease in the amount of deer available for harvesting by two Alaska natives. Second, she was stunned that the ANILCA, which she had read, could be so misapplied. June Christle is never one to remain silent.

"You guys shouldn't take this lying down," she told the men on the crummy. "Section 404 isn't just for native Alaskans, it is for rural Alaskans. You 200 men and the 400 members of your families have just as much right to the economic activity crucial for your existence as the two people the Sierra Club is representing."

Soon word of what June Christle was saying on the crummy reached the owners of the company. They came to June Christle. "What can we do?" they asked. "Form a loggers' group and fight back," she told them. When they asked her if she would do it, she said, "Yes." From that very simple and straightforward beginning came the Loggers' Legal Defense Fund, which, under June Christle's leadership, quickly enrolled more than 7,500 loggers.

June Christle worked with attorneys to file a "friend of the court" brief on behalf of the Loggers' Legal Defense Fund, while putting pressure on the federal government and the State of Alaska to take a tough stand, not only on behalf of the loggers and economic activity, but also on behalf of a correct reading of the ANILCA. At the same time, June Christle allied the loggers group with fishermen in the area who were drawing the opposition of various environmental groups.

As to the allegations regarding the deer population, June Christle and her friends documented the actual cause of whatever deer depredation, if any, was occurring. They discovered the cause wasn't the logging. It was poaching and unregulated hunting, activities that should have been under the watchful eye of the Alaska Fish and Game Department. When the Loggers' Legal Defense Fund came to court, it came with photographs documenting that the Sierra Club's case was founded on a falsehood. June Christle and the loggers won.

June Christle wasn't done. She was furious that one of the key players in the case had been Alaska Legal Services (ALS). Funded with taxpayer dollars, including dollars from the people of Hoonah, ALS had joining with the Sierra Club to shut down timber harvesting. June Christle wanted to learn more about ALS. She obtained ALS's charter and discovered that, while subsistence lawsuits were the least important of the 15 types of lawsuits in which ALS could engage, 21 of the 27 lawsuits in which ALS had engaged were subsistence lawsuits. Furthermore, these lawsuits were basically "environmental lawsuits" in which ALS challenged economic activity.

"What really fried me was that while Alaska Legal Services was telling the legislature that it was helping the poor, it was using these lawsuits to shut down economic activity and to make more money, through court-awarded fees, to file even more lawsuits. I decided to cut their funding and I did it. Here in Alaska people know if you are politically active. The people in Juneau know me, they know I'm credible and they know I will not shut up."

That's when June started a newsletter she called *Old Growth* and began sending it out to everyone she thought was involved in issues similar to hers. She began to reach out to find experts who could help her, and she began to respond to calls for help from others—including a young woman fighting the National Park Service in Virginia, Alice Menks.

In 1990 June learned of a conference being held in Denver, Colorado, sponsored by Grant Gerber's Wilderness Impact Research Institute. She knew she had to be there to make more contacts and to network with new friends and potential allies. The only thing that kept her from boarding the plane for the Lower 48 was an emergency she had to handle: one of her firm's tugboats sank in Los Angeles harbor. Nonetheless, two of her members made the trip.

"I realized that we needed help, that we needed to work with others. Just because we had won one battle didn't mean they wouldn't come back again. I remember what had happened to the oil business and to mining. I knew I had to get personally involved, so I went to one of the Wise Use Leadership Conferences. Part of the answer for all of us is to communicate about our successes, to share what we know and to move ahead in our local areas."

June Christle was soon named President of Alliance for America, "by default," she claims. The real reason, she admits, is the fact that everyone knows her because of her efforts to spread the word, to be available to anyone who needs help and to learn everything she can about winning the battle against radical environmentalists. "My thing is making sure people know you can do this, knowing that you are right, that you can fight and win this battle ethically.

"When I got to the first Alliance meeting, I had no idea what was going on with private property. I thought it was basically a western battle involving federal lands. Today I know this is a national battle that involves the use of any land. What I want people to know is that there are tools they can use. They can get the information they need and they can make use of it to fight back. It's simple stuff, but most people don't know it."

True to her ideals, when the western-led, 1993 bipartisan filibuster erupted in response to one of Secretary Bruce Babbitt's first forays in the Clinton Administration's War on the West, June Christle was there. Earlier she had been contacted by filmmaker Roger Brown of Summit Films in Gypsum, Colorado, about a video he was producing on the contributions cattlemen make to the economic vitality and environmental well being of the West. June Christle helped to ensure that the video was finished, helped put it on 18 state-wide public broadcasting stations, and then had the film premiered in Washington at the annual Fly-In for Freedom, a premier attended by a virtual *Who's Who* of Congressional friends of property rights. The event was the kickoff for the victorious filibuster.

Meanwhile, June Christle was behind the scenes, working with congressional staff, drafting language and talking points, while assisting with the development of tactics, all of which helped to lead to a major first victory in the defeat of Babbitt's damaging grazing and western water language. June Christle relishes that victory. "In the past the trip to Washington, D.C. has been about timber, as it had to be. For the first time we reached out to deal with the other issues facing us. We demonstrated that we can work together, that we can fight back and we can win."

In Hoonah, Alaska, where June Christle lives, there is no priest for the tiny Catholic congregation. Thus, it is with June's leadership that the bake sales and the clothing drives are conducted. It is through her—June has been trained as a eucharist provider—that the host is received, and it is June Christle who delivers the sermon. On Thanksgiving Sunday, before preparing the meal she and her husband would enjoy, June Christle was at church, serving her faith and the men and women in whom she believes.

When friends mention such things, June snorts "I'm no saint!" Perhaps not, but certainly a hero.

ROBERT E. GORDON, JR., AND BENJAMIN W. PATTON
Washington, D.C.

Groucho Marx is reputed to have once resigned his membership in an organization asserting, "I don't care to belong to any club that will accept me as a member."

In March 1989 Robert E. Gordon, Jr. and Benjamin W. Patton found themselves in much the same position as Groucho Marx. Both were committed naturalists, nature enthusiasts and lovers of the out of doors. However, they were also conservatives. They believed in limited government, in property rights, in Constitutional guarantees and in the free market system. As they explored the realm of left-leaning if not downright socialist nature and environmental groups they discovered groups to which they didn't care to belong.

Rob Gordon and Ben Patton realized that if they wanted to combine their love of nature with their belief in mankind, their belief that people are the most important resource, that people are not the problem, but uniquely the solution, they would have to create their own organization. They did—The National Wilderness Institute (NWI).

Rob Gordon, who grew up in New York and Oklahoma and received a B.A. in Soviet Studies and Russian from Vanderbilt University after studies at Moscow State University and the Pushkin Institute in St. Petersburg, knows the out of doors as few environmentalists ever will. An avid mountain climber, he has scaled Mount Rainier (14,410 feet) in Washington State and Cotopaxi (almost 20,000 feet) in Ecuador. He has traveled alone by dugout canoe and on foot into the wilds of Ecuador's Amazon Basin where he studied butterflies, other insects and monkeys.

In fact, Rob Gordon was in Ecuador during the volcanic eruptions and devastating mud slides that killed 10,000 or more. It was there that he acquired a healthy skepticism regarding the

73

capability of government when, as a result of government in-
competence, he was presumed dead, his parents notified and
asked to come to Quito to identify his body.

Ben Patton, who received a B.A. from Georgetown University in Washington, D.C. in government and Spanish, with a
concentration in Latin American studies, is also an outdoorsman.
He is an ardent duck hunter, a devoted (is there any other kind?)
fly fisherman, an experienced offshore sailor, and a fixed-wing
pilot.

While Ben Patton was never presumed dead in the rain
forests of South America, as a "military brat" he traveled throughout the world. As the grandson of General George S. Patton and
the son of a major general he is also the inheritor of a legacy of
service, heroism and leadership. In his grandfather's words, "Wars
may be fought with weapons, but they are won by men. It is the
spirit of the men who follow and of the man who leads that
gains the victory."

In 1989 Rob Gordon and Ben Patton founded The National Wilderness Institute as a common sense grassroots environmental group committed to presenting a different world view,
a view that sees humans as the solution and not as the problem.
In Rob Gordon's words, the "NWI view of the world is one that
allows us to be concerned about the environment and still believe in science, in technology, in economic growth and, most
importantly, in people."

The NWI approach takes the long term view, in which its
philosophy is achieved not by a lot of sensational acts but by a
methodical placing of one brick atop another. It is also a philosophy that involves the nitty-gritty painstaking nuts and bolts
researching and gathering of the facts and figures necessary to
take on NWI's opponents. For example, it is to NWI and its
groundbreaking research on the Endangered Species Act that most
people turn for accurate information of the impact of the statute.

As Rob Gordon has noted, "I have come to believe that
one of the greatest forms of pollution is the useless, inane or
deceptive environmental information, stories and propaganda
being heaped upon our society. There is so much of it that it's
often hard to pay attention." Rob Gordon and Ben Patton work
hard to replace nonsense with common sense and the deceptive
with the forthright, simply because the facts are on their side.

"All of the indicators we might care to examine—whether those regarding air quality, water quality, birds, fish, or wild game—run contrary to the central tenets of status quo environmentalism. That is the case because the learning curve is green. We are constantly learning more and improving current technology and thus our ability to utilize and to conserve available resources.

"Dr. Julian Simon's victory in his famous wager with Paul Ehrlich, butterfly specialist and well-known planetary doomsayer, proves the point. Simon bet that any basket of goods selected by Ehrlich would decrease in price from 1980 to 1990. Ehrlich took the challenge, called Simon a 'Space Quacko Economist,' and said that the bet was laughably easy. Simon won hands down because Ehrlich failed to account for the most important resource of all—progress brought about by human ingenuity and creativity. We have the ability to alter our environment for the better. We are more efficient thanks to progress, which is inspired through the incentives of a free market and private property. That's what makes the learning curve green."

Ben Patton, whose grandfather's heroics sought to achieve the freedom we are only now seeing in the USSR and Eastern Europe, marvels that "while the rest of the world is rushing away from government control because it has failed both the economy and the environment, this country is rushing toward it. There is little evidence to support the idea that government ownership of a resource is good for the resource; in fact, there is quite a mountain of evidence to the contrary."

Rob Gordon and Ben Patton seek to slow that rush not only by providing the information that those who share their view need to fight back but also through publications (including *NWI Resource* magazine and *Fresh Tracks* newsletter), numerous television, radio and magazine interviews, consultation and testimony to the Congress and federal agencies, as well as numerous press briefings and appearances before audiences throughout the country.

Rob Gordon is optimistic. "Clearly we are demonstrating that we do have an impact. We started NWI with virtually no backing simply because we believe as we do. We have found that there are millions who share our view and we are growing fast."

At last, Rob Gordon and Ben Patton, naturalists, lovers of nature, believers in the intrinsic worth and ability of human beings, and philosophical conservatives have found the club in which they wish to be accepted as members.

TERESA PLATT
Coronado, California

When Teresa Platt says, "The last few years have been quite harsh on our tuna industry," it is the epitome of understatement. For the American tuna fishermen, like western ranchers, timbermen, miners, the oil and gas industry, furriers, owners of private property and others, have been the target of a vicious and premeditated assault.

It is an assault that combines the seemingly endless funding of radical environmental groups, an apparently unlimited supply of audacity and gall by the leaders of those groups, the gullibility, carelessness and even negligence of the national media and the willingness of Hollywood's elite to embrace the latest trendy politically correct cause.

For the assault upon Teresa Platt and her colleagues in the American tuna industry—which is made up largely of Americans of Italian and Portuguese descent—had nothing to do with saving the Earth, or even the dolphin. It had everything to do with the anti-human agenda of environmental groups, which require hype and hysteria to retain their power and to raise their money.

Teresa Platt, her family and friends fish for tuna in the Eastern Tropical Pacific Ocean (ETP) an eight million square mile area stretching from California to Hawaii and then to Chile. The ETP produces 25% of the world's supply of canned tuna. It is the world's largest yellowfin tuna fishery, producing 30% to 40% of the world's supply of that marvelously flavorful fish.

It is yellowfin tuna, because of its high yields, wonderful taste and quality, that makes it possible for U.S. fishermen and U.S. cannery workers to compete toe-to-toe with low-wage workers worldwide. In Teresa Platt's words, "We are truly blessed to have access to this fish in such abundance in the Eastern Tropical Pacific Ocean.

"There is one hitch, though: the larger mature yellowfin swim beneath herds of dolphin and we have to encircle both the dolphin and the fish to catch the yellowfin. But there are many

77

benefits from fishing for the large tuna which swiim in association with dolphins. By concentrating the fishing on the schools
of primarily large yellowfin, allowing the young fish to repro-
duce, the fishery is bept beautifully healthy. Also, since the tuna
and the dolphins compete for the same food source, removing
the aggressive tuna from beneath the dolphins free up food for
the dolphins, keeping them healthy. It is a system in which
management by man offers balance and a positive impact."

Fishermen are careful to release the encircled dolphins
unharmed, since it is unlawful to harm them and fishermen need
dolphins to help them find and hold the yellowfin. You don't
hurt your scouts.

In fact, according to a report by the National Academy of
Science, "Dolphin and the Tuna Industry," commissioned by the
U.S. Congress, the U.S. fleet is currently releasing unharmed an
almost perfect 100% of the dolphins encircled during fishing.

Not surprisingly for Teresa Platt and others who have been
where she is today, that is not enough for radical environmentalists, whose goal is to "stick it to the U.S. tuna industry." That
is what they have done.

Using an eleven minute, highly-edited, video filmed
aboard a renegade fishing boat, radical environmentalists hood-
winked the gullible unquestioning American media into asserting that what was shown on the video was not only "representative of the U.S. fleet," but was filmed aboard an American vessel.
In fact, as Teresa Platt and her colleagues with the non-profit
Fisherman's Coalition discovered, almost nothing the anti-tuna
crowd said about the video and how it came to be was true.

Why it took tiny Teresa Platt and her friends to uncover
the lies and deception involved in the video that destroyed more
than 10,000 jobs and left the U.S. tuna industry a shadow of its
former self is a story in and of itself. Instead of doing its job of
investigating and questioning, the media became part of the rush-
to-judgment, legislation-by-headline and facts-be-damned mentality of those with an all too obvious axe to grind.

In fact, the boat upon which some 100 dolphins were
killed was not registered in the U.S., but Panama, carried nets
that are not to be used in the ETP since they do not permit dolphins to escape, was operated by a crew untrained to ensure
dolphin release, and was operated in a manner that had it been
a U.S. boat would have drawn heavy fines and jail time for its
crew. Yet the media bought the radical environmentalists' line

that this was not only a part of the U.S. fleet but was "representative of the U.S. fleet." Not surprisingly, legislation that decimated and almost destroyed the U.S. tuna industry soon followed.

Yet, if Teresa Platt and others like her have anything to say about it, the U.S. tuna industry may be wounded but it is not dead. Teresa Platt and her friends are fighting back. Why did Teresa Platt get involved?

"Because I couldn't stand it anymore. My back was up against the wall and I had to fight back. The environmentalists had been getting away with murder—the murder of our jobs, our heritage, our families, our fishery, our ocean. Our statements to the press were censored. Our video footage on fishing the correct way was never shown.

"There are fishermen who have been out there for thirty years who know that tuna fishermen do their best to protect, the tuna fishery, the health of the ocean and the dolphins. Who got paid off to get video footage that tries to prove otherwise? I want to replace the manufactured lie with an image of what tuna fishing is all about: good people going to sea, leaving family, sailing thousands of miles, catching hundreds of thousands of tons of fish, transporting that fish across the oceans of many countries, processing that fish around the world for people to enjoy worldwide.

"I am proud to be fighting for fishermen who want control over their lives again, who want to be able to fish in their traditional fishing grounds. We have been on the receiving end of this hate too long. We just couldn't take it anymore."

Teresa Platt and her friends will no longer be victimized. While the years ahead are uncertain ones, tuna fishermen are facing them with courage and hope rather than with timidity and fear.

CHARLES S. CUSHMAN
Battle Ground, Washington

Every morning at the mine you could see him arrive,
He stood six-foot-six and weighed two-forty-five.
Kind of broad at the shoulder and narrow at the hip,
And everybody knew you didn't give no lip to Big John!
                                        —Jimmy Dean

The fictional "Big Bad John" of Jimmy Dean's imaginary coal mine was nowhere near as imposing as the real world's Chuck Cushman. However, like Big John, there's no missing Chuck Cushman's arrival at a mine, a ranch, a farm, a working forest, or, more likely, in the small towns of America—to lead the fight against oppressive government and for property rights.

When the National Park Service threatens to sweep more private property into an ever-expanding park, when the U.S. Forest Service threatens to eliminate economic activity, or when local politicians cave in to pressure from national environmental groups for more land lockup, the call often goes out to Chuck Cushman's American Land Rights Association in Battle Ground, Washington.

In a meeting hall filled with frustrated and furious local citizens, Chuck projects a confident and cheery presence. A large powerfully built man, he brings to his audiences not just the skills of a masterful political tactician, but also a sense of humor that allows people to turn anger in creative directions.

Cheerfulness and enthusiasm are Chuck Cushman's greatest gifts to those who turn to him. He helps others respond to oppressive hurt with outrageous humor. He has helped frightened residents and business people fight back with such success that opponents have dubbed him "Mr. Rent-A-Riot." It is an insult he wears like a badge of honor.

Recognizing intuitively the truth in Saul Alinski's *Rules for Radicals* that "ridicule is man's most potent weapon," Chuck Cushman's publicity stunts have made the media howl with laughter while exposing the duplicity and deceit of radical environmentalists.

When a Congressman introduced legislation putting loggers out of work but offering to retrain them as service workers, Chuck Cushman sent a 300-pound logger into the Congressman's office carrying a chain saw and a reader-board which declared: "I want to be retrained. I want to be the Congressman's brain surgeon." The television cameras loved it. Environmental groups loathed it. The Congressman was stunned.

Yet Chuck Cushman did not grow up in the small town settings he now calls home, surrounded by the rural Americans who regard him as a friend and neighbor. He was born and raised in Los Angeles. As a young Boy Scout he rowed Audubon Society members to Anacapa Island for bird-watching. He was even a member of the Sierra Club.

As a young man he hawked peanuts at Dodger Stadium, then, during the 1960s, he exchanged his vendor's tray for the briefcase of a highly successful insurance executive. Thirteen times he qualified for the prestigious Million Dollar Round Table. He also got involved in his community helping to teach disabled children, eventually chairing Los Angeles Mayor Tom Bradley's Education Committee.

In 1970, following his father's example, Chuck Cushman purchased a cabin in the village of Wawona inside Yosemite National Park. The cabin wasn't much, but it was a home away from home, a restful retreat far from the hectic pace of Los Angeles. When Chuck bought his cabin he thought the National Park Service was the "good guys." After all, his father had been a seasonal ranger at Yosemite for years, and as a teenager Chuck had served as a Student Conservation Corps volunteer in Olympic National Park.

One day National Park Service bureaucrats told his father he had to sell his cabin to the government or he would never work for them again. Sadly, Chuck's father moved out and stood silently as his cabin was burned to the ground. Each weekend Chuck returned to find another neighbor's cabin destroyed by fire. Finally, the same bureaucrats tried to muscle Chuck out of his cabin.

Chuck Cushman fought back. He discovered a well-disguised National Park Service plan to force private property owners out of the parks "to protect the resources." He soon discovered something even worse, a program of endless expansion, growing all the national parks bigger and bigger and continually creating new parks by confiscating a hundred homes here and a dozen businesses there.

The arrogance and coercion he found within the National Park Service, as well as the deception and outright lies, left Chuck Cushman a changed man. He organized his fellow property owners in Wawona. Their campaign forced the National Park Service to end its plan to destroy Wawona.

Other communities suffering from the same government oppression learned about the property owners' victory in Wawona. They wanted to learn how to fight back. In 1978 the National Park Inholders Association was formed with Chuck Cushman as its volunteer Executive Director.

"We organized property rights groups in 50 parks that first year," says Chuck, "and took horror stories right to Washington. Congress was incensed. They heard us, and revoked the National Park Service's condemnation authority."

Chuck Cushman soon learned that other federal agencies were destroying private property rights all over America. In 1980 he expanded and renamed his organization the National Inholders Association to address all hostile takeovers of private property by the federal government.

"We are not anti-park," he said. "We're pro-people. Parks and wilderness areas can be positive where they do not damage the socio-economic fabric of rural America. Just like two aspirin, parks can be very beneficial. But a hundred aspirins will put you in the hospital. Many rural communities are in need of economic hospitalization because their infrastructure has been destroyed by removing too much land from the tax base."

Chuck Cushman found himself invited to hundreds of counties, local communities, school districts, landowner groups and multiple-use organizations eager to learn his tactics in fighting back. He established a lobbying presence in Washington, D.C. and pioneered political opposition to unbridled environmentalism, winning victory after victory.

Chuck Cushman's stature as a defender of private property rights grew to the point that President Ronald Reagan named him to the National Park Advisory Board. His opponents didn't like him, but they couldn't ignore him.

From his old farmhouse in Battle Ground, Washington, Chuck Cushman uses computers, modems, fax machines and other tools of the modern age to call out floods of letters and telephone calls to Congress. His tactical ability is legendary. While in the field, his mastery of the imaginative non-violent protest demonstration led *Time* magazine to recognize him as "The tank commander of the Wise Use Movement."

Yet Chuck Cushman is not just the master tactician and inspirational and enthusiastic leader. Like the "Big Bad John" of song, he is down in the "muck and the mire" of the grassroots battle. For people and communities fighting the arrogant power of the federal government and the billion-dollar-a-year strength of environmental groups, Chuck Cushman is the one, who like Big Bad John, gives a "sagging timber a mighty shove," that allows besieged citizens to cry out, as Big John's miners did, "There's a light up above!"

MARGARET ANN REIGLE
Cambridge, Maryland

"The devil," it is often said, "is in the details." Margaret Ann ("Peggy") Reigle, who began her professional life as a Certified Public Accountant with Arthur Young & Company, is a master of even the smallest detail. Not surprisingly, it was her attention to detail, plus persistence and hard work, that ensured Peggy Reigle's rapid move up various corporate ladders in New York City. Her career culminated when she became Vice President of Finance of *The New York Daily News*, the largest daily circulation paper in the country.

Yet she and her husband discovered that their demanding executive careers left precious little time to be together. Both were on the fast track, but they didn't like where that track was taking them. They concluded that there was more to life than big bucks and boardrooms. In 1987 they gave up more than two decades in New York City for rural life on the Eastern Shore of Maryland. Peggy Reigle, granddaughter of a waterman and a farmer, wasn't just visiting, she intended to put down roots deep into the fertile soil of Maryland. She invested her life savings in an abandoned farm along the Choptank River to restore it to farming, but also, in due course, to subdivide and to sell 14 lots ranging from 5 to 22 acres to fund an "early retirement."

In March 1989 following then-Vice President Bush's thoughtless campaign promise of "no net loss" of wetlands, four federal agencies, with the stroke of a pen, changed the manual used to delineate wetlands. As a result Peggy's 138 acre farm was no longer "uplands," but instead were "wetlands," and thus "waters of the United States" as defined by the Clean Water Act, and thereby subject to the control of the U.S. Government, primarily the U.S. Army Corps of Engineers. Yet because she had no immediate need to change the use of her property, Peggy saw no need to challenge the federal designation of her lands as "wetlands."

Peggy Reigle's land was not the only land affected by the "wetland" policy change. The same pen used by the faceless

85

bureaucrats to change the status of her farm tripled the amount of "wetlands" in Peggy's Dorchester County—from 84,000 to 259,000. As a result, more than 68% of this very rural county along the southeastern edge of the Chesapeake Bay fell under federal control.

Neighbors of Peggy Reigle, Irma and Joe Phillips, were from West Virginia, and like Peggy, had invested their life savings in 22 acres of land that they had divided into two lots. It was on one of those lots that they intended to build their retirement home, financed by the resale of the other, so that they might live the rest of their lives near their daughter and grandchildren.

For Irma and Joe, the new wetlands manual had devastating consequences. When Irma and Joe applied for a permit to use their land, the Corps and the EPA told them in writing that they had not satisfied federal wetlands requirements and arrogantly and callously suggested they look for property outside Dorchester County upon which to build. Thus, as a result of the Corps' new manual and the resulting restrictions, Irma and Joe's property was rendered worthless, thereby obliterating their life savings.

In May 1990 Irma came to Peggy in tears, no longer able to cope with the fact that a bureaucracy on the far side of the Chesapeake Bay had suddenly taken their life savings. That's when Peggy stepped in. "Irma, don't think about it anymore. I'll deal with it." Peggy set out to provide the detailed technical response required for resubmission of Irma and Joe's permit request. The more she learned of how the bureaucrats had written their own agenda into federal policy, a policy that had been neither reviewed nor endorsed by Congress, the angrier she became. "I was outraged at what the agencies were doing to Irma and Joe."

Peggy Reigle's anger needed an outlet. Moreover, she believed that there was no way that President Bush, in his commitment to a "kinder, gentler" nation, could be aware of the impact of his administration's wetlands policy on rural senior citizens and "mom and pop" landowners. Peggy wrote a five-page letter to President Bush. Knowing that he would never see it, she sent a copy to 80 Members of Congress and various news outlets.

When the story got into print, "my phone started ringing off the hook. Most of the calls were from people in situations similar to Irma and Joe's, people who wanted me to see their permits through the regulatory quagmire." Peggy urged landowners to get active in the political process. Then she formed an organization called the Fairness to Land Owners Committee (FLOC). On July 3, 1990, at a meeting of the Dorchester County Commissioners, FLOC erupted on the scene with 150 landowners urging county officials to issue a proclamation of crisis to President Bush. The following week the county commissioners signed and mailed that proclamation. Subsequently, Peggy traveled throughout rural Maryland and got nine other counties to do the same.

Peggy Reigle began traveling around the country, testifying at hearings and meeting with landowners who had similar stories to tell. In the process, she discovered whole communities at risk as a result of the plans of covetous bureaucrats for a park, wildlife refuge or some other "environmental" purpose. Today, FLOC has over 13,000 members in 46 states, mainly "moms and pops" who have been abused by the government. "They're not real estate developers or oil and timber interests, entities that have well-paid lobbyists in Washington, D.C. These are little people who lack political clout and who are not represented by their elected officials."

Peggy's purpose in creating the Fairness to Land Owners Committee was simple: to do for thousands of others throughout the country what she had done for Irma and Joe. She would be there when what she calls the "eco-fascists" came crashing through the castle door. She would give the unrepresented a voice. Today, Peggy Reigle receives between 40 and 60 calls a month from people seeking guidance on dealing with over-zealous bureaucrats. For those who need more help than she can provide, Peggy works with attorneys and consultants who provide assistance *pro bono* for the most egregious cases. In addition, she receives hundreds of calls each month from others seeking information or simply a shoulder on which to cry.

Peggy has drafted model legislation for private property rights protection acts, filed *amicus curiae* briefs in several important property rights cases, including *Lucas v. South Carolina Coastal Council* and *Dolan v. City of Tigard*, testified before the U.S. Congress and various executive committees, and addressed audiences of hundreds of landowners throughout the country.

Peggy Reigle has also sprung to the defense of those targeted and victimized by the "hang 'em high" tactics of wet-behind-the-ears-Department of Justice lawyers intent upon making an example of alleged "environmental criminals" and a name for themselves. She devoted a substantial portion of her time over the last two years to letting the nation know the outrage of the imprisonment of men like Ocie and Carey Mills of Florida, John Pozgai of Pennsylvania, and Bill Ellen of Virginia.

The injustice done Bill Ellen, while working as a project manager on land near Peggy Reigle in Dorchester County, was particularly appalling. Bill Ellen, a lifelong conservationist and environmentalist, was in the midst of his work to create a 103-acre wildlife sanctuary within a 3,200-acre estate when he was charged with and convicted of disturbing "wetlands," despite the fact that the Clean Water Act, under which he was prosecuted, never mentions "wetlands." Bill Ellen was imprisoned for six months. Peggy's only regret in her work for Bill was that, despite her effort and that of thousands of Americans across the country, she failed to obtain a pardon from President Bush for him.

Peggy believes in getting the message out. "If we are to turn this country around we must inform the American people of the abuse of the moms and pops." Peggy Reigle knows what it takes to get the story out. Her work on behalf of Bill Ellen brought coverage on *PBS's MacNeil-Lehrer Newshour, CBN's 700, Fox Network News, The Wall Street Journal, Insight* and 200 pages of national and local print coverage.

On other issues, she and FLOC have been featured in *Forbes, The New York Times, Insight on the News, CBS News, NBC News, Voice of America, The New York Newsday, The Washington Post, Tomorrow, The New American, MacNeil/Lehrer Newshour,* and *ABC Nightline.* The *MacNeil/Lehrer Newshour,* featuring 14 precious prime time minutes, pitted The Fairness to Land Owners Committee against the National Audubon Society. However, of all the coverage Peggy has obtained in the print media, she is proudest of an article that appeared in the September 2, 1991, issue of *Forbes* magazine written by the late nationally syndicated columnist, Warren Brookes.

"Warren educated and inspired me and, best of all, he made me laugh when I was angry and too serious. Warren became a great friend and he and his wife Jane were to spend Christmas 1991 with us. He became ill and passed away December 28, 1991. His death was a very personal loss to me and a profound loss to the property rights movement. No one understood economic and environmental issues better, could see through the mendacity of environmentalists more easily, or could communicate all of it more directly."

Peggy Reigle, a frequent witness before Congress and other federal entities, greatly fears the ever-growing abusive power of the government. "Legislators and overzealous regulators, fueled by the apocalypse rhetoric and junk science of the radical environmental movement, are waging the greatest war on private property rights in the history of this Nation. As a result, the most endangered commodity in this country today is private property, a basic right and freedom of the American people, which is protected by the Fifth Amendment to the Constitution of the United States. It is a principle upon which our Nation was founded, a principle which built this country and made it great.

"Under the guise of saving the environment, environmental zealots are fleecing landowners of their rights to the prudent use and enjoyment of their land. Legislators, bureaucrats and environmental hucksters are waging war against the real environmentalists—those who own and tend the land; those who produce the food and fiber for this great Nation."

Peggy draws a distinction between conservation—to which she believes most Americans, including herself, are committed—and confiscation, the weapon of choice for environmental groups. "I believe in conserving our natural resources. I don't believe in stealing people's private property. There's no reason we can't have clean air and clean water and good dirt in this country without stealing land. If the people believe we should not have development on the waterfront or elsewhere, they should be willing to pay for it because if it's in the public interest, the public should share the burden. If they want to make the whole Eastern Shore of Maryland a state park, let them. But let them reimburse the property owners for their investment."

When all of this started back in 1990, Peggy Reigle told her husband it would be over by Thanksgiving. Clearly there are things she would prefer to be doing, the things that brought her to the Eastern Shore of Maryland, things like family, farming, fishing, canning, quilting and gardening. Yet until the battle is over, until the onslaught against private property rights is turned back, Peggy Reigle, the master of detail, of persistence and hard work, will continue to answer her phone, provide advice to troubled land owners, publish the FLOC newsletter and play her part in defeating the diabolic plot to deny Americans their most critical civil right—the right to own and use their private property prudently.

Robert O. Voight
Lubec, Maine

Well I'm on the Downeaster Alexa,
and I'm cruising through Block Island Sound.
I have chartered a course to the Vineyard.
But tonight I am Nantucket bound.

*   *   *

I was a bayman like my father was before.
Can't make a living as a bayman anymore.
There ain't much future for a man who works the sea.
But there ain't no island left for islanders like me.
> —*The Downeaster "Alexa"* by Billy Joel.

B illy Joel's melancholy imaginary fisherman may have sailed out of Lubec, Maine, a historic fishing village of some 1,950 people on the easternmost point of the United States. "Downeast," as its hardy residents call it, is a land of raw, harsh beauty, of gnarled fir trees, of scrubby blueberry barrens, of rugged rocky coastline. Yet the independence of its people is as fierce as the landscape and the winters that have shaped it.

Billy Joel's fisherman, with his 28 lines of verse, is positively loquacious compared to the typical laconic "downeasterner." Friendly but restrained and almost unapproachable, cooperative but often unyielding in matters of principle, downeasterners give each other a wide berth. Tradition, family, community, heritage are all-important to the men and women of Lubec. Even though Bob Voight is one of them—a trusted friend and a good neighbor—they still call him "the new fellow from Washington."

"New" as his neighbors use the term is relative, since Bob Voight came to Lubec more than 25 years ago, came to Lubec to make his home after a 22-year career in the United States Air Force during which he had a number of tours in Washington, D.C. In Lubec, Bob worked as a consultant and writer of a monthly national economic forecast. Later he and his wife bought a motel that they still own and operate. In Bob's words, "I was looking for a different and larger challenge."

He could never have anticipated the challenge that awaited him. In May of 1988, when Bob returned to Lubec from a visit to Florida, a friend pulled him aside: "Have you heard? They want your land for a national park." Bob laughed it off. "They" might want his land. But, after all, it was *his* land, and he wasn't selling. Case closed!

In less than two years, Bob Voight was "up to my hips in a battle with the State of Maine Planning Office and the National Park Service." By then he recognized that the covetousness that he had brushed aside so cavalierly two years earlier posed a very serious threat that his land would be taken from him. He realized how serious it was when he learned that the State of Maine Planning Office and the National Park Service had been studying and surveying his land without his knowledge let alone his permission for ten years. They had been surveying Bob's land as part of an 18-mile stretch of coastline that they wanted to declare a National Natural Landmark.

Bob Voight, who considered himself an environmentalist, had watched the dramatic transformation in Washington, D.C., during his frequent tours of duty there, had watched as environmental concerns had become part of the political landscape and as statute after statute had been adopted to protect the quality of the human environment. His reading of the *Washington Post* had led him to conclude what most Americans believed: that the Audubons were saving birds, and that the other environmental groups were dedicated to doing good.

However, when he discovered what the National Park Service had been doing behind his back, when he discovered the plotting and the sneaking and the treachery, he knew he had to find out what was up Downeast. He became an active member of the Washington County Alliance and became educated in the hidden agenda of the environmentalists and their bureaucratic surrogates in what Bob Voight calls a "very destructive religious cult."

Bob found out that what he had learned from reading the *Washington Post* had not been right, or had ceased to be right, for he discovered that the environmentalists didn't want to simply clean up pollution. The environmentalists wanted to convert Maine into what they called a "wilderness museum."

It wasn't just the attempted creation of a National Park in Downeast Maine—in the course of which they had trampled upon the civil and property rights of local land owners—but the implementation of an entire "vision" of Maine's future, a "vision" that required a huge wilderness surrounded by limited areas of access for some forest products activity, some tourist activity, and small clusters where people could live.

A crucial component of the environmentalists' "vision" was the establishment of the Northern Forest Lands Council, the insidious prelude to the creation of a new federal-state governmental entity that would control some 26 million acres of privately owned land in Maine, New Hampshire, Vermont and New York State. Under this ambitious scheme, an area the size of Ohio would be removed from the control of four of the original Thirteen Colonies and would be placed in the hands of a superbureaucracy which—subservient to the federal dollars that would keep it alive and beholden to the environmentalists who served as the midwife at its birth—would be managed, not for people, but as part of the environmentalist "vision."

Bob Voight, a sturdy 70-year-old with a silvery mane, and a quiet, contemplative manner, realized he could not sit this one out, realized that too many of his fellow Maine residents did not know what was being done to them, were unaware of the threat being posed to their freedom and to their traditional way of life.

Bob took threats to freedom very seriously, for as a bomber pilot during World War II, he had not just fought against tyranny over Europe, he had spent years in a German prisoner of war camp. If he learned one thing during those years, it was that freedom is very precious and well worth fighting for.

He realized that what was needed in Maine was a way of fighting back, an organization to go toe-to-toe with the rich and powerful environmental movement. In early 1990 he and Erich Veyhl, a neighbor and friend, created the Maine Conservation

Rights Institute, an educational research organization dedicated to property rights and private conservation. As Bob says, "nothing in my life has been the same since."

He is involved in the Maine Conservation Rights Institute seven days a week at all hours of the day and night. His office is the electronic command post for a statewide organization of more than 400 members, disseminating mailings, communicating by telefax and modem and telephone, networking with people and organizations throughout Maine and the nation.

Bob Voight's organization has changed the political landscape in Maine. Described by the media as "a major counterforce to the land preservation movement of the 1980s [which] could change the course of public policy," it has, in Bob's words, "raised the awareness level of people across the state on the basic threat to their way of life."

He and his organization have done much more than that, stopping dead in its tracks the National Park Service plan to create a Downeast National Park out of private land along the coast of Maine, derailing the plans for the Northern Forest Lands Council, and seriously undercutting the credibility of the National Park Service's National Natural Landmarks program.

Like Billy Joel's lonely fisherman, Bob Voight continues his quiet quest of the elements, using the Constitution as his compass, led through the stormy seas of the political battles he fights daily by his belief that the constitutional rights of the individual must be respected and protected.

Like Billy Joel's fisherman, Bob Voight might be inclined to say, "I've got people back on land who count on me . . . [a]nd a good captain can't fall asleep."

DIXY LEE RAY
SEPTEMBER 3, 1914—JANUARY 2, 1994

In 1981 Dixy Lee Ray stepped down as the first—and still only—woman Governor of the State of Washington. She was 68 years old. She had enjoyed a remarkable career: twenty-nine years as an associate professor of zoology at the University of Washington, nine years as director of the Pacific Science Center, Nixon appointee as Chairman of the Atomic Energy Commission, then the first Assistant Secretary for Science in the U.S. Department of State and finally as Governor.

After years in the rough-and-tumble world of politics, Dixy Lee Ray was "wrung out" and "exhausted." She needed a rest, but she also needed to provide for herself. Dr. Ray let it be known that she would accept speaking invitations.

Selecting the topic was easy. Although she was nationally known as a public official, she had spent nearly four decades as a scientist, and more specifically, as a marine biologist. She would give speeches about science.

The year 1981 was a good year to be talking about things scientific. Increasingly the media was focusing on such matters, particularly environmental issues. However, Dixy Lee Ray had a unique perspective on these issues. She was feisty and independent. Her independence showed even in her name: she was born Margaret Ray but renamed herself after her favorite region—the South—and Civil War General Robert E. Lee. Most of all she valued her absolute integrity. She took nothing at face value and made up her own mind only after carefully sorting fact from fiction.

Years earlier, in the late 1960s when most Americans were first becoming aware of the environmental movement, Dr. Ray had already been offended by its extremism, its attacks on all

95

things technological, its assaults on modern civilization and its shrill return-to-nature advocacy.

Part of the reason was philosophical. Dixy Lee Ray was an old fashioned conservationist—a believer in good steward-ship, in the wise use of natural resources, and in the ability of mankind to live in productive harmony with nature. She had felt the bond with nature all her life: at age 12 she became the youngest girl to climb Washington State's highest stratovolcano, Mount Rainier, 14,410 feet.

Part of the reason was professional. Dr. Ray was a scien-tist who took great pride in her profession. She earned her un-dergraduate degree at Mills College in Oakland, California and a doctorate in zoology at Stanford in 1945. For years she hosted an educational television program teaching youngsters about the biology of the Puget Sound. She was greatly troubled by the "political science" being used to "prove" alleged environmental calamities and to justify environmental "cures." She had seen too much of that first-hand as a committee member of the Na-tional Academy of Sciences and National Science Foundation.

Part of the reason was personal. The "good old days" for which the environmental movement yearned and to which it wanted the nation to return were the days in which Dixy Lee Ray grew up in Tacoma, Washington, the second of five girls, days that were, in her words, "dirty, disease-ridden and smelly." "That's one of the advantages of living a long time," said Dr. Ray, "you know about such things."

When she returned to the lecture circuit in early 1981, it was to discuss one of the hot topics of the day: the state of the human environment and the future of the planet. What she had to say shocked and surprised those who heard her, for it was contrary to everything they had been hearing or reading in the media. She was outspoken and unafraid to state the truth, how-ever unpopular and politically incorrect it might be.

Dr. Ray's audiences wanted to know more. They wanted her speech in writing. They wanted to carry it around, to read it over and over, to study it, and to quote from it. In 1987 she sat down to write her book. Two years later, it became the first scientific book ever published by Regnery-Gateway. It grew into something more: the company's biggest seller ever!

The result was the marvelously readable yet thoroughly documented *Trashing the Planet*, which, despite not being marketed by a big New York publishing house, sold more than 100,000 copies and was republished in paperback. Thousands of those sales have been by word of mouth as Americans eagerly welcomed a book that challenged much modern mythology on environmental issues. It became a favorite reference of talk-radio icon Rush Limbaugh.

Dixy Lee Ray, the feisty biologist, had become a trendsetter. In large part due to the incredible success of *Trashing The Planet*, other much younger authors were inspired to address the topic first broached by Dixy Lee Ray. Yet Dixy Lee Ray had not exhausted the subject. She wrote another book: *Environmental Overkill: Whatever Happened To Common Sense?*

Dixy Lee Ray was the nation's best known conservative speaker, writer and thinker about environmental issues. Her opinions were sought by the nation's most influential leaders and respected by millions. Everyone who met her held her in highest esteem. She was beloved.

With a speaking schedule that would challenge the stamina of someone half her age, Dr. Ray pressed on, traveling from audience to audience—whether in person or via radio and television—to carry her message of truth, of hope and of a belief in the future of mankind.

She died at her island home at the age of 79 on January 2, 1994, of a severe bronchial virus contracted during a winter speaking engagement. True to form, she could be heard on a radio talk show blasting the Clinton administration's environmental policy just three days before she died.

Today she has her rest—the rest she refused to take in her all too short time here. We who grieve her passing also celebrate her life. The world is a richer place for her having come this way.

Dixy Lives.

LEON FAVREAU
Gorham, New Hampshire

Just up the road from Leon Favreau's Bethel, Maine, business, some 85 miles north of Portland and just east of the Maine - New Hampshire border, along Highway 26, lies the site of Grafton, Maine. Early in the nation's history, Grafton was a timber town that thrived upon the abundant timber resources of the White Mountains of New Hampshire and Maine. However, when the original white pine timber supply was exhausted, the community disappeared. Today all that remains of Grafton is an impressive wooden monument in the midst of a now-abundant forest. It honors the men and women of courage and vision who carved a community out of the harsh frontier.

Grafton, Maine, serves as a constant reminder to Leon Favreau. Grafton reminds him both of the need for the wise use of natural resources—to ensure a reliable supply of wood products—and of the need to strive constantly and mightily to avoid obsolescence.

It is because Leon Favreau not only understands such things but puts them into practice that 82 people in tiny (2,000) Bethel, Maine, are gainfully employed. For Leon is the embodiment of "Yankee ingenuity" and living proof that the greatest resource is the human mind, which, when combined with abundant and well-managed natural resources, can yield a quality human life and a healthy environment.

Hard work and long hours have always come naturally to Leon Favreau. He was only two years old when his father and mother moved their family from a small town in Canada's Quebec Province to the United States. His father, who wanted to be his own boss, had heard much of the American dream and how a person, if he but had the will and the willingness to work hard, could prosper. Those early years were not easy, and Leon remembers the many demands upon the family and the many sacrifices it made.

At an early age Leon worked at his father's mill where no job was too tough or too menial for him to perform. If his father believed in hard work and a quality product, he did not believe in more than minimal pay for his sons. In his father's philosophy, work was its own reward. In a way it was, for when Leon left home for college, he knew his father's business.

Leon Favreau worked his way through the University of Maine in Orono, earning a degree in civil engineering. For several years he worked for an engineering company, first in Pennsylvania, then Ohio, Alabama and finally, for another firm, in Berlin, New Hampshire. Although his father would have welcomed his return to the family business, it wasn't until after his father's death in 1979 that Leon returned to manage the mill his father had opened in 1959.

The mill—which manufactured components for furniture (railings and seats for stools, for example)—was doing well, but Leon was worried about the future. More and more companies were entering that segment of the market. Leon worried that his older mill would not be able to compete. He began to look around.

Leon Favreau, the civil engineer, and Leon Favreau, the man who had spent his youth working at the equipment in his father's mill, quickly spotted a niche. For years, the bending of hardwoods for such items as chair arms, backs and legs, had been an expensive and time-consuming process. Leon knew that some European mills had been experimenting with the use of electricity to accomplish the same feat.

After traveling to Europe and seeing the process first hand, Leon knew that it could be done in America. Just as quickly, he became frustrated with the bureaucratic and logistical difficulties involved in importing the European machines. So he designed his own.

The next years were busy. Leon Favreau modernized and expanded his father's business. He replaced equipment with his new designs, built new buildings, added new product lines, sought new customers, and hired additional employees. Today, Leon's approach to this age-old procedure is unique in the United States. Although very successful, it demands perfection. Yet despite such demands, Leon feels very lucky. He is doing exactly what he has always wanted to do.

In 1984 his life took another twist. One of his father's long-time business advisers gave Leon a copy of a book length document called, "The Draft Management Plan for the White Mountain National Forest." Leon was urged to read it.

Published by the U.S. Forest Service, the Plan set forth various management alternatives for the White Mountain National Forest for the next 50 years. Many of the proposed alternatives called for drastic reductions in the amount of timber available for harvesting. Leon Favreau worried first about the decreasing availability of raw materials for his business. However, as he became more involved in the Plan's review process, he was shocked to learn that the proposed decrease in timber harvesting had little, or nothing, to do with concern about forest health or good conservation practices, and almost everything to do with the lobbying efforts of nationally funded environmental groups.

Although a quiet and reserved man, hardly the stereotypical activist, Leon Favreau has never shied away from what he sees as his responsibilities—to his family, to his employees, and to his country. He chose to become involved. He participated actively and aggressively in commenting on and helping to ensure revision of the White Mountain plan. He knew that would not be enough. Thus, in 1987, Leon co-founded The Multiple Use Association, located in Gorham, New Hampshire, over which he presides to this day. The MUA's primary goal is to promote healthy forest management practices and sensible land management policies on public and private land. It accomplishes its objectives by hosting conferences, educational symposiums and by networking with other wise use groups across the country.

"I fully expect to be working part time as a pro-use forest activist until I retire. I see it as nothing more than a cost of doing business. I believe environmental zealots will be around virtually forever. I do not see the issue, as the media likes to portray it, 'a jobs-versus-the-environment issue.' Rather it is 'a wise use of resources versus non-use of resources issue.'

"America has a problem and it's called the environmental movement. Bringing sense to today's environmental movement is a job for everybody. People must educate themselves about both the environmental and wise use groups. If they make contributions to environmental groups, they better make sure they know what those groups stand for. Do not be fooled by a terrific looking exterior."

Leon Favreau, who believes he can learn something from each person he meets, has spent the last ten years looking beneath the exterior of both environmental and wise use groups.

"The wise use movement is true grassroots activism at its best. The one thing wise use groups have in common is a belief that people can work and recreate in harmony with nature. On the other hand, the environmental movement is about money and power and elitism and about using misinformation and bad science to scare the public."

Leon admits that he has come a long way in the last ten years: from an uninformed business owner to an activist always in search of new opportunities to educate people. A prolific writer of letters to the editors and commentaries that have been published throughout the country, he urges others to join with him in his battle.

"The danger is that not enough of us will act in time and because of this, we will continue to lose our rights, in small ways such as land use regulations or in large ways such as the formation of greenline areas and biological diversity reserves."

Leon Favreau knows that the loss of that freedom will destroy the economic incentives that now exist for those whose hard work, creativity and ingenuity make a better world for themselves and for others. He fears what would happen then—that of the hundreds of towns that depend upon the wise use of timber resources the only remaining trace would be a wooden monument like the one that stands at the site of Grafton, Maine.

PAULETTE PYLE
Lebanon, Oregon

In October 1992 Paulette Pyle was on her way east to Monument, Oregon, from her home on the west side of the Cascade Range in Lebanon. Traced on a map, the route stretches halfway across Oregon, the nation's tenth largest state. Unfortunately, that's not the half of it, since most of the route is designated as "scenic." While the view may be a feast for the eyes, the roadway itself demands much of the driver: it twists through two national forests, skirts several wilderness areas, and runs along narrow, winding roads with hairpin turns. On this day the switchbacks were very wet and slick.

Somewhere past Prineville, but short of Mitchell, Paulette Pyle rounded one of those switchbacks to encounter four deer leaping from both the left and right toward the middle of the road. Instantly she hit the brakes and one of the deer while the other three bolted for the woods to her right. Out of control, the car veered to the right and headed for the canyon. Only two cement posts supporting wire cables lining the edge of the road kept Paulette from plummeting hundreds of feet.

Characteristically, miles from nowhere, isolated in the middle of rural Crook County, Oregon, the next car by was driven by someone Paulette knew. Standing slightly dazed in her red suit and her ripped nylons, Paulette flagged down her 70-year-old friend, who had been out bird hunting. Marveling at the sight of her car, with what turned out to be more than $7,000 in damages, teetering on the edge of the road, her friend asked what she wanted to do.

"I'm due in Monument to give a speech to 200 people at the Grange Hall. They'll be there waiting for me. I told them I'd be there and I have to be there." Paulette was on a mission: a long time state senator who only half-heartedly supported the legislative needs of his rural natural resources district—Wayne Fawbush—was up for reelection. "Fawbush always wins by 50 or 60 votes and I know there'll be 200 voters in that hall. If I don't show up and Fawbush wins again, I'll never forgive myself."

So, for another two hours Paulette sat in her friend's pickup while he drove her to Monument to give the speech she'd promised to give. As for Fawbush, "We kicked his butt."

For Paulette Pyle, the battle against environmental extremism, against big government, against oppressive regulation, for private property rights, for the free enterprise system and for natural resources businesses is not just a job. It's a way of life, a passion, a tenet of her deeply-held religious faith. She comes by such tenacity and perseverance naturally—it was an essential element of her growing up.

Paulette is the oldest of eight sisters and brothers raised in an orphanage after their mother left a note and her children behind one winter morning in the piney woods of Georgia. When their logger and truck driver father returned to find the note he realized he couldn't take care of the children. He took them west to the grandparents and then to two Catholic orphanages, one for boys, another for girls.

"My folks were like something out of *Coal Miner's Daughter*. We were dirt poor, but we knew about hard work. All we had to do was watch our father. My earliest memory— in fact, we have the photograph—is of my sister and me sitting on our two mules, Maggie and Kate, as they pulled the logs out of the woods."

Paulette Pyle was in the sixth grade when the family moved west, where she lived at St. Joseph's Children's Home in Culdesac, Idaho, until she graduated from the eighth grade. She then went to live with John and Lillian Lustig—dairy, chicken and wheat farmers—while attending Saint Gertrude's Academy in Cottonwood, Idaho. She cannot remember a time, even then, when she was not deeply interested in and fascinated with politics. Yet in the 1960s her conservative inclinations were still dormant. She thought President Lyndon Johnson was "great" and U.S. Senator Barry Goldwater was "nuts."

From the time she was 16 years old Paulette worked at St. Mary's Hospital. On graduation from high school in 1965, she began working full time as a medical records technician. She took college correspondence courses to become certified in her field, got married and had four babies.

About the time her first child was born, her interest in politics had her paying close attention to then-Congressman, later U.S. Senator, James A. McClure, particularly his speeches about private property rights. "He had a profound effect on my early political thinking," says Paulette. "For the first time I began to understand the relationship between private property and the creation of wealth.

"By the time my twins were born in 1971, I had decided to get actively involved in politics. I remember carrying a twin on each hip to go door-to-door in Idaho's largest county, Idaho County, to campaign for candidates. There is no better way to learn grassroots. My real motivation came following my attendance at a candidates forum in Grangeville, Idaho, to hear some 30 different office seekers. One stood out: Steve Symms, a former Marine who owned an apple orchard in Nampa. He stood up there on the stage, with one of his apples in his hand and said, 'Join with me. Just like I'm going to do with this apple, help me take a bite out of government.'

"From then on I had the fever. I had found what I wanted to do. It was like the calling I had never found until that day. From then on I was involved in grass roots. That's the way it's always been for me. I've never been involved from the top down, only from the bottom up."

"Following the campaign, my husband and I moved to Lewiston where I worked at St. Joseph's Hospital until Steve Symms asked me to join his staff. I had five of the toughest counties in Idaho, but Steve carried every one of them nearly every time he ran. It was because of grassroots."

In 1976 Paulette remarried. Her husband, who had been working on a construction project in Lewiston, returned to Albany, Oregon, and Paulette went with him. In Oregon, she dropped out of politics. After all, she had her hands full raising the six children she and her husband shared.

Not surprisingly for someone with the "fever" of politics, her retirement didn't last long. In 1979 she helped Mike Fitzgerald, a conservative, take on a liberal wilderness advocate and timber opponent, Congressman Jim Weaver.

Shortly thereafter the herbicide battle broke out as the life-causes-cancer crowd, energized by the popularity of the fear-mongering of Rachel Carson's *Silent Spring* and other similar tracts, not to mention the panic that followed the cranberry and then the cyclamate scare, declared war on the use of herbicides in Oregon, the nation's most fertile and most diverse natural resources state.

That was when her friends began calling Paulette, urging her to apply for a job with the newly established grassroots organization, Oregonians for Food and Shelter (OFS). Paulette didn't know. With a name like OFS, she was hesitant. It sounded pretty liberal to her.

Ultimately, after learning of the organization's goals and objectives, her friends won her over. Paulette Pyle was interviewed, offered the job, and accepted only after being assured that the job would only last until July or November 1980 at the latest. If herbicide opponents failed to get enough signatures to put the herbicide ban on the ballot, the fight would end in July. If it got on the ballot, the campaign would end in November.

Paulette's employers had guessed right. Unfortunately, they had also guessed wrong. As they had hoped, the initiative failed to get on the state-wide ballot. As a result, it was over in July. However, unexpectedly, the Lincoln County Medical Society's proposed ban on forestry aerial and roadside use of phenoxy herbicides got on the ballot in Oregon's Lincoln County. Paulette and a young lawyer named Dave Dietz were assigned to run the campaign to defeat the initiative.

Their first survey was a shocker. Had the vote been taken on the day of the survey, Paulette and friends would have lost by a two to one margin. Knowing she had her work cut out for her, she called her husband. She probably wouldn't be home for the next six weeks, she told him. Over the next month and a half, Paulette and friends spent $80,000 on a grassroots campaign in support of timber and against the county's most prestigious citizens—the medical doctors. On the day of the vote, Paulette and her friends won by a two-to-one margin.

Paulette Pyle has been with Oregonians for Food and Shelter (OFS) ever since. Shortly after the Lincoln County campaign the organization became a nonprofit public interest education organization committed to ensuring the survival of Oregon's vitally important natural resources industry. Over the years, in one of the "greenest" states in the country, OFS, in Paulette Pyle's words, "has never lost a lawsuit, never lost a ballot initiative, and never had a bad legislative session. Because we're successful, people automatically turn to us for help."

Paulette believes OFS is successful because "it is like a part of my religion. I'm in this thing heart and soul. Some people say you shouldn't become too political, that it will come home to bite you. I don't believe that. I'm here to make a difference and if I have to take risks, then I'll take risks. If you don't take risks you can't accomplish anything."

As anyone involved in natural resource activities in Oregon will readily attest, Paulette Pyle has accomplished a lot. In addition, she is highly regarded and respected across Oregon's diverse resource constituencies. One reason: "We never miss one of their meetings." Another reason: "When there is a problem, the person doesn't have to be an OFS member. If that person is part of our natural resource base—a rancher, a logger, a wheat farmer, hog farmer, mint farmer, grass seed grower, whatever—we'll be there."

Paulette Pyle doesn't want to win just for her members and her constituency. Because she is committed to natural resource activities she works tirelessly for all those involved in them. That kind of commitment has led her to the type of strategic thinking crucial to long-term victories.

"We began to realize that no matter how many votes we won in the legislature, we were always fighting an uphill battle because we had lost the first vote—the vote for speaker of the house and president of the senate. We also realized that many of our rural friends—people who are suffering most directly because of the legislation favored by environmental extremists—were electing the very people who were putting in anti-rural leaders. We decided to turn that around.

"It became a whisper campaign, 'win the first vote,' all around the state, in rural community after rural community. If people wanted to be successful during the legislative session, we told them they had to win that first vote." That campaign, and an agriculture political action committee Paulette helped organize, enabled her and her friends in agriculture to take over the State House and to come within two members of controlling the State Senate for the first time in more than 20 years. All this while President George Bush was losing to Governor Bill Clinton.

"We took a page out of the book of the environmentalists. For years they have been deciding what candidates support their views and working to get them elected or keep them in office. I started going to their meetings to discover who those folks were so we could go after them."

Paulette Pyle is always available, whether campaigning with walking pneumonia or calling out the troops while flat on her back recovering from surgery. If something needs to be done, Paulette is there.

"Honest to God, you have to have that kind of commitment. You have to have the fever. You have to believe, to know it is the right thing to do and to do it with all of your heart and soul. I don't have much patience with those who operate from any other premise, that's why I love the Bruce Vincents, the Jackie Langs, the Valerie Johnsons, the Rita Kaleys, the Mike Millers, the Evelyn Badgers, the Sharon Becks, the Mack Birkmaiers, the Paul Moreheads and the Andy Andersons.

"I always remember what one of the nuns in the orphanage said to me. 'How you turn out is entirely up to you. It all depends how much you are willing to put into the effort."

For Paulette Pyle, who stood alongside the road next to a car she had just destroyed, wondering only how she would get to Monument, Oregon, to speak to friends to whom she had made a promise, the answer is simple. She puts in everything she's got and intends to keep it up. "As long as I can be what I believe, I'll be politically involved."

BRIAN UNNERSTALL
Frohna, Missouri

The crudely made sign erected along side the road read in bold letters, "DEATH TOLL," and then in smaller letters, "Total Number of Log Trucks out of Fairview." Two pegs permitted the double digits posted to be changed. On this day they read, "87." Beneath the number, the sign read: "EACH TRUCK IS A HEARSE FOR 10 TREES."

Such was the rhetoric regarding an almost insignificant timber sale in the nation's second smallest, and Illinois' only national forest—the Shawnee National Forest south of Murphysboro, Illinois. Notwithstanding its size, what happened on the Shawnee is a microcosm of the national battle over prudent management policy by the U.S. Forest Service.

This timber sale on the Shawnee had it all. First, conflict erupted over a straightforward U.S. Forest Service sale that had been designed using thoughtful timber management practices. Then, environmentalists filed a seemingly endless stream of administrative appeals followed by federal lawsuits, which culminated in the rejection of the case by the U.S. Supreme Court. Protesters—mostly college students with too much time on their hands—chanted and sang, went on hunger strikes, perched in trees, buried themselves up to their necks in roads, chained themselves to logging trucks, and finally got themselves arrested. Criminal suits were followed by civil suits. Congressmen in districts hundreds of miles away—and in total ignorance of the facts—voiced outrage over the proposed logging. The media generated one-sided and largely fictional coverage of all these events. Finally, U.S. taxpayers lost a whopping quarter of a million dollars as a result of all these shenanigans.

It started out as a simple purchase of hardwood lumber slated by the U.S. Forest Service for sale. The Forest Service recognized the need to prepare the site for oak regeneration in an old and decaying part of the forest that had grown increasingly unsuitable as wildlife habitat. In 1985 the oak, hickory and pine on a 141-acre parcel of the Shawnee National Forest was pur-

109

chased for the East Perry Lumber Company of Frohna, Missouri, by its procurement forester, Brian Unnerstall.

"Although we most often purchase our timber from private lands throughout Missouri and Illinois, we thought this small sale from the Shawnee offered an opportunity to acquire some quality timber, while working for the long term health of the forest. By harvesting the trees in patches you are allowing sunlight to hit the forest floor. Oak needs full sunlight to grow. After we cut the timber, the Forest Service will go in and cut the little maple and beech trees down, leaving more room for the oak trees to grow. From every standpoint—economics, forestry, jobs, local revenues—it made sense. It seemed like a good idea at the time."

U.S. Forest Service procedures, permitting an appeal to be filed by anyone in the United States for the cost of a 29 cent stamp and stationery, yielded a number of objections to the sale. However, after reviewing the documents the Forest Service found the appeals to be without legal merit and denied them. Pausing just long enough to change the caption and the format on the appeal documents, opponents of the sale proceeded to federal court. At each stage in the litigation process the sale was upheld. When the U.S. Supreme Court refused to hear the case, the matter was closed. It had only taken four years.

In 1991 East Perry Lumber Company prepared to harvest the trees it had purchased. With the help of college students recruited from the University of Southern Illinois at Carbondale, opponents of the sale protested at the site. They built platforms high in the trees and perched there with their signs and their shouts. With "U" shaped bicycle locks fastened about their necks, they bolted themselves to logging trucks. They dug holes in logging roads and buried themselves up to their necks.

The protesters drew the attention of the local media, and soon the major media outlets in Chicago, including the *Chicago Tribune*. Their protests reached Washington, D.C., where various anti-resource Members of Congress threw in with the opposition, demanding investigations and a delay of the sale by the Forest Service. To its credit, the Forest Service held firm. "A deal is a deal." it said. "A sale is a sale." However, the Forest Service reconfigured the sale, eliminating the unattractive and thereby controversial "clearcuts" replacing them with well-shaped selective cutting units.

Finally, in 1991, four years from the time when the Forest Service sold the timber, the Forest Service was ready to proceed. So was Brian Unnerstall. "I don't see where the earlier delay helped anything or changed anything. We can't wait any longer. We need the wood to keep the mill running. They're asking us to hold off until they can find a reason to stop us. We're not stupid. We've given them enough opportunities."

Once again, the youthful protesters skipped class to drive to Fairview to protest the sale. This time it wasn't just college kids from the local area. Protesters came in from as far away as Washington, D.C. and Oregon. However, Brian Unnerstall recognized between one half and two thirds of the protester as "old hippies, local society outcasts who live in the backwoods or in two local artist communities, members of a ragtag group that calls itself RACE—Regional Association of Concerned Environmentalists." There was one other difference: this time the Forest Service was ready for them.

The Forest Service brought in reinforcements, including rangers from throughout the region. Local law enforcement personnel were notified and more than a dozen sheriffs and deputies from Jackson County were present. The roads leading to the sale were roped off, and areas for peaceful protest designated, so as not to interfere with the passage of East Perry's logging trucks.

Nonetheless, there were disruptions. Calling themselves the "Fairview Freedom Fighters," dressed in matching T-shirts, with long hair and beards being the norm, they screamed and waved signs at the loggers as they drove past into the sale area. "We think you are stupid," was the mildest of the epithets.

There were also arrests. Seventeen sale opponents were arrested, mostly for criminal trespass. However, four were charged with more serious crimes, including violating a closure order and aggravated battery of a police officer. In addition, the Forest Service discovered 29 spikes in the trees marked for harvest, spikes of the kind used as booby traps.

There were not just timber sale opponents. A handful of members of the pro-timber Conservation Coalition met at the Murphysboro Ranger Station for an "anti-demonstration" endorsing the Fairview sale. Chuck Daugherty, spokesman for the Coalition, which supports multiple use of forest land, said, "What these protesters are doing is wrong. We thought if we didn't say something soon, they might get their way."

Brian Unnerstall was there for all of it, overseeing the East Perry Lumber Company men and equipment while coordinating with Forest Service personnel. He had real concerns for his fellow employees. "The loggers' job is dangerous enough without having to worry about protesters. Our people don't need to be looking over their shoulders." Ironically, it was Brian Unnerstall himself who was involved in an episode that would reverberate long after the last log had left the mill.

As Brian Unnerstall drove through the protest area a scruffy protester ran alongside the East Perry Lumber Company pick up truck dragging a six-inch diameter log. Brian Unnerstall saw him coming and pulled his foot off the accelerator and began to tap the brake. Just as he did the protester leaned forward and heaved the log beneath the wheels of the pickup. Brian Unnerstall hit the brake but it was too late. The log spun beneath the pickup's wheels, snapped, and then swatted the protester. Off balance, he tumbled to the ground far behind the pickup.

Brian Unnerstall stopped at the Forest Service communication station just 100 yards down the road and reported the incident, asking that medical assistance be sent back. By the time help arrived, the protester had a very different story to tell. He had crawled beneath Brian Unnerstall's stopped pickup, he said, intending to use his body as a sacrifice to stop the sale. He said that the driver of the pickup saw him, made eye contact, and despite his presence beneath the truck, drove over his prone body with the truck's rear tires. He was seriously injured he said, although hospital officials could not verify his assertion that his torso bore tire treads.

The majority of the arrested protesters were booked and released after signing court documents swearing that they would not return to the sale area. Others charged with more serious crimes were booked, jailed and later tried. Meanwhile the logging trucks continued to roll.

Protesters scheduled a fast, not to stop the sale, they said, but to "make a strong political statement without fear of arrest or armed guards." One protester thought she was doing more than that, according to a local newspaper. "Although she dropped from 95 pounds to about 87, she felt she was able to eliminate some toxins that were stored in her body, free up the energy normally spent on digestion and become more in touch with her inner system."

Congressional rhetoric reached new heights. Congress-man Sid Yates of Chicago—whose only connection with a forest are the trees of Lincoln Park that face the high rise condomini-ums of Lakeshore Drive—demanded a halt to the harvesting. "I made it clear that it shouldn't take place. I tried to stop them, but I couldn't do it."

Even the local congressman, ignoring the economic ben-efits of the timber sale and the jobs being created, asked for more delay. Later, after the sale had been completed, the Forest Ser-vice gave him a tour of the area. He asserted, "You never are prepared for all this stuff lying on the ground. From a visual perspective, it looks awful." He concluded that the areas cut were "obviously too large," and said he would seek to bar such timber harvesting in the future until such time as everyone can agree on how large a cut is proper.

Subsequently, the Forest Service announced the results of the sale. While the environmental impact had been very posi-tive, the economic impact to federal taxpayers had not been. In the end, the Forest Service spent more than $315,229 bringing in rangers from other states to help control the protests. Origi-nally theForest Service's costs had been under $20,000, compared to receipts of $50,762. The Forest Service had projected a profit of $31,000. Now, because of the obstructionist tactics of the environmentalists, the sale was an economic loss, but not a sil-vicultural one.

Says Brian Unnerstall, "Our experience demonstrates the lie that is the so-called 'below-cost timber sales.' People who oppose any timber harvesting whatsoever tie these things up in the appeals process and before the courts and force the Forest Service to spend tens of thousands of dollars defending its deci-sions after spending tens of thousands of dollars in environmental studies to make the decision. Then they engage in civil disobe-dience at the sale site and force the Forest Service to spend even more. No wonder the Forest Service can't make money on some of these sales. But if they lose money on these sales, in truth it's not that logging is being subsidized by taxpayers, it's the fault of these environmentalists whose protests are being subsidized by the taxpayer."

The sale also carried a price for Brian Unnerstall. For four years he had worried over the sale and whether or not it would ever take place. During the sale itself he was on the site for 10 hours a day, shuttling back and forth between Forest Service officials and his fellow employees. His constant fear was that something would happen that would send his company into court or that would result in adverse national publicity. His fears were justified. The scruffy protester who ran at him with the six inch log filed criminal charges. Brian Unnerstall had tried to run over him, he said. In the end, the grand jury refused to issue an indictment.

Brian Unnerstall had been confident that he would not be indicted. "There was never any doubt in my mind that they would not indict me. We know for sure that the man was never under my vehicle or in front of it." However, the process was not without its stress. "I was worried. I kept going over and over it in my mind. Frankly, I couldn't believe that someone would lie like that. I thought that the grand jury wouldn't believe him but I wasn't sure. I lost a bunch of sleep over it, I can tell you that.

"I learned a lot from the experience. I learned that these people will stop at nothing to achieve their objectives. They will lie, cheat and steal, engage in violence and attack people verbally and physically." Following his experience in the Shawnee National Forest, Brian Unnerstall helped form a local timber group to educate people about the environmental debate.

"Most people who earn their living from the timber and lumbering industry have no idea what is going on and what is at stake. We are attempting to get them informed and involved. I believe there is a real groundswell of support for our point of view. Of course it helps that we're right in the middle of Rush Limbaugh country. He was born just down the road in Cape Girardeau."

Brian Unnerstall also learned something else. "I thought that timber sales were controversial in the Pacific Northwest because they are large, or because so much of the land is owned by the U.S. Government and sales spread over entire counties. Our experience on the Shawnee taught me that even the smallest sale, even the tiniest timber harvest will be subjected to the same nonsense that we had seen for years in Oregon and Washington.

"People are getting lost in the entire debate over timber issues. There is absolutely no discussion of the needs of the people for wood products or the fact that wood products are the most environmentally sensitive of all products that we could use. There is something else too. According to the anti-timber folks, people are not as important as other life forms. These people carried spikes into the sale area, and although, thank God, we didn't run into any spiked trees, the fact that they were apparently willing to use a weapon that could kill a timberman to 'save' a tree shows a total disregard for human life.

"Here these people were talking about the harvesting of trees as a 'death' comparable to the end of a human life. To speak of our logging trucks as hearses is to demonstrate a disconnect between the real world and the imaginary world in which these people appear to live. If we think trees are as important as people or that harvesting a tree that has no feelings or emotions or soul is 'death' comparable to the loss of human life then civilization is in deep trouble."

PAULA PENCE EASLEY
Anchorage, Alaska

Early on, growing up in Louisville, Kentucky, Paula Easley realized that she was not "your typical sedate, diffident southern belle." What Paula Easley wanted just wasn't "done" in those days, and especially not in genteel and refined Bluegrass Country, in a land of colonels, courtliness, courtesy and curtsies. For what Paula wanted was the excitement and challenge of a career. She wanted to be in business, so she started one.

Paula Easley's mother often said, "Be careful what you wish for, you might get it." She was right. In 1962, with a baby in her arms, Paula and her husband left suburbia for a family business venture running a lodge, a trading post and small industrial project in Stony River, Alaska. It sounded idyllic and exciting. It was certainly the latter.

Paula Easley traded life in Kentucky with telephones, natural gas heat, modern appliances, flush toilets, running water, electricity, supermarkets, and freeways for Alaska and bush radio, wood stoves, "honeybuckets," a wringer washer, hand-pumped water, a generator, shopping from catalogs and muddy trails.

Paula Easley discovered the true meaning of her mother's cautionary advice. She also discovered what true excitement can mean when she was once left "in charge" for two weeks to run the entire operation, teach school, run medical schedule, and survive a series of unexpected calamities with no time for sleeping. She discovered something else: she could do anything she wanted to do.

Paula Easley, who came from a part of the world where the next town was but a short drive away, discovered that in Alaska, even if there was a next town—and usually there wasn't—no roads existed to get there. She had never been in a place where work was almost a privilege, so scarce were the opportunities. For the first time in her life she realized how absolutely essential it was for people to be able to find work.

The despair and hopelessness she saw on the faces of the men and women around her in bush Alaska was something she

117

never forgot. It drives her to this day. For the contrast between Alaska's potential and its present, during the double-digit unemployment days of the 1960s, was brutally stark. Paula Easley knew Alaska's future lay in its wealth of natural resources and in its scenic assets.

"My dream was for Alaska to have an economy and jobs based on wise use of its resources. We had 'world-class' everything, but we had no infrastructure." That realization and that dream took Paula into the public policy area. She became head of the Resource Development Council for Alaska, a nonprofit public interest educational association committed to sensible economic growth. Once again her search for challenge was rewarded.

"In the 1970s we fought Washington for the right to build the trans-Alaska oil pipeline through Alaska rather than Canada. We fought environmentalists' efforts to stop mining to turn Alaska into a national park, and we sought federal support for a gas line from Prudhoe Bay."

In Haines, a town with 78% unemployment at the time, Paula Easley fought to keep a tiny sawmill open against the demands of the Audubon Society that the area be turned into an eagle preserve. A growing group of grassroots activists, realizing at last what the environmental movement was all about, fought back, struggling for the right to earn a living against people "outside" who had their jobs and didn't care whether Alaskans did. Paula and her group's leaders traveled the country speaking out, warning Americans that if they let environmental groups take over Alaska, their states would be next.

"Our opponents were the wealthy members of groups such as Sierra Club, Wilderness Society, Friends of the Earth, National Wildlife Federation and Greenpeace. They would stop at nothing to 'save' Alaska from Alaskans. They are just as dedicated today. During my 12 years with the Resource Development Council for Alaska, I witnessed every trick in the book by representatives of these groups. With no shame whatsoever, some simply defended their actions by saying, 'the ends justified the means.' I vowed, no matter how hard the battle got, not to stoop to their ruthless and irresponsible tactics."

At least Paula Easley was never bored. As she reports, running a 10,000 member grassroots organization, "qualifies you for a suite in the Home for the Bewildered. You're always on the hot seat. Your time is never your own. You're constantly struggling to raise money for critical projects at the very time you're doing the project, and the issues never go away. Instead, they multiply." Paula heard of countless threats to freedom and property rights during eight years on the National Public Lands Advisory Council and she came to know how devastating poorly conceived environmental policy is to communities and their residents.

In 1988 Paula Easley shifted from being a public policy advocate to a maker of public policy as Director of Government Affairs for Anchorage Mayor Tom Fink. For Paula it was *deja vu*. The issues hadn't changed, only the clients. Now, instead of fighting for the men and women of Alaska who struggle against the "land lockup" demands of environmentalists, Paula battles on behalf of local and regional governments laboring under exorbitant federal mandates imposed by an environmentalist-controlled Congress—mandates to meet impossible environmental standards at local expense.

There is another similarity. As in the early days of grassroots activism against the environmental juggernaut, most local and regional governments are not well-organized, not activist, are uncomfortable in the political arena and therefore hesitant to work with congressional delegations and federal agencies. Paula Easley wants to change all that. She would ignite beneath officials in city and county offices across America the same fire she lit under others. To alert her bank of activist mayors when actions are needed on federal policy, she manages a FAX network she calls, tongue firmly in cheek, "NEPA" (Network for Environmental Policy Awareness).

Whether it's policies on wetlands, the Endangered Species Act or unfunded federal mandates to push already-clean water to ultra-clean, she believes individuals have the power to change them. However, they need good information on their number, value and costs. They need it on a per-household basis—such as "this regulation to remove radon from drinking water will raise your water bill by $85 a month."

"People would be outraged if they realized many federal mandates can be unnecessary, misapplied, too costly for the benefit gained or lack any semblance of sound science to justify them. If it takes a Constitutional Amendment to stop the onslaught of mandates, then that's our next project."

Anchorage is not alone in its concern over federal mandates that destroy a community's ability to guide its own destiny, to set its own priorities. The City of Cheyenne, Wyoming must spend $25 million over the next five years in its effort to meet federal environmental mandates. Unfortunately, the entire budget for the City of Cheyenne for one year is only $22 million. In October 1993 the mayor of Cheyenne joined with 43 other Wyoming mayors in writing to President Clinton and the Wyoming congressional delegation demanding an end to unfunded federal environmental mandates. While Wyoming municipalities clearly understand the nature of this looming crisis for American cities, thousands of other U.S. cities appear unaware. Paula Easley has her work cut out for her.

Those who know Paula Easley have no doubt that she will get the job done. For the southern girl from Louisville, Kentucky, by way of Stony Creek, Alaska, there isn't anything she can't do—especially when what she's trying to do isn't "done."

ERICH VEYHL
Concord, Massachusetts

In the 1970s Erich Veyhl began to dream of owning a home on the New England coast. He would often bicycle up the north shore of Massachusetts looking for the right place, even pedaling as far as the New Hampshire border. "I just couldn't get out of the city fast enough. I always wanted to be able to get to a rural area—the coast in particular." In the mid-1980s his search intensified, reaching all the way to the Canadian border. Eventually he discovered a spectacular 43-acre property on Moose Cove in South Trescott, Maine, with 400 feet of ocean frontage. He bought it, planning to build a permanent home on the site. However, a home that would do justice to the site would be expensive. Later Erich found a small affordable house on six acres a dozen miles north in South Lubec. He had found the coast of his dreams.

It wasn't long before his dream became a nightmare. Erich Veyhl discovered that the nonprofit National Parks and Conservation Association was lobbying Congress to create a new national park that would include his property. He was stunned. Everybody around Lubec was stunned.

"Ours was one of several areas the environmental group was targeting in New England. At first we tended to think that this wasn't real, that this couldn't be us. But it didn't take long to dawn on us that we were wrong. We had no idea, in fact, just how far it had gone at that point. Now years later we're still finding out things about what they were up to."

Erich Veyhl knew nothing about the National Parks and Conservation Association. In fact, he had never heard of it. He knew precious little more about the National Park Service. His only contact with the National Park Service had been with the friendly young men and women in their khaki uniforms at a historic site in the Boston area. He vaguely recalled people losing their property at Cape Cod National Seashore, and that made him uneasy.

In his search for more information about what was happening to his coastal home site, Erich spent a day on the phone

121

calling friends to locate anyone who might have information on the National Park Service. He wanted to know if the threat to his property was serious. Erich eventually found Chuck Cushman, executive director of the National Inholders Association. Cushman told him the threat to his property was serious indeed. As he told everybody, Chuck told Erich Veyhl that he'd better get organized and that he ought to get his friends and neighbors involved in the process as well.

Erich networked by phone with everybody he could find around Lubec. They invited Chuck Cushman to hold a meeting—attended by a hundred locals—where he shared his experiences fighting the National Park Service. As a result, local landowners formed the Washington County Alliance (WCA) to mobilize opposition to the National Park Service's land grab.

They even held their own press conference in the state capital at Augusta, something so alien they would never have dreamed that normal people could do such a thing.

However, Erich Veyhl wasn't satisfied. He wanted to know more. He wanted to know exactly what was going on, why it was being done, who was behind it and how it could be stopped. He called people, dug out documents, networked, did any kind of investigation he could think of, an arduous task at best.

He soon found another tool, the federal law that permits access to government documents—the Freedom of Information Act. Over a two year period Erich devoted a major portion of his free time to conducting a massive records search, a search that yielded a library of land-use documents called by Keith Schneider of *The New York Times,* "the best library on environmentalism I've ever seen."

It was certainly the most complete library outside the National Park Service of an obscure policy that permits the designation, by the federal government, of so-called National Natural Landmarks. Erich Veyhl learned that 587 landmarks had been designated throughout the country, and that thousands more were in the crosshairs of the National Park Service's regulatory weaponry, egged on by the National Parks and Conservation Association and other environmental groups. Erich knew that one of those areas was his own piece of the Maine coast, now threatened by national park classification and NNL designation.

Erich and his colleagues found that when the National Park Service told landowners that the federal NNL designation was honorary and did not restrict the use of the land, it was only a half truth. The whole truth was that state and local governments can restrict designated landmarks through a web of complicated laws and regulations. When Erich asked Chuck Cushman about the NNL program, Chuck replied, "I never heard of it, but if it has anything to do with the National Park Service, I don't trust it."

Erich's search through the files of the National Park Service revealed something else: National Park Service employees had been violating their own regulations by surveying private property without notifying the landowner, much less obtaining his or her permission. He also discovered the smoking gun—the National Park Service knew it was violating its own policy and had known it from the beginning. Said one document, "The question of secrecy and publicity is a hot topic which will undoubtedly come back to haunt us over the years if this document becomes generally available to the public."

Erich Veyhl and a Lubec colleague named Bob Voight took the smoking gun and other documents to Congress, which eventually enacted a moratorium upon the landmark program. However, Erich wanted more. He wanted an investigation of the National Park Service and its landmark program. In 1992 the Maine landowners got what they wanted, a stinging indictment of the National Park Service by the Inspector General of the Interior Department that revealed that the U.S. Government had been surveying 2,800 locations encompassing more than 90 million acres for potential landmark designation. The report also took a look at the smoking gun and declared the obvious: "Land may have been evaluated, nominated, and designated without the landowners' knowledge or consent." The hottest smoking gun, however, was the revelation that the National Park Service had been using the NNL program as a secret hit list to turn private land into new national parks.

Erich, having for the moment saved his dream retreat on the rocky coast of Maine, has not folded up his tent in the New England land campaign. He and his colleagues in the Washington County Alliance and the Maine Conservation Rights Institute have returned to the fray time and time again in opposition to the U.S. Fish and Wildlife Service's effort to expand Maine's Moosehorn National Wildlife Refuge by confiscating unwilling landowners' property; in opposition to an multimillion dollar expansion of the Minute Man National Historical Park; and in opposition to the attempt by environmental groups and federal bureaucrats to lock up 26-million acres of private land in four New England states.

Erich, who has devoted hundreds of hours over the past several years to fighting the private property rights battle in New England, is not just generous with his time. He is magnanimous in his willingness to share what he knows with others. He is a frequent contributor to Ann Corcoran's *Land Rights Letter*.

Erich Veyhl would like nothing more than to pursue his career as a computer engineer without the intrusion of environmental extremists. "I don't enjoy fighting bureaucrats." He'd also like the chance to sit quietly in his Concord home listening to jazz and admiring his collection of miniature cars. Instead, he found himself in the property rights battle because of what he feared would happen to his property in Maine. "We weren't looking to pave over the wilderness. We like it the way it is. That's why we bought our land in the first place. We just don't want the government or anybody else to take it away."

The reluctant warrior has remained active because he sees much more than his small piece of coast land as being at risk. "The problem is there are people out there who believe we have to keep nature free of human intervention. They use this poetic 'don't-touch-nature' rhetoric. But when they say they want to protect natural resources, that's really a euphemism for taking over private property.

"The basic issue here is one of private property rights. The preservationists want to characterize us as a bunch of Birchers. But those are obvious distractions away from the real issues. There are a lot of us who want to protect the environment from toxic waste dumps and pollution. But we also want to keep our land. The problem is, the preservationists believe we have to preserve the land and nature, free of man."

LOUISE LISTON
Escalante, Utah

Born in a log cabin in tiny Escalante, Utah, a remote southern Utah town, during the midst of the Great Depression, Louise Liston had a very personal introduction to how hard life can be in the rural West. When she was two years old her family moved to Idaho in an attempt to save her father's family homestead. Four years later her mother died.

When her father remarried three years later the family moved to Milwaukee, Wisconsin, where Louise grew up. Yet, from the time she was 13, each summer she returned to Escalante to live with her late mother's parents. It was there she met her future husband and some years later married him and returned to live where she had been born.

A rich pioneer heritage had imbued in Louise Liston a deep love and appreciation for the land that surrounds and protects Escalante. Thus for her to return to Escalante was to return home in more ways than just to return to the place of her birth. It was with complete contentment that she settled into the life of a rancher's wife and mother to the six children she and her husband brought into the world.

To make it in the ranching world, Louise and her husband agreed that she would return to college to finish her degree and become a school teacher. Two years and a summer later she had her degree and that fall began teaching in a one-room school house (grades one through six) in Boulder, Utah. When a teaching job opened up in Escalante she returned home once again.

Louise Liston's first encounter with the environmental movement occurred a number of years later when she was teaching at Escalante High School. The leader of an environmental group wrote an article for the local paper protesting a proposal by the Utah Highway Department to reroute a portion of the existing highway from Boulder to Escalante.

Louise knew that road like the back of her hand. For the two years she taught in Boulder, she had driven it in all kinds of weather, night and day. She remembered in particular one por-

125

tion of that road: a very dangerous sharp blind turn above a dropoff of several hundred feet. There had been a number of near-accidents on that turn. Everyone who knew that section of highway thought it a miracle that no one had ever died there. That was the road the school bus, filled with the children of her friends and neighbors, traveled every day.

The environmental leader argued that road construction would destroy forty feet of a beautiful limestone formation. Louise was compelled to respond. Yes, she wrote, forty feet of the formation would be gone, but 30 miles of that same formation would still be there for the traveling public to enjoy. "In no way," she wrote, "can that forty feet of limestone be equated with the young children whose lives may hang in the balance."

Louise Liston wasn't content to write the letter to the editor. She wrote a petition on behalf of the schools in support of the road construction and circulated it through the community. After she had obtained more than 500 signatures she presented it to the Utah Highway Department. Shortly thereafter the road was built.

As a rancher's wife, Louise Liston was often asked to lend her voice to the public debate regarding regulation of federal range land. Those activities led to her appearance in support of a much needed east-west access road across Garfield County—the so-called Burr Trail. Her appearance at a hearing in Escalante led to her appearance in Washington, D.C. before a U.S. Senate Subcommittee.

Within the year she was asked to run for Garfield County Commissioner. She won. After 25 years of teaching, Louise was ready for a change. What a change it was.

A month after she was sworn in, four environmental groups sued Garfield County to prevent the county from improving the Burr Trail. It was then that Louise joined with her fellow commissioners in seeking to utilize a federal law that authorizes western counties to take over roads across public lands. Control over the Burr Trail would at last give Garfield County its vital east-west link. As Louise puts it, "One more time it was a battle where people and their needs were less important than scenery."

The Burr Trail battle turned Louise Liston, the rancher's wife, the school teacher, the mother of six, into one of Utah's most articulate advocates for multiple use. Over the years she gave speeches, participated in televised debates, wrote articles, and appeared before congressional hearings and federal judges on a breadth of western issues including grazing, rural roads, national park expansion, and eco-terrorism.

One reporter called Louise the "pit bull of multiple use" for her role as one of Utah's and the nation's most formidable voices against wilderness designation—including a proposal that would have designated 5 million acres of wilderness in Utah and cost more than $13 billion a year and tens of thousands of jobs. She became known as an articulate opponent of single-use land management and an ardent advocate of private property rights and grazing.

Louise Liston's national reputation as an advocate for the West and Westerners resulted in her elevation to the chair of the National Association of Counties (NACo) Public Lands Steering Committee and to NACo's Western Interstate Region's Board of Directors. She helped lead the charge to get NACo to designate ten natural resource dependent communities as "endangered" as a result of federal policies and regulations. One of the named communities was Louise's Escalante.

Many environmentalists speak and write of their love for the wide open spaces of the American West, for the land and its charms and rugged beauty. So does Louise Liston. However, unlike so many high rise environmentalists, she doesn't just talk the talk, she has walked the walk.

DAVID LUCAS
Isle of Palms, South Carolina

The phrase, "I'll take this all the way to the Supreme Court," is a cliche. Everybody says it. People say it to demonstrate commitment to a cause, to a principle, to their belief that they are right—and willing to pay the price in money and in time to prove it.

Yet the phrase is more, for it reflects an underlying belief in the United States Constitution, in our system of government, and in the guarantee that, if you are willing to pay the price, you can find, as the marble above the U.S. Supreme Court entrance reads, "Equal Justice Under Law."

However, to seek a ruling from the Supreme Court is not a journey to be undertaken lightly. The trip is long, arduous and expensive. Sometimes when one knocks at the door of the Court there is no answer.

One who made that journey, who paid the price and won the victory—not just for himself, but also for millions of others—is David Lucas.

David Lucas was born in North Carolina, but at a "tender age" his family moved to Turkey Creek, South Carolina, where he grew up learning about the land from his granddaddy who started with "40 acres and a mule." One of David's earliest memory was of walking along a hot dusty road in search of the pop bottles that would provide him a pocket full of change for candy and maybe a Coke.™

David Lucas grew tall and strong, and, during his days with the University of South Carolina Gamecocks, was named an all-conference player for his gridiron heroics as a fleet-footed but powerful defensive end. Yet as big and strong and as used to powerful adversaries and thunderous blows as David was, he was unprepared for his confrontation with the arrogance of the environmental elitists who coveted his land.

In 1986, after years of hard work as a developer of quality real estate properties in his native state, David bought two

129

beach front properties with the dream of building a home for his family on one and a home for sale on the other.

In 1988 the South Carolina Legislature enacted a law permitting setback lines to be drawn along the South Carolina coast, seaward of which no structures could be built. The line drawn by the South Carolina Coastal Council was behind David Lucas' lots, preventing him from any use of his property. The government told him he could not build upon his land—although he could continue to pay taxes.

Ironically, homes had stood for years on the beach upon which David intended to build. A house had stood on the lot adjacent to his since 1975. As David noted, "The conception that these people are fighting for pure water, pure air, is not true at all. The attack upon me was for no real environmental reason. It was an attack upon individual liberty and individual property rights."

David Lucas sued, charging that the actions of the South Carolina Coastal Council violated the Fifth Amendment of the U.S. Constitution by converting his "private property" to "public use" without "just compensation." The trial court found a "taking" and awarded Mr. Lucas $1.23 million. However, by a three-to-two decision the South Carolina Supreme Court reversed.

When David Lucas asked the U.S. Supreme Court to hear the case there was no guarantee that it would. In fact, less than 4% of petitions requesting a hearing by the Supreme Court are granted. Nevertheless, on November 18, 1991, the U.S. Supreme Court agreed to hear the case.

On Monday, March 2, 1992, the U.S. Supreme Court heard oral arguments in what is surely one of the most important property rights cases in history. David Lucas sat in the front row to hear the highest court in the land ask about his dream.

In June 1992, the Supreme Court ruled that it appeared that an unconstitutional "taking" had occurred. The Supreme Court instructed the State of South Carolina that it could not simply declare something to be a nuisance and prohibit it. South Carolina would have to find a precedent under common law for calling something like building a home a nuisance. The U.S. Supreme Court sent the matter back to the

South Carolina Supreme Court for a ruling in accordance with the U.S. Supreme Court's decision.

Subsequently, the South Carolina Supreme Court held that David Lucas had been denied use of his property unconstitutionally and ordered him compensated. Ironically, after paying for and acquiring his beach front property, South Carolina decided to sell the land—for development.

After David won, he received hundreds of calls from "all over the country." Yet the calls did not come from CEOs of large corporations or big financial institutions that had a lot of money tied up in real estate. The calls came, he said, "from private individuals in just about every state in the union."

Thus, when David Lucas won, he prevailed not just for himself and his family, but also for millions of property owners whose land is coveted by those who, in the name of environmental policy, would "take" but would not "pay." As the Supreme Court declared, "[a] strong public desire to improve the public condition is not enough to warrant achieving the desire by a shorter cut than the constitutional way of paying for the change."

MARY F. WIRTH
Kane, Pennsylvania

In northwestern Pennsylvania, about one hundred fifty miles northeast of Pittsburgh and seventy-five miles east of Lake Erie lies the Allegheny National Forest. Spreading south and east of the Allegheny River, the forest envelops the larger part of four counties: Warren, McKean, Elk and Forest. In fact, more than 75% of Forest County lies within the boundaries of the Allegheny National Forest.

The Allegheny National Forest, like most forests managed by the U.S. Forest Service in the eastern United States, is different from national forests in the American West. In the West, most of the land that makes up a national forest has been owned and controlled by the U.S. Government since the land entered the Union. While inholdings, the results of early homesteaders, may exist, they are the exception and not the rule.

With regard to the Allegheny National Forest and other eastern components of the U.S. Forest Service, the converse is often true. Most of the land was settled and claimed in the early days of the Republic. However, following the Great Depression, under the Weeks Act, the U.S. Government bought up much of the land, although certainly not all, and drew a management boundary around it.

That is why within the Allegheny National Forest lie such communities as Endeavor, Hickory, Whig Hill, Truemans, Cherry Grove, Rogertown, Tiona, Wetmore, James City, Highland Corners, Pigeon, Lantz Corners, Westline and Marshburg. The Allegheny National Forest is not just a green-colored piece of federal domain on a map of the Eastern United States. It is home to tens of thousands of Pennsylvanians. It is also where they play and earn a living, a living that is today under attack.

Just to the east of the Allegheny National Forest, at the intersection of U.S. 6 and Pennsylvania State Highways 66 and 321 lies Kane, Pennsylvania. Kane is known for two things. One is as the Black Cherry (*Prunus serotina*) Capital of the World, a title the people of Kane have worked hard to promote. The other

133

is as the Icebox of Pennsylvania, a reputation that is well earned but just as soon forgotten.

Kane, Pennsylvania, is also the home of Mary Wirth, first Executive Director of the Pennsylvania Forest Industry Association, and Executive Director of The Allegheny Hardwood Utilization Group, which are fighting against the efforts of environmentalists to end productive use of the resources of the Allegheny National Forest.

Mary Wirth, with a degree in horticulture from Pennsylvania State University, wanted nothing more than to remain at home to raise her children. Yet, as she read her husband Jonathan's forestry journals and professional magazines, she knew that she "could not just sit back silently while forestry professionals were being maliciously slandered."

However, it is not enough, says Mary, to become aware of an issue, to realize that the issue is important to you, and to be knowledgeable enough about the issue to know what you are supporting. "There must be a conviction, a realization that this is not just something you agree or disagree with, but something that touches your values and beliefs and is worth standing up for."

Mary reached that point several years ago and has been a forestry activist ever since. She was first spurred into action by an article in one of her husband's journals, to which she responded with a letter to the editor. That letter was only a start.

Her reading and research led to more writing, this time articles for a variety of forestry, farming and local publications. One of the first battles she undertook was on "wetlands" regulation, when she learned that, as a result of the 1989 U.S. Government manual, 50% of Warren County could be considered "wetlands."

There were other battles as well, as environmentalists sought to prevent, not just timber harvesting, but hunting, off-road vehicle recreation and other uses of the lands managed by the U.S. Forest Service. Particularly galling to Mary was the attack on forestry, since Pennsylvania is the nation's leading producer of hardwood lumber.

Although 79% of the forested land in Pennsylvania is privately owned, that did not stop environmental activists from targeting forestry. Although the hardwood forests of Pennsylvania depend, in fact, thrive upon clearcutting, environmentalists sought to put an end to that activity, even on private land.

Mary Wirth had her work cut out for her. Yet she was driven by a deeply felt conviction, a conviction which came when she first understood the very foundation of what environmental groups were saying. As Mary explains, environmental elitists assert "that mankind is not a part of nature and that man and nature cannot coexist." They recommend "the embrace of socialism so as to minimize the significance of individual rights thereby leading to a deterioration of private property rights and an erosion of our constitutional rights." They advocate "the degradation of religious beliefs to the point where a human life is of no more significance than a tree, or an animal or even a bug and nature itself is worshipped."

Today, Mary is as busy as ever, mobilizing local support and traveling the country to tell her story. Reflecting, she says she has experienced the full range of emotions. She feels "anger that an entire profession of hard working, honest people is under such a vicious and unfounded attack." She is fearful "that our freedom, way of life, livelihoods and our community will cease to exist." Sometimes she succumbs to hatred "for the terrorist acts of spiking trees, sabotaging equipment and otherwise terrorizing innocent families." Often she experiences sadness "that there are so many forestry professionals who are not motivated enough to even bother to respond," but then happiness, "that I have met so many hard-working, dedicated people who have responded and who are making a real difference."

Above all, Mary Wirth has hope: "hope that through education America will realize our contribution to society; hope that the anti-human philosophy of environmentalists will be seen for what it is and changes will occur; and most of all hope that our efforts are not in vain.

"Come judgment day, I would much rather have to explain why I cut down trees to help people than why I cut down people to help trees."

JAMES D. PETERSEN
Medford, Oregon

J im Petersen was born and raised in the mining town of Kellogg, Idaho. His father began digging ditches for the Bunker Hill Company after the Great Depression for 25 cents an hour. Eventually, he retired as the company's construction superintendent.

Like his dad, Jim Petersen worked in the mines. He went underground to pay his way through college. It wasn't just the insistence of his college-educated school teacher mother or his father, who dropped out of school in the eighth grade, a casualty of the Great Depression. Jim Petersen wanted to be above ground, to breathe the air and to see the sky and the trees— especially the trees.

Jim Petersen obtained his degree in journalism from the University of Idaho and then worked for several newspapers in Idaho, Montana, Oregon, and eventually Illinois. In 1972 he left the newspaper business to return to the mountain west where he opened a small advertising agency in Kalispell, Montana. In 1980 he tried his hand at a regional business publication.

In 1985 Jim Petersen became Executive Director and co-founder of The Evergreen Foundation, which later became a nonprofit tax-exempt charitable corporation. The Foundation was created for two reasons: to help restore public confidence in forestry, and to help advance public understanding and support for scientifically-based forest policy and forest practices.
According to Jim Petersen, "the foundation does not lobby, and we do not sue people. We are in the information business, nothing more and nothing less.

"There is one reason why the Evergreen Foundation exists today: the unwavering financial support of forest products manufacturers in southern Oregon, especially the members of the Medford-based Southern Oregon Timber Industries Association—our first sponsor. Later came the Roseburg-based Douglas Timber Operators.

137

"These are mostly small family-owned businesses with a long history of community involvement in southwest Oregon's timber communities. In the early going, their contributions kept us alive. They had the wisdom and the patience to give us a chance to try to do something that had never been done before. We are a success today because they stuck with us in the early years, in spite of criticism from skeptics who considered *Evergreen* to be a waste of money."

Jim Petersen is creator and editor of *Evergreen*, the full-color bi-monthly journal designed to keep Foundation members and others up to date on issues and events that impact forestry, forest communities and the forest products industry. At 100,000 readers, *Evergreen* has become the largest forest-related publication in North America.

Evergreen published its first issue in March 1986. Its primary function in 1986 was simple: involve people in the U.S. Forest Service's recently-initiated ambitious forest planning process. Jim Petersen believed that if the people in the communities understood the issues, understood how decisions regarding the forests that surrounded them affected their lives, they would become involved.

As a result, for eight national forests in the West, Jim Petersen's *Evergreen* provided alternatives that focused on multiple outputs: harvesting, reforestation of areas where earlier plantings had failed, trail development, eradication of insect infestations, expansion of campgrounds, and construction of roads that opened more of the forest to greater public use. Jim Petersen's alternatives generated wide public support.

As a result of *Evergreen*, the Forest Service received a wealth of substantive comments from local residents and users of the forest, particularly in the Umpqua, the Siskiyou, the Winema and the Rogue River National Forests. "Our Umpqua National Forest 'Family Forest Plan' generated more letters of support than any other planning document in Forest Service history—more than 14,000 cards and letters. The people took the Forest Service at its word, that it wanted to know what the people wanted, that it wanted the people most affected to become involved. The good news is that the people became involved. The bad news is that the environmentalists derailed the process.

"I believe the environmentalists took a hard and cynical look at the forest planning process and concluded they couldn't control it. As a result, the environmentalists and their lawyers moved from the forest planning process and the Multiple Use and Sustained Yield Act, where the needs of the people were relevant, to the courtroom and the Endangered Species Act, where the needs of the people were totally irrelevant."

As a result, *Evergreen's* mission changed. "Once the forest planning process was over it became very clear that *Evergreen's* mission was much larger and the time frame in which it had to under take that mission much longer than we had thought. When you discuss timber, there is never a shortage of issues or a scarcity of confusion on those issues."

Jim believes that "the greatest threat to the nation's future is the cultural gap which now distances rural America from its cities. We have become a nation of city dwellers a generation or two removed from our distant rural heritage. There is not much about city life that hints of where things come from or where America began.

"We are the richest nation on earth, but in ever-increasing numbers we have absolutely no idea where our wealth comes from. Worse yet, we do not know the people who bring us these riches in such abundance. If more of us knew more of them, we would probably view logging, farming and mining in a more favorable light."

While Jim Petersen is the creative force behind the efforts of timber-producing communities to inform the American public regarding timber issues and although he has won many awards for his creativity and behind the scenes work, he is proudest of The Evergreen Foundation's most successful venture to date: "The Truth About America's Forests." What was to have been a single press run of 75,000 copies became eight press runs. Today, more than 600,000 copies of this slender booklet have been distributed across the United States. A children's edition is soon to be published along with a series of brochures that highlight its key points.

According to Jim, the incredible success of "The Truth," in which every piece of information is footnoted as to the public sources from which it is derived, demonstrates "how desperate people are for credible, documented information regarding the state of forests in America today."

For Jim, "The Truth" was "an extraordinary leap of faith. But as David George once observed, 'Don't be afraid to take a big step if one is indicated. You can't cross a chasm in two small jumps.' We saw a chasm, the cultural gap, the one which now distances this nation's rural resource producers from its urban resource consumers and we sought to cross it."

Thanks to Jim the truth is starting to get out and the chasm is beginning to be bridged. Jim finds some irony in the attempt to prevent the use of America's vast timber resources since, "wood is a green product. It's renewable, recyclable, energy efficient, and friendly to the environment.

"However, in America there is growing public pressure to take productive forest land out of production. For some it is simply a matter of wanting more of America to be wild again. Others fear we are running out of forests and out of time in which to save what is left. Many distrust industries in general and the profit motive in particular. A few even fear technology itself.

"The plain fact is that we cannot have the things we need in abundance if we do not use our natural resources for their intended purpose. Can we live with less? No one knows, because no nation has ever survived that asked its citizens to accept a permanent lower standard of living and no government has endured that did not provide its citizens with the opportunity for a better life."

Jim Petersen, who began his working life in the mines of Idaho and now travels the forests of the Pacific Northwest, knows about America's rich natural resources and how vital they are, not just to a higher standard of living but also to the hopes, the dreams and the aspirations of the American people.

Jim has a picture of his hero, his father, taken at CCC Camp 7 on Cataract Creek on what was then the Coeur d'Alene National Forest. The photograph reminds him of stories his father told of cutting firewood during the Depression, of how he felled dead snags on the hills behind Kellogg, bucked them into lengths he could handle, and dragged them to town where he cut them into stove wood lengths. He sold his wood for a nickel a cord.

Jim Petersen knows how bleak things would have been if that's all the future had held for his father or for him. Jim Petersen wants for every father and their sons and daughters the dream that motivated his father and that inspires him.

RUTH KAISER
Bountiful, Utah

One of the first meetings was in Boise, Idaho, where the large conference room at the Red Lion Inn was filled to overflowing. No glad-handing conventioneers, this gathering of shiny, lean cowboys and their wives, they were there to work and to learn.

They came from all over Idaho, from Oreana and Rogerson and Terreton and Culdesac and Corral, and other towns of which most people have never heard. They came in from Oregon—Halfway and Drewsey and Riverside; from Nevada—Ruby Valley and Denio and Orovada; from Utah and Washington too.

In polished boots, pressed levis, spotless white shirts and huge hats, they sat at the tables, their notebooks out, their pencils poised. Faces ruddy from the sun and wind, they listened intently, taking copious notes in tiny strokes, straining to glean the information they needed to win the fight against the environmental machine that meant to doom them.

Behind it all, managing the details, checking in the late registrants, taking the money, selling the tapes, the books and the study guides, meeting and coordinating with the speakers—in a phrase, doing all that had to be done to make it work and smiling all the while—was Ruth Kaiser.

Ruth Kaiser was born in Oklahoma, the daughter and granddaughter of sharecroppers who had suffered through the Great Depression. She grew up hearing the stories of friends and neighbors who were driven from the land they loved and the homes they cherished.

As a very young and impressionable girl she had seen the desolation of the wind swept farms her family's neighbors had been force to abandon. Years later, writing an essay for her college English class, she reflected upon that time. Who were the people who used to live in the boarded up homes that dotted the prairie? What were they like? What had become of them?

The image of those empty places where people used to be, where families once gathered around the dinner table and where children at one time laughed and played was one she never forgot. There was something else that stayed with her: the understanding of the dedication, hard work, relentless energy and drive that it takes to make a living raising animals and crops.

When Ruth Kaiser was young, the family moved to California, following the path thousands of "Okies" had trodden before them. She ended up better than most: she obtained her degree in history, political science and business administration. Yet her love was American history, especially that regarding the Founding Fathers.

After more than twenty years in the insurance industry, Ruth wanted something more. She was troubled by the direction she saw the nation heading and she wanted to do something about it. She began to do part-time volunteer work for a nonprofit organization that taught the constitutional principles as espoused by the Founding Fathers.

In 1986 she moved to Utah to help spread the word about the Constitution, its origins and its application to modern problems. Yet, once again, her work seemed irrelevant, especially in light of the real world difficulties being faced by the men and women of the rural West.

When Ruth was approached by several western cattlemen seeking guidance on how to solve the problems they and others like them faced from the heavy hand of government and well-funded special interest environmental groups intent upon driving them off the land, she knew what had to be done.

"We needed to educate people on how to protect their rights. We needed to offer solutions, not just get people together to retell their horror stories." So that's what she, and the cattlemen who first came to her, did. They developed solution-oriented information and began holding seminars.

Ruth was asked to sign on as the Executive Director, being what she calls the "chief cook and bottle washer" of the National Federal Lands Conference. Cattlemen say, "Ruth Kaiser is the glue that holds it all together. She makes it go."

Ruth Kaiser demurs. "I ain't a hero. This is my job. It's what I do. I believe all of us, working together, networking with other organizations, are going to run the other side off the map, or die in the effort."

Her organization has taken the lead in the County Movement, an effort by local governments to take control over their lands and their lives back from federal bureaucrats. The National Federal Lands Conference has had stunning success in awakening dozens of counties to their rights and powers. That success may well help to ensure the willingness of local and regional governments to become more involved in fighting for the economic rights and future of their citizens.

What Ruth Kaiser does is not without disappointment. "My frustration comes from people who, like sheep, think they need permission from the law to express their freedoms. People are afraid to take charge of their destiny. We have got to change that mentality."

So Ruth Kaiser, who remembers those empty homes in Oklahoma and doesn't want to see the same specter across the American West, sets out to do just that.

DAVID A. RUSSELL
Crestview, Florida

David Russell was born in a tiny rural community in Santa Rosa County, Florida, in the early days of the Great Depression. In the 1930s David Russell, who today fights for the Constitution and property rights, had a more basic challenge: to stay alive.

David Russell's parents, poor share-croppers, were divorced when he was six, leaving him, in his words, "without the stabilizing influences of family." He lived with a succession of aunts, uncles, a brother, a sister, and any other relative who would take him in while he attended school. From the age of 10 he supported himself selling newspapers on the street, selling greeting cards door-to-door, and working as a "printer's devil" in a local print shop. At the age of 16, never having attended a full year of classes at a single school, David Russell dropped out.

The next year he joined the United States Air Force where he served his country for 20 years. During that time he obtained a high school diploma and completed two years of college-level business studies. In 1968 he retired as a Technical Sergeant after several years with one of the U.S. Air Force's Inspector General Teams and three overseas tours.

David Russell returned to the Panhandle of Florida and settled in Crestview, a rural town of 20,000 and the county seat of Okaloosa County, where he became a realtor. Within two years he had his own real estate firm. Two years later he opened another office in adjoining Walton County. He also became a mortgage broker, a general contractor, a securities dealer, a developer and the teacher of the Real Estate License Law Course for the Florida Real Estate Commission. Three times he was voted Realtor of the Year by his fellow realtors.

David Russell is a firm believer that anyone who takes his livelihood from a community should put something back. For him that has meant being active in a plethora of local charities as well as serving on the Crestview City Council and as President of the Crestview Chamber of Commerce.

145

In 1991 during the development of the Okaloosa County Comprehensive Plan, a plan mandated by Florida's Growth Management Act, a plan touted as a 10-year plan for growth, David Russell made a startling discovery. Instead of planning for growth, the plan was an artifice to stop practically all growth and to consolidate people in enclaves—the cities.

"It left little or no choice for the individual who might not want to live in the city," says David Russell. "It literally robbed the property owner of the value of his or her land. If an owner's land was not in the so called 'growth zone,' the value of the property was obliterated."

David Russell had two concerns. First, "the growing use of 'wetlands' and 'endangered species' to target private lands, to turn control of that land over to environmentalists and bureaucrats, and to confiscate the lands without 'just compensation.'" Second, "the apparent objective of bureaucrats and environmentalists to crowd more people into the cities, to depopulate the land, and to leave it for creatures, thereby severely limiting people who love the rural lifestyle."

David Russell, five-time President of the Board of Realtors, took his concerns to the local realtors. They were unwilling to take a stand. But David Russell, who remembers the oath he took upon his entry into the Air Force ("to support and defend the Constitution against all enemies, foreign and domestic"), could not sit silently by while the government took the property of his friends and neighbors. He decided "to try to organize a force to counter the onslaught of bad legislation and refute some of the propaganda being presented through the media."

In August 1990 David Russell established Citizens for Constitutional Property Rights, Inc. (CCPR). In an effort to form chapters in each of Florida's 67 counties, David embarked upon a crusade, criss-crossing the state eleven times. The objective was simple: "to give the common man, the individual property owner, a voice in the decisions being made that affect his land, a voice that has been ignored because property owners were not organized." Today, CCPR has members in 45 of Florida's counties as well as 27 states. Sixteen counties have formed individual chapters and coordinators are at work in ten more.

In May 1991 during negotiations between Santa Rosa County and the Department of Community Affairs (DCA) over the local comprehensive plan, the DCA negotiators tried to pressure the county into surrendering its rights. CCPR members from five surrounding counties demonstrated their support for the Santa Rosa County Commissioners and their opposition to the DCA. Outside the building a cart filled with boiling roofing tar sat bubbling while more than a thousand CCPR members waved feather pillows. The crowd carried signs reading: "We're ready, Mr. Commissioners, if you are." The DCA negotiators and their battery of lawyers exited from a back door and returned to Tallahassee. As a result, Santa Rosa County has the most flexible comprehensive plan of any county in the state.

In February 1992 David led a thousand property rights advocates in a "Caravan to the Capital." On the steps of the Capitol CCPR presented a black coffin filled with copies of the Constitution and the Bill of Rights. The outside of the coffin read: "Here lies the Constitution and the Bill of Rights, killed by the DCA, DER, and the DNR" (Florida's regulatory agencies).

David Russell, although not an attorney, wrote the first version of The Private Property Rights Act of Florida. Passed by the legislature, it was vetoed by the Governor. David Russell and his colleagues are not to be denied. They have redrafted the legislation and have put together one of the greatest coalitions in Florida's history to push for passage of the Private Property Rights Act.

In reality, despite the end-of-life-as-we-know-it predictions of environmental zealots, David Russell's property rights legislation would simply require state regulators to determine whether their rules may violate the Constitution by causing a "taking," and if so, how much that "taking" will cost the citizens of the Sunshine State.

The call for such legislation follows President Ronald Reagan's signing in 1988 of Executive Order 12630, the "Takings Implication Assessment" (TIA) order. Under EO 12630, federal agencies are required to determine whether proposed regulations will result in an unconstitutional taking of property and, if so, to determine the cost to the U.S. Treasury.

President Reagan acted following the decision of the U.S. Supreme Court in *Nolan v. California Coastal Commission*, 483 U.S. 825 (1987), a case litigated by Ron Zumbrun's Pacific Legal Foundation. In that important case, the Court held that when regulations go "too far" they convert "private property" to "public use" requiring "just compensation" to be paid. The Court's decision was hardly a new view as to the meaning of one of the Bill of Rights' most important provisions. Justice Oliver Wendell Holmes reached the same conclusion in 1922.

Recognizing a need for federal bureaucrats to act with an appreciation for the potential impact on the U.S. Treasury of Fifth Amendment "takings," Justice Department attorneys, led by Mark Pollot and Tom Hookano, asked Attorney General Ed Meese to push the TIA concept with President Reagan. During meetings conducted by Pollot and Hookano with federal regulators in the early days following the signing of E.O. 12630, estimates of potential costs to the U.S. Treasury exceeded $1 billion.

Pollot and Hookano were prophetic. Within a matter of years, a federal court held the U.S. Government liable for more than $200 million, including interest and attorneys fees in a single case involving private coal lands in Wyoming. Although the Government "taking" resulted not from a federal regulation but from an Act of Congress that declared that certain western coal was never to be mined (that beneath so-called alluvial valley floors), the result was the same. Private citizens had lost the use of their property.

Arizona was the first to adopt a state version of the Reagan Executive Order. Efforts to enact what became known as the Private Property Protection Act began when a handful of angry farmers drove into Phoenix to meet with then-President of the Arizona Farm Bureau, Cecil Miller. It soon became the primary legislative goal of an unusually broad and diverse constituency.

Hardly unusual, the legislation was good government at its best. It simply required Arizona officials to inform the people of the state as to the anticipated or potential cost of proposed regulatory action. Nevertheless, the outcry from environmental groups was extreme. They labeled the legislation the "polluters protection act" and worse. Arizonans were told its adoption would mean the end of all state health and safety regulation. (The same radical rhetoric was heard in Florida and every other state that proposed property rights legislation.) Legislators, however, were not to be fooled. They passed the bill.

For a brief period, Governor Fife Symington threatened a veto. Then he heard from the people of Arizona. In the end the bill was signed into law with a powerful message from the Governor.

[Does] environmentalism require its adherents to denigrate the principle of private property as it has been known in America from the very dawn of our national existence? If so, then they have embraced an environmentalism that is foreign to me .... The right to property is a civil right, no less than the rights to freedom of speech and worship, and the rights to due process and equal protection under the law.

The groundbreaking effort begun by the people of Arizona continues throughout the nation. David Russell and other property rights advocates will not be denied. "When state and federal bureaucrats and environmental zealots control a person's land, they control all of the activities of the individual. All the rights of our Constitution are rendered worthless when the most basic right, the right to own and use property, is taken."

David Russell has completed two careers already. Today he forges boldly ahead on his third. What keeps him going? "Of all the things I have done, nothing has given me greater satisfaction than knowing that in a small way I am following in the footsteps of the Minutemen—doing what I can to preserve this great nation of ours. It would be a betrayal of all our Founding Fathers stood for to let the government subvert the freedoms they held so dear. I believe the love of freedom still lives in most of us. Once aroused, we can be an awesome force and return the government back to where it belongs, to the people. One person can make a difference if he or she has determination and commitment."

David Russell, who, growing up in poverty in Florida, must surely have thought he had been forgotten, has become one of the nation's unforgettable leaders, a modern-day Minuteman.

SUE SUTTON
Maxwell, California

In his best-selling dogmatic diatribe, *Earth in the Balance,* Vice President Al Gore "question[s] the fairness of a relatively small group of farmers using the vast majority of [California's] water." Sue Sutton of Maxwell, California, less than 75 miles north of Sacramento in Colusa County, did not need to read Al Gore's book to learn his views on farmers in the fertile Sacramento Valley.

For Sue Sutton and her friends and neighbors have been on the receiving end—not of the water that they desperately need to grow their crops—but of a prolonged and vicious attack on their way of life. It is an attack that originated in the Endangered Species Act—a law for which Gore claims substantial responsibility.

On December 13, 1991—a Friday the Thirteenth—a federal judge ordered the total shutdown of irrigation water to 141,000 acres of farmland and wildlife refuges in the Glenn-Colusa Irrigation District. The shutdown was required, ruled the judge, to protect the endangered winter-run salmon. For Sue Sutton and her husband, John, the news was devastating. Their 1,200 acres of rice, wheat and vine crops depend on water from that irrigation district.

If permitted to stand, the judge's decision will devastate 1,200 farming families in Glenn and Colusa Counties who annually grow crops valued at $85 million. Like a pebble in a pond the ruination will ripple throughout the valley to some 12,000 farm-related jobs and $255 million in economic activity. As a result of the Endangered Species Act, the unemployment rate in Sue Sutton's valley soared to 31%.

It is not just the economy that suffers. So too does the environment. Twenty thousand acres of refuges and 5,000 acres of private wetland will lose their water. As much as $26 million in hunting revenues will be lost. Ironically, other endangered species will also suffer: the Swainson's hawk, the peregrine falcon, the giant garter snake, the bald eagle and 21 other species.

151

Sue Sutton—the daughter of an engineer who took his family throughout the United States and Mexico in pursuit of work, and wife of a man whose family had spent four generations on the land—was unwilling to take the news lying down. Her "school of hard knocks" upbringing and her education in conflict resolution told her that something could be done. She quit her job as a school counselor at tiny Elk Creek Elementary School in Glenn County and went to work saving the farms of the Sacramento Valley.

Within five days, Sue Sutton and a few neighbors organized the Family Water Alliance (FWA), a grassroots education organization. In a little more than two months FWA held its first rally at which more than 4,000 angry family farmers were in attendance.

It was Sue Sutton with her cry of "Wake up Sacramento! Wake up California! Wake up America!" that energized the crowd on the steps of the California State Capitol. It was that rally, and the work of Family Water Alliance (whose motto is "Every day is Earth Day on the Farm"), which brought Sue to the attention of the nation. Soon she was speaking for the farmers of northern California on Ted Koppel's "Nightline," ABC World News "American Agenda," and Public Broadcasting Service's "To Quench a Thirst."

Today the FWA is a nationally recognized organization which networks with over 150 other organizations across the state and country. The FWA has taken on a variety of issues: private property rights, home rule, regulatory takings, as well as the economic impact of the long list of creatures that, under the Endangered Species Act, threaten and endanger Sue Sutton's community: the winter and fall run salmon, spotted owl, tri-colored blackbird, Swainson's hawk and the giant garter snake.

Sue soon discovered that the issue did not just involve the farmers of the Sacramento Valley. Millions of others throughout California were being adversely affected by the distorted implementation of the Endangered Species Act. Sport and commercial fishermen, the Central Valley Project, cattlemen, miners, foresters, builders and many others were also affected.

With Sue Sutton as its spokesperson, the FWA appeared at a variety of hearings, both at the state and federal level. The FWA also sought to educate the federal and state bureaucrats responsible for making the day-to-day decisions that affect the families in Colusa County.

A trip to Washington, D.C. netted federal funding to study alternative means of protecting endangered species, including sonic and light, interim flat plate screens and temperature control devices.

Sue Sutton's FWA seeks, through its "Food for Thought" program, to ensure that the public realizes that farmers are the original conservationists and that farming is "green." Farmers provide wildlife habitat, ensure the presence of open space, and turn water into food—all the while creating jobs and supporting a strong economic base for California.

FWA, like all grassroots groups, realizes that facts, figures and attempts to persuade officials are not enough. FWA recognizes the truth of the bumper sticker often seen in northern California, "If the people will lead, the leaders will follow." Thus Sue Sutton's FWA has emblazoned 2,000,000 grocery bags with the FWA message, and has installed more than 200 messages along Interstate 5 from Sacramento to Redding.

Sue has advice for other grassroots groups. "First, we identify and emphasize our commonalities, we stop competing and we share the power. Second, we build ownership of the organization through involvement and by identifying each other's strengths and focusing on them. Third, we communicate constantly and spend the majority of our time with those people we are likely to win over to our side."

Sue admits, "It hasn't been easy. Even though the judge recently modified his order—to a severe reduction in our water allocation—the future is still, at best, only blurry." Sue and her colleagues work hard to keep their spirits up.

"Over the last two years we've come up with a number of mottoes so we don't burn out. We're in this for the long haul." Sue emphasizes "taking baby steps, turning every rock, recharging often, celebrating victories no matter how small, realizing that families are important, rigorous adherence to the truth, back up emotion with facts, and do our homework."

Sue Sutton believes that the key to success for any grassroots group such as the FWA is "to educate local people, to build coalitions and to network like mad, to identify common sense solutions, to approach Congress united, and to stress citizen involvement." Today she has brought together the leaders of the timber industry, fishermen, miners, farmers and others who have one thing in common: the Endangered Species Act, which, if left unchallenged, will destroy their lives. "Since the U.S. Government settled a lawsuit with environmentalists by agreeing to list 400 new species as endangered, since 40% of those species are in California, and since those species will not be found in the cities, rural Californians are in grave danger.

"Fundamentally, the Endangered Species Act and the manner in which it is being implemented are wrong. It is primarily a tool to manipulate citizens, corporations, cities, counties and other entities for the gain of government agencies and preservationist environmentalists. It is often punitive, many times has nothing to do with protecting the allegedly endangered or threatened species, and is selectively enforced. Finally, it is a tool to confiscate private property in violation of the Constitution.

"Vice President Al Gore ignores the fact that we feed America. Despite the small number of farmers, everyone benefits from our work, because we supply cheap, wholesome, nutritious food. No one goes hungry in this country. But you take away the food that we put on the table and the nation will soon understand our vital contribution. America must support its farmers. All the great countries of the world support their farmers. Why not America?"

Are you listening Vice President Gore?

TROY R. MADER
Gillette, Wyoming

A few years ago my son Luke and I went to see the Walt Disney Company's adaptation of the Jack London novel, *White Fang*, the tale of a young man's adventures in gold rush Alaska and his friendship with a wolf.

Afterwards as always, we sat through the credits. Yet these credits were different, for at the end was a disclaimer:

> Jack London's *White Fang* is a work of fiction. There has never been a documented case of a healthy wolf or pack of wolves attacking a human in North America.

Something about the *White Fang* disclaimer stuck in my craw. Perhaps it was that the disclaimer was followed by a statement bemoaning so-called "persecution" of the wolf and calling for the introduction of the wolf into "wilderness areas." Perhaps it was that the disclaimer was attributed to Defenders of Wildlife. Yet I had to admit that I knew precious little about wolves.

That's when I first met Troy R. Mader of the Common Man Institute. For six years Troy has been reading, researching, interviewing, observing and otherwise gathering any information he could about wolves in North America. Incredibly, at a time when the U.S. Fish and Wildlife Service, aided and abetted by a host of powerful environmental organizations, is attempting to reintroduce the wolf in eighteen different regions in the lower forty-eight, Troy is just about the only one with the facts and figures for those who oppose wolf reintroduction.

According to Troy Mader's Common Man Institute, attacks by healthy wolves upon humans, although uncommon, occurred in North America as early as the 1830s. Recently a wolf bit a 16-year-old girl camping with a youth group in Algonquin Provincial Park in Ontario, Canada. In Minnesota, wolves kept as pets attacked two children, killing one. Troy Mader has documented numerous other wolf attacks.

155

After reviewing Troy Mader's information I concluded that the *White Fang* disclaimer was wrong. I took my concern to the Walt Disney Company, asking that the disclaimer be revised or abandoned before the film was released in video format. A representative of Defenders of Wildlife (DOW), not Walt Disney Company, responded advising me that DOW had recommended the disclaimer to the Walt Disney Company and that DOW stood by its "disclaimer."

DOW asserted that all previous attacks by wolves upon humans in North America had not been "scientifically" documented. Furthermore, many "attacks" were by "tame" wolves, or were not really "attacks" since DOW "did not characterize" instances where wolves bit people as "attacks."

In asserting the absence of "scientific" documentation, DOW ignored some available information and, in a bit of weird science, presumed that attacking wolves are not healthy unless their health had been documented "scientifically." DOW's weird science became even weirder when it presumed that attacking wolves were tame unless it had been documented that they were never in captivity.

The conditions, qualifications and assumptions implicitly made a part of the DOW disclaimer necessitate the following ridiculously convoluted revision of the original *White Fang* disclaimer in order to be accurate:

> There has never been a *scientifically* documented case of a wild wolf—*that is, a wolf that was never at any time owned by a human*—or a healthy wolf or pack of wolves *with a written certificate of health* attacking *in a serious manner— attacking does not include biting*—a human in North America.

Thank goodness for people like Troy Mader who show us how to read between the lines of environmentalist rhetoric.

Predictably, given the embrace by Hollywood elitists and the dominant liberal media culture of federal proposals to put wolves into other peoples' backyards, Troy Mader is not the most popular speaker at public forums on wolf reintroduction. It takes a real toughness to step before a hostile crowd, as most of them are when Troy arrives, and go toe-to-toe with an "expert" from the U.S. Fish and Wildlife Service. Yet that is what Troy does.

However, when he leaves he takes with him the grudging admiration of his debating opponents and the support of those who have just had their eyes opened for the first time.

Troy Mader attributes his toughness to his cowboy father who was born just south of Broadus, Montana, and left home at the age of fourteen with his only change of clothes in a paper sack. Troy says his father taught him the importance of "principle and hard work." He taught Troy something else, the importance of learning. As his dad said, "leaders are readers."

Yet it was Troy Mader's sixth grade teacher who provided the spark for a life of activism. Mr. Howard had served in Europe during World War II and lived through some of the war's bloodiest battles. However, it was not Mr. Howard's recounting of those days which Troy remembers but the day Mr. Howard handed out tiny Liberty Bell-shaped pins with the words: "Freedom is not free." At last Troy understood the purpose behind his teacher's tales of heroism in battle and the price paid by those with whom he had served.

After years in business with his father, Troy Mader became a deputy sheriff in Campbell County, Wyoming. It was during his years as a law enforcement officer that he discovered his life's work: research and investigation.

Shortly after his father persuaded him in 1987 to start what became known as the Common Man Institute, Troy Mader began his study of the wolf. Ironically, he did so following a bitter argument with his father in which Troy advocated returning the wolf to Yellowstone National Park. To settle the argument, his dad urged him to find out the facts.

That simple agreement has led Troy Mader on an incredible and seemingly endless journey to the National Archives, the U.S. Department of Interior, the U.S. Fish and Wildlife Service, the Library of Congress, and hundreds of other libraries, archives and museums. Troy has traveled more than 25,000 miles throughout North America, including Canada and Alaska. He has conducted more than 180 interviews with biologists, game wardens, conservation officers, predator control specialists, professors, outfitters, trappers, hunters, Native Americans and others with experience in dealing with wolves.

Today, following years of research and study, Troy Mader travels the West speaking wherever he may be heard regarding the risks, not just to livestock, but also to humans, of a return of the wolf. Incredibly, he is most unwelcome by his own government, which once denied him the opportunity to distribute his pamphlets on wolf reintroduction at an open house sponsored by the federal government. When it comes to government meetings on the wolf, freedom of speech is generally only for environmentalists who support reintroduction.

The experience reminded Troy of what Mr. Howard had said about freedom not being free. It also reminded him of something his father often said, something about "eternal vigilance" being the "price of liberty."

ALICE MENKS
Madison, Virginia

T he photograph on the back cover has a grainy, long-ago look. The faces are blurred and indistinct. In the background, in the midst of a barren snow-covered field, sit two empty broken-down wooden wagons. The men in the foreground are obviously officials, dressed in suits, wearing hats. One wears a long heavy overcoat. They are struggling through the snow, their legs bent awkwardly under the strain.

They are struggling, for between them they carry a woman stretched out stiff like a corpse. In the shadow between them she is but a dark mass except for the triangular shape of her thin gaunt face. Her head is lifted slightly, her eyes no more than black circles. A dark gash delineates her downturned mouth. Perhaps she is weeping.

Inside the back cover, the photograph is explained:

> Nellie Jenkins Woodward witnessed two area sheriffs remove her mother, who was five months pregnant, from their home in 1937. All their belongings were piled on horse-drawn wagons, and the chimney of their home was pulled down. This was to be the legacy of Shenandoah National Park.

The book is *US vs. NPS—Virginians Defending The Bill of Rights,* and it is only one indication of the all-consuming addiction that drives its author, Alice Menks. It is a most worthy manifestation of her passionate campaign, for she and her co-author, Leri Thomas, have documented a shocking indictment of the National Park Service for its activities in the Old Dominion.

The Commonwealth of Virginia is rich with the legacy of courageous battles for freedom. Every school child knows the names of Virginians who, in one way or another, cried out "liberty or death." Yet it was not just a faraway king that

159

they feared and against whom they railed. They feared too an over-zealous government.

It was for that reason that they—George Mason, Patrick Henry, Thomas Jefferson and others—demanded a Bill of Rights as the price for Virginia's approval of the Constitution. James Madison, who had opposed a Bill of Rights until a confrontation with his Orange County constituents, became a leader in the fight for a Constitution that contained enumerated freedoms. In the end, it was the ratification by Virginia that incorporated the Bill of Rights into the Constitution.

For Alice Menks, who lives in a city and county named after James Madison, his words of more than two centuries ago have a special and timeless significance. Said Madison in calling for a Bill of Rights: "I believe there are more instances of the abridgment of freedoms of the people by gradual and silent encroachments of those in power than violent and sudden usurpations."

Alice Menks has seen first-hand what Madison only feared, for the "gradual and silent encroachments" of government against which he sought to guard with the Bill of Rights is the history of the National Park Service in Virginia.

Virginia is rich with history. It is not just the birthplace of eight presidents, but also the most fought-over state of the Civil War. For some history buffs and almost all federal bureaucrats, such historical significance engenders a covetous response. As one of them once said, "I find Virginia a fantasy land. I wish I could make the entire state a scenic and historic area."

They have tried. However, since the National Park Service does not have sufficient funds to purchase property outright, bureaucrats have resorted to a variety of subterfuges: "greenlining," "buffer zones," "scenic rivers," "national landmarks," "historic landmarks," the Register of Historic Places, and Memoranda of Understanding (MOU) with local government.

Alice Menks says the duplicitous approach of the National Park Service to controlling private lands is at its noxious worst in "Green Springs Historic District" in Louisa County. As Alice Menks and others wrote in *US vs. NPS*, what the National Park Service did there "exemplifies the arrogance and shamelessness of National Park Service efforts to ignore and trample on the rights of private property owners and local democratically elected governments."

Louisa County—which lies between Richmond and Charlottesville—is where the National Park Service, using the pretext of historic preservation, locked up 14,000 acres—an area the size of Manhattan. The National Park Service action was opposed not just by an overwhelming majority of local residents and by local government, but also by the Louisa Historical Society. The reason was simple: the only thing historic about Green Springs was the amount of litigation that would take place over the National Park Service's brazen lockup.

In order to stop economic development that was opposed by a local preservationist, the National Park Service used the presence of five homes of *bona fide* historical significance to burden the 14,000 acres with a national historic designation. Thereafter preservationists had the acreage labeled a State Historic Landmark, followed quickly by federal listing on the National Register of Historic Places. When the preservationists learned that the "scenic easements" they had been quietly buying up could not be turned over to the federal government, they had the area elevated to National Natural Landmark status.

It was over almost before the locals and their elected representatives knew it had begun, but it was not too late to go to court, so to court they went. Finally, a federal district judge agreed with the locals, vacating the federal designations. Unfortunately, in the wake of the Reagan landslide of November 1980, the rascals who had been thrown out by the voters returned to Washington, D.C. in December for one final indignity to the people.

Congress reversed the judge's ruling, thumbed its nose at the people of Louisa County and reinstituted National Park Service control over the 14,000 acres. While acknowledging that the National Park Service had acted improperly, Congress argued that if it did not act and the judge's ruling stood, all historic preservation actions by the National Park Service might be similarly set aside.

Nonetheless, in an unusual rebuke Congress ordered that henceforth no land could be placed on the National Register of Historic Landmarks without the permission of a majority of local property owners. Yet that did little to stop the

National Park Service, since Congress also provided that no landowner approval is required to designate property as "eligible" for placement on the Register.

So the National Park Service proceeded with designating "eligible" areas, working hand-in-glove with a small band of local preservationists while making use of a variety of federal laws and, when federal funds were unavailable or inadequate, using tax-exempt millions from private land trusts.

That is, until Alice Menks and her colleagues, angered by the arrogance of the National Park Service, moved on the State Capitol in Richmond seeking, like their forefathers, a bill of property rights for Virginians. Despite the powerful forces rallied by the National Park Service—including its federally funded state surrogate and out-of-state-land-lock-up money—the people prevailed. Their property rights were protected. A threatened veto by Virginia's governor never materialized.

Ironically, it was not historic designation that drove Alice Menks from her quiet existence—home-schooling her two small children, picking and pressing wildflowers into works of art, caring for her home—and into the "down-and-dirty" of grassroots politics. Rather it was the frightening roar of an awakening dragon, near whose home Alice Menks and her husband had unwittingly settled.

Originally Alice Menks and her husband were delighted to have Shenandoah National Park as a neighbor. As Alice Menks now says, "I never thought about how the park had been created. I just assumed it was all from public lands."

Alice Menks' innocence was destroyed when Shenandoah National Park, like a dragon slumbering after consuming a huge meal, awoke and began to look around at what private parcels it might next devour. Using a public relations campaign which had served it well in the past, the National Park Service began to decry "threats" to Shenandoah, threats that, when one sorted through the hype, hysteria and hyperbole, came down to one phrase: private land. The "solution" offered up by the National Park Service and its preservationist allies was simple: get rid of or gain control of the private land. Feed the dragon.

Although prohibited from expending federal funds for land acquisition, that did not prevent the National Park Service from using its private sector allies to lock up more land that might become future "gifts" to the federal government. In the midst of what Alice Menks regarded as a rather frightening process, she discovered the maps at the offices of the Madison County Administrator contained the names, addresses and occupations of many private land owners near Shenandoah National Park.

On April 1, 1990, Alice Menks and her neighbors gathered to discuss what they might do about the restless dragon. It was at that meeting that Alice Menks first saw the Jessica Savitch *Frontline* television news story of the taking of Cuyahoga Valley National Recreation Area in Ohio, *For The Good of All,* showing how the National Park Service drew new boundaries, condemned homes and communities, ran the people out and then burned down their houses. "Lord preserve us," she prayed silently as she watched in horror, "they are still doing it today!" What the National Park Service had done in Ohio caused Alice Menks to question her original assumptions regarding the creation of Shenandoah National Park.

Alice Menks learned that what is now Shenandoah National Park had once been privately owned lands, lands that had borne people's homes, lands that had supported farms and orchards, and more importantly, communities. Shenandoah National Park had once been home not to the hundreds its promoters had asserted but more than 15,000 Americans, people who lived in rural isolation, and solitude. Yet their isolation was not great enough, for being mere hours from the urban sprawl of Washington, D.C., they became pawns in Washington's search for a future source of water, and for a rural setting in which the people of the city could retreat—for a day—to be refreshed.

When National Park Service officials went to the area expecting to find "virgin timber, primeval forests, and pristine wilderness," they found homes, orchards and farms. It made no difference. So what of the people who lived there? Park proponents defamed them as "selfish, stubborn and avaricious," as "fundamentally uncivilized people," as "cultural primitives," as "lazy," "filthy," "ignorant," and "inbred." So, for the greater public good, the federal government took their land, pulled down their barns and homes, and sent them packing.

"When I first saw the photograph of Nellie Woodward's mother, Mrs. Jenkins, I wept," says Alice Menks. "I thought how degraded and humiliated she must have felt. I couldn't help thinking how I would feel having my children watch me being carried away from our home.

"Then I realized that somewhere in Washington, D.C., or some other big city where these decisions are made, people were now talking about doing this very thing to us, were looking at the boundaries of the park and were wondering how to get rid of the Menks, or their neighbors.

"There's an incredible elitism among them," says Alice Menks, "an elitism that permits them to at once conclude that we are worthless and that they know better what should be done with us and with our property. We saw it more than 60 years ago when they carried Mrs. Jenkins away. I'm here to see that it doesn't happen again. If being a Virginian, being an American, means anything, it means that."

James Madison would have been proud.

BEN LOVE
Marathon, Texas

"The sun has riz, the sun has set, and here we is, in Texas yet." With 840 miles from El Paso to Port Arthur and 927 miles from the Panhandle to Brownsville, it is little wonder that the miles seem longer in Texas. That is particularly the case out where the sun sets on Texas, in the wide open country of Terrell, Pecos, Jeff Davis, Presidio and Brewster counties.

Brewster County alone comprises some 4 million acres of rugged Chihuahuan Desert. The average rainfall varies from less than 9 inches annually to 18 inches in the higher elevations in the northern part of the county where the Del Norte Mountains approach the Davis Mountains of Jeff Davis County. The southern boundary is the Rio Grande. Brewster County's population is about 8,500 with 80% residing in the county seat of Alpine. Just 31 miles east is the only other town of size in Brewster County, Marathon, with a population of 800.

Brewster County, like the counties that surround it, is cattle country. The ranches, like the open country where they are located, are large. The largest city in the area is Fort Stockton in Pecos County, a city of some 10,000 largely supported by oil and gas production in the area.

Brewster County is the home of Ben Love and has been for more than 20 years. Ben is a fourth generation cattleman. The LV brand carried by his cattle was first registered in Texas by his great grandfather in 1873. Ben was born and grew up on the family ranch near Llano, Texas, along the Llano River some 50 miles northwest of Austin.

Ben Love graduated from the Texas Military Institute in 1964, completed his B.A. at Texas Tech in Lubbock and obtained his J.D. degree from St. Mary's School of Law in San Antonio. He served in the U.S. Army and was discharged in 1972 as an Infantry Captain. That same year he was admitted to the Texas Bar and moved to Brewster County.

In addition to running his ranch, on which he has raised a magnificent herd of registered Red Brahman cattle, Ben Love

165

also maintains a successful law practice in Marathon, where he has focused upon real estate, environmental and oil and gas law. Ben and Kay Love and their three daughters live an isolated life: the ranch is 36 miles from the nearest town, 70 miles from the nearest doctor, 200 miles from a shopping mall, and 8 miles from the nearest neighbor. While they're too busy to be lonely, it's a good thing Ben Love is a lawyer. One of those neighbors is the National Park Service.

Big Bend National Park was created in the 1940s on the oft-heard promise that the park would enhance the local economy. While the dream of an economic boost is little more than a hazy memory, the hard feelings of the families of those forced out of what became the park remain.

Since Ben Love's family acquired the Brewster County ranch some years after the creation of Big Bend National Park, Ben arrived in Southwestern Texas with an open mind. That soon changed as one episode after another caused him to become wary of the ways of career bureaucrats who frequently seemed insensitive to property rights, traditional land usage and the needs of local communities. Ben's contacts with the National Park Service became something of a graduate course in bureaucratic affairs.

In the late 1970s a portion of the Rio Grande—from the west side of Big Bend National Park to Amistad Recreation Area near Del Rio—was designated a Wild and Scenic River as a result of a deal cut by Congressman (later short-term Senator) Bob Krueger. Despite Krueger's promise that there "will never be a Wild and Scenic River in my district," he changed his mind and the people of arid Brewster and Terrell counties were saddled with federal control of an important water source. As galling as was the flip-flop of their congressman was the National Park Service response.

Fearing the worst, Ben Love contacted the National Park Service to ascertain the regulatory response to the designation of the Rio Grande as Wild and Scenic. He was assured that the Draft Plan in no way affected the Love ranch. Later, when he got a copy of the Plan he was shocked to learn that the National Park Service proposed a visitor center at the very heart of his ranch, upon its most commercially valuable site.

Despite the assurance of the National Park Service that all of Ben Love's neighbors were for the plan and that Ben and Kay were the last to sign the cooperative agreement, Ben decided to talk to his neighbors. Many were unaware that the river had even been designated. Others were apprehensive about any federal plan to control the lands near the Rio Grande and none favored the plan.

They were right to be apprehensive. The land grab planned by the National Park Service was nothing if not audaciously ambitious. In designating a river as Wild and Scenic, Congress authorizes the government to acquire a set number of miles along the river. The challenge and opportunity presented the National Park Service by the Rio Grande designation was that the river is an international border with much of its banks already owned by the federal government (Big Bend National Park) or the State of Texas (the Black Gap Wildlife Management Area). The National Park Service's response: it would calculate the total land acquisition that would have been permitted had the Rio Grande not been an international border. Then it would acquire that amount of land along only one side of the river. Worse yet, in order to get the amount of land it desired, the National Park Service planned to acquire private land along the Rio Grande.

Literally overnight, Ben Love and a few neighbors organized Texans for the Preservation of the Rio Grande (TPRG). This was before "preservation" became a distasteful word to landowners. Ben's telephone bill for the group's first month of organization was nearly $4,000, but it paid big dividends. The organization grew rapidly and gained statewide support.

In hopes of gathering public support for its plan, the National Park Service held meetings throughout Texas to permit participation by the Sierra Club and other environmental groups. What the National Park Service had not counted on was the popularity of Ben Love's group and the strong ties of other Texans with west Texas and Texans for the Preservation of the Rio Grande. The debate came to a head at the Alpine, Texas meeting where a standing-room-only crowd of angry TPRG members forced the National Park Service to consider a "no action" alternative. In the end, as a result of the overwhelming public sentiment and hundreds of comments, the National Park Service adopted TPRG's "no action" alternative.

The Rio Grande Wild and Scenic River fiasco was a wake-up call for thousands of West Texans. They had learned how the National Park Service works and that their government could not always be trusted. The federal government learned something about West Texans: they might be rural, but with organization they could band together and be heard effectively. They also had a lot of friends outside West Texas.

In 1989 the National Park Service announced its plans to study a 4,000,000 acre area in Brewster, Jeff Davis, and Presidio counties for possible inclusion in the national park system. When affected ranchers formed the Davis Mountain Heritage Association, the first call they made was to ask Ben Love to serve as a board member and legal advisor. At the National Park Service public meeting in Fort Davis, more than 500 angry West Texans packed the community center with hundreds more leaning in through the open windows. When one local commentator asked for a show of hands of support for the proposal, the only hand raised was that of the elderly wife of a retired National Park Service employee. Her husband kept his hands in his pockets.

In 1990 Ben Love was elected president of the Davis Mountain Heritage Association. Under his leadership the two groups expanded to represent over 13,000,000 acres of privately owned land and changed its name to the Davis Mountains Trans-Pecos Heritage Association (DMTPHA). In 1991 Ben Love became Chairman of the board. Today he continues to serve the group as informal counsel. In 1992 DMTPHA helped form the Trans Texas Heritage Association to take the DMTPHA message statewide to fight for property rights and sensible environmental regulations.

The DMTPHA brochure depicts a local landmark surrounded by the words, "Land of the Free, Home of the Brave." Only brave and independent individuals would have dared to do what this band of hardy West Texans has done.

Under Ben Love's guidance the Davis Mountains Trans Pecos Heritage Association and its new statewide ally, the Trans Texas Heritage Association, review hundreds of government plans, acquisitions and activities that potentially affect property owners. The associations' leaders attend scores of meetings and hearings each year, comment on countless proposed government actions and regulations, monitor federal and state legislation and provide vital information to members and to the public.

Through Ben Love's tutelage, the members of these grassroots organizations are learning that the system still works, but only if citizens make it work. The key is information, knowledge and the courage to stand up in meetings and be heard. West Texans have also learned to stand up for one another. Their battle cry is, "If it affects my neighbor, it affects me!" Ben notes, "For years West Texans have lived a life of acceptance of government. Whatever an agency wanted, it got without meaningful local challenge or even input. In four short years that has all changed drastically. Any agency proposing almost anything in West Texas does so with the knowledge that its plans will be reviewed by DMTPHA, and now with the emergence of TTHA, a statewide presence is being felt. One of my greatest feelings of accomplishment is the knowledge that these two associations don't really even need my help any longer because so many others have learned to be effective."

Ben Love serves on the Board of Directors of the National Cattlemens Association, the Texas and Southwestern Cattle Raisers Association, and the Texas Wildlife Association. He also serves on the Board of Legal Advisors to Defenders of Property Rights, a Washington, D.C.-based public interest legal foundation specializing in the protection of property rights. He has carried his message of the defense of property rights throughout Texas and the nation in speeches, seminars, and congressional testimony. He also writes for a variety of statewide and national publications.

A private pilot with more than 2,000 hours of pilot-in-command time in high performance aircraft, Ben finds it difficult to sit still and watch a bully take unfair advantage of people who don't have the means to defend themselves. It is only his commitment to Constitutionally protected freedoms that allows him to take leave of that which he loves the most, his family and ranch, to travel more than 2,000 miles to Washington, D.C. Ben Love knows how important it is that he go to Washington, D.C. For as great as are the distances in Texas, they are nothing compared to the gulf that separates Washington's power elite from the real people who populate this country.

JOANN ETIENNE
Saint Croix, Indiana

"We've been on the outside looking in a whole lot longer than we've been on the inside looking out, so we've got a little different perspective than most folks," says Joann Etienne of St. Croix, Indiana. "My husband, Phil, was raised on a hog farm, one of 12 children. I was raised at the other end of the county on a dairy farm. We know what it is to be poor. As for the sawmill, it was only by accident that we wandered into timber."

Joann and Phil Etienne may have become involved in timber accidentally, but it is no accident that they have stayed over the past 20-some years, becoming one of the most successful small operations in the country. How they "wandered" into timber is the story of many of the nation's family-run small businesses, particularly in the natural resources industry.

"Phil had been working construction. He bought a bulldozer and was doing hourly contract work for folks. Then his younger brother, Greg, talked Phil into buying an old used John Deere 4-40 log skidder. At the time, I was running a country story in Derby, Indiana.

"All we had then was a little place here on the river. For several years, the crew was just the three of us. Phil was the cutter. Greg drove the skidder. I drove the log truck. Then about 10 years ago, we sold all the equipment to Greg and bought a sawmill. It just about consumed us for several years, but we made it."

One of the things that has made the Etiennes' operation a success is Phil's and Joann's attitude toward their public. It helps that a lot of them are friends and neighbors. Nonetheless, they realize that they must do all that they can to build public support for what they do for a living. Providing 30 jobs and making a sizable contribution to the financial well-being of the local community in payroll, health care and taxes is not enough.

"We always make sure that our log yards are cleaned out and smoothed down. We remove any mud we track onto the county roads. We're courteous to our neighbors. A lot of the

171

roads we go down to cut timber are just narrow country roads we share with everybody else. So we teach our drivers to be courteous to the other folks who use those roads. We're always careful to install water control systems like ditches, culverts and water bars on all skid trails and haul roads to prevent erosion. Today the regulators call what we do "best management practices" (BMPs), and they want to put it in the rule books and hire bureaucrats to enforce it, but we just call it common courtesy.

"Of course, no matter how hard we try, we're going to make mistakes. We had an operator get too close to the edge of a swamp one time and, thinking the skidder was going in upside down, he jumped clear. The truck didn't roll over. It just slid on down into the water and with those big flotation tires floated away. You can bet that photograph made the newspaper. Same as the time when one of our fully loaded trucks hauling bark and saw dust rolled over. There's nothing as pitiful-looking as an 18 wheeler laying over on its side. Sort of like a turtle on its back.

"So when we had our open house in July 1993, we ran a full page ad with pictures like that, real attention getters, with the words—in big, bold print—NOW COME SEE WHAT WE DO RIGHT!" More than 800 folks did."

The open house hosted by Phil and Joann Etienne was a textbook example of public outreach to build support and to inform others about the benefits of good forestry management practices. The tone was set by the sign at the front gate which led, the scenic way, up through the woods to the mill: "WELCOME TO PHIL ETIENNE'S TIMBER HARVEST INCORPORATED, WHICH WITH OUR FAMILY AND FRIENDS PRODUCES RAW WOOD PRODUCTS FOR 80,000 AMERICAN CONSUMERS EACH YEAR."

The mill was spruced up as if ready for the very first logs to go through and Phil and Joann's family and employees were stationed throughout to give talks and to provide information on the operation. Two-inch tree cross sections—"tree cookies," Joann Etienne calls them—were placed on the ground for people to follow from one informational stop to another. One of the warehouses was cleaned out and set up to resemble a small forest with wildlife exhibits provided by a local taxidermist. Foresters and wildlife specialists were brought in to talk about forestry and about the benefits of good forest management practices to wildlife.

There was also food. "The guys at the mill roasted a couple of hogs, sliced potatoes until they were nearly blind, cooked a ton of beans, roasted hot dogs, and served up a couple thousand Cokes.™ The kids may have come for the food, but they were fascinated with what we were doing. Kids love technology, they love big machines and when they found out what we were doing was good all the way around they were really excited. It was the classiest thing we'd ever done. I was about blown away by it all."

Joann Etienne isn't just involved locally. In the past, she devoted a considerable amount of time to state and national battles on timber policy, beginning with her involvement with the Hoosier National Forest. Like most eastern components of lands managed by the U.S. Forest Service, the Hoosier National Forest was created in the 1930s from lands that had been settled and then lost due to unpaid taxes and foreclosures.

Today the Hoosier National Forest spreads across several Indiana Counties, including Joann Etienne's Perry County. Of Perry County's 150,000 acres of timberland, the U.S. Government owns more than a third—the federal lands battle is by no means an exclusively Western States problem. Despite an abundance of rich timber resources—primarily red and white oak, as well as hickory—for several years there hadn't been a single sale on the Hoosier National Forest.

"An environmental group called the Hoosier Environmental Council brought a lawsuit saying the Forest Service failed to do a proper forest plan. The Forest Service rolled over, said it hadn't obeyed the law, and agreed to amend the plan. Unfortunately for us, since we were dependent on timber from federal lands, that new plan didn't include any timber sales. Despite all of our efforts to get the Forest Service to adopt a reasonable harvesting plan, the Forest Service went the path of least resistance and did what environmentalists demanded. I don't look for the Forest Service to cut timber in the Hoosier National Forest in my lifetime."

Joann Etienne's efforts to preserve a multiple use approach to the Hoosier National Forest made her a very visible figure in, and eventually Chairman of, the Indiana Forest Industry Council (IFIC). Phil Etienne had long been one of the original directors who had founded IFIC, which is made up of some 120 sawmills and logging companies.

"During the fight over the Hoosier National Forest, I took the position that we here in southern Indiana needed to make wise use of the timber resources of the federal lands which predominate in some of our counties. This is high hill country here, but for the grace of God and a 90-degree turn in the Ohio River we'd be living in Kentucky. We've got some coal and some limestone, but mostly we've got timber and a lot of woodworking industry, cabinet makers and so forth. Unfortunately, the national forest got locked up.

"It hurt a lot of people. Anytime you stop harvesting from as much land as the Forest Service controls down here something is going to happen. Some people are going to go out of business. We vowed that it would not be us. We tried to become more competitive. Overnight we started going farther and farther out for timber."

Today, the Etienne mill is, as it began, a family business. Phil's brother Greg—who started it all—runs a logging crew. Phil and his brother Doyle, who also has a logging crew, buy the standing timber and arrange for it to be harvested and delivered to the mill. Phil and Joann Etienne's four children also work at the mill. Daughter Felisa, a computer whiz almost from birth, keeps the records, while her husband Dan is a loader operator. Daughter Cindy also works in the records department while her husband Jason works in the "short board operation," a high technology attempt to find ways to use slabs cut from butt logs for something other than wood chips. Son Wade, age 14, works in the short board operation after school; while son Robin, an 11-year-old businessman, runs the vending machine concession.

After her work at the state and national level, Joann Etienne returned to local grassroots activity. "We are not going to win this battle at the national or the state level, although we have to maintain a presence there. We will win it here at home—thousands of us all over America. Environmentalists are winning today because for the past 20 years they worked to capture an entire generation of young adults trained in the preservation way and not the conservation way. Everyone hopped on board the preservation train because it's supposed to be so wonderful. No one ever told them about the costs. We have to start all over and get the word out, to change things from the grassroots up.

"The folks here at the mill gave me a plaque which has my motto on it: 'Whatever it takes.' It also has a poem, something about the people who get ahead in life are those who get up everyday looking for ways to excel and if they don't find them they create them. Let's face it, no one is going to knock on my door each day saying, 'Here's your opportunity to show off your industry.' We have to create that opportunity ourselves and we have to be imaginative. If everyone in the timber industry would do that we could turn this thing around in 10 years."

For someone who has spent more years on the "outside looking in" than the "inside looking out," Joann Etienne sounds like someone who spent a lot of time thinking about what she would do if she ever got "inside." She also sounds like someone who is not going to waste the opportunity now that she is there.

WILLIAM "FOSSIL BILL" KRAMER
Silver Bay, Minnesota

William "Fossil Bill" Kramer was not always what he now calls himself—"The Angry Environmentalist." For years and years he was simply an environmentalist and he was proud of it.

From 1943 until 1946 Bill Kramer served as a navigator in the Army Air Corps in Europe. In 1949 he received a B.S. degree in journalism from Northwestern University. In 1951 he was recalled to active duty, this time with the U.S. Air Force in Korea, where he served until 1953.

For a number of years Bill Kramer worked as a journalist, publisher of a trade magazine, and then public relations head of a national trade association. For years his articles were carried by most U.S. dailies and consumer magazines.

Then in the early 1960s Bill found a new love—rock hounding. He returned to college to study geology, mineralogy and paleontology. In the mid-1960s he started his own business and earned the nickname "Fossil Bill" the hard way: camping out, digging rocks and fossils.

Bill Kramer's love of the out-of-doors was the perfect companion for his newfound fascination with the incredible history concealed within the rocks and stones that most folks ignore. Soon, the career he had started on a whim became a passion. He became the leading U.S. promoter of gem-mineral-fossil shows, and within the decade owned stores throughout the country.

Naturally, as an outdoorsman and as someone whose study of the earth was both a vocation and an avocation, Bill had much in common with those who, in the late 1960s and early 1970s called themselves "environmentalists." He didn't know much about them, but he knew he was one. After all, he loved the out of doors, he was immersed in a study of the planet and its history, and he believed in a reasonable balance between economic progress and environmental protection.

177

"For years my wife Tec (short for Thecla) and I were caught up in the web of fairy tales spun by Audubon, the Wilderness Society, the Sierra Club and all the rest: Man is wrecking the planet. Nature knows best. Acid rain is killing our forests. Wolves are endangered. Nuclear power is bad. Rain forests are the lungs of the earth. Biodiversity is vital to medical progress.

"Being believers, we passed this nonsense on to our four children. We'd be preaching it today had it not been that a vicious attack on our lifestyle and private property shocked us to awareness. It took the roof falling in on us personally to wake us up."

The roof to which Bill Kramer refers is a rather humble and isolated one, located as it is "on the Canadian side of a remote border lake—eight miles by boat or snowmobile to a dirt road and pay phone, another 60 to a small town." It was there that in May of 1983 Bill and his wife retired to "rough it and get back to nature."

Bill insulated their rustic cabin, replaced the large propane heater in the living room with an air-tight wood stove, and insulated and heated the outhouse. They took their water from the lake and took sponge baths in a tub in the kitchen. To keep the wood stove going they spent a great deal of time cutting wood with a chain saw and hauling it via a powerboat or snowmobile.

Isolated on their three-acre island with no telephone, no mail, and no way to get anywhere, they were truly "getting back to nature. In January it got to be 40 to 45 degrees below zero and the wind blew and it snowed so hard we couldn't see the woodpile. At times like that we'd put more wood on the fire and commune with nature and read how man was destroying the planet and all."

Bill Kramer read about acid rain. When he and Tec read that their island was "square on acid rain alley," they became quite upset and traveled to various hearings being conducted by the State of Minnesota on the subject. It was at those hearings that Bill met some "real nice fellows from Audubon and Sierra and other big environmental groups. They were worried about acid rain, too, so we got along just fine."

Then one day their friends came to visit Bill and Tec on their island. Their friends were horrified at what Bill and Tec were doing to the "wilderness." As far as their friends were concerned, their island was virgin wilderness and shouldn't be messed up with such things as motors and modern "conveniences." His "friends" believed that for Bill and Tec "to coexist with animals, we had to live and behave like them!"

Shortly thereafter, Bill learned that their "friends" had gone to both U.S. and Canadian authorities to have motors forbidden in the area Bill and Tec called home. Furthermore, their "friends" were trying to get rid of all private property for hundreds of miles around the Kramers so that 12 million acres could be made into uninhabited wilderness. Ironically, there was already more than three and one half million acres of wilderness just a mile from his island.

Bill Kramer started a property owners group—The Association of North Woods Property Owners—to fight back, "tooth and nail." He became its first president and today serves as its Executive Director. He spearheaded successful efforts to prevent a green takeover of the area.

That wasn't enough, however. Bill Kramer began to research environmental groups. He discovered that they are "obscenely well-heeled," with some of them taking in hundreds of millions of dollars a year, that "they've become giant bureaucracies with staffs in the thousands," all with one goal: "more power and bigger budgets," that they are "unconcerned about people, private property or constitutional rights." He concluded that "environmentalists are using and suckering the American people."

The more Bill Kramer learned, the angrier he became. In April 1990, he decided it was time to put some truth into environmental reporting. He reached out to editors across the country, picked up some subscribers and launched a weekly column called "The Angry Environmentalist."

Weekly mailings and talks to concerned citizen groups from Florida to Alaska have made Bill Kramer and Tec abandon their idyllic island life. They made the sacrifice because, "we are dedicated to a great cause: preserving American freedom."

During his research Bill Kramer was appalled to learn that major corporations and their foundations, the very entities that should be leading the defense of free enterprise and private property rights, were funding their enemies—extreme environmental groups. According to Willa Johnson's Capital Research Center and its annual *Patterns of Corporate Philanthropy,* the vast majority of public affairs dollars contributed by major corporations goes to "liberal or radical organizations." Meanwhile, groups of what Bill Kramer calls "freedom fighters" were in desperate financial straits.

"I'm a relative newcomer in the battle against green madness, but I feel compelled to state the obvious. It's important to halt the support big business gives to its own destruction—the destruction of all of us. Before we know it, freedom and private property will be relics of the past. The interests of corporate America are obviously best served by the ideals we espouse since Big Green has always been hostile to business. Today it is even more threatening. It should be possible for us to convince business leaders where their vital interests lie, where the interests of this great nation lie. We must mount an intelligent intensive program to do just that."

Not surprisingly, Bill Kramer is not just talking, he is doing something about it: actively advising businesses to support friendly grassroots groups through presentations and fund-raising campaigns.

Bill Kramer is not proud of what he was. He feels foolish that a smart man like himself could have been so taken in. He is proud of what he has become. He still thinks of himself as an environmentalist—but now he's an angry one because of what those with an anti-people, anti-property, anti-progress agenda have done to his movement. Bill Kramer will probably stay angry, at least until people become a part of the environmental equation.

CHERYL JOHNSON
Campton, New Hampshire

A t one time or another I have belonged or contributed to just about every environmental group you can name," says Cheryl Johnson. "That ended in 1991."

That was the year Cheryl Johnson traveled to Washington, D.C. for the first time. She was fresh from her early battles over proposed "wild and scenic" designation of the river that flows through her home town of Campton, New Hampshire. She went to the Nation's Capitol for the Fly-In For Freedom, the annual gathering of grassroots activists in the nation's capitol. She was looking for ideas, for support, for solutions. She found friends—and herself.

"I met and talked with Oregon loggers about what was happening to them and to their families. I had read the National Wildlife Federation stories about the northern spotted owl. Having heard both sides, I believe the loggers." Cheryl was changed forever.

"When I got home, I packed up an eleven-year collection of National Wildlife magazines and mailed them directly to Jay Hair, thirty pounds of magazines which, as a wildlife artist, I often used. I included a note: 'Since I don't have a recycling facility in my town, I would appreciate it if you would take care of them for me. I suggest that recycling them into something more useful—paychecks for Northwest loggers—would be appropriate. If you are too busy to do it yourself, perhaps your chauffeur can drop them off.' He never wrote back."

Cheryl Johnson was "so angry. I felt duped, cheated and robbed. All those years I thought I was helping wildlife, and most of the money was going toward fancy office buildings, exorbitant salaries and political agendas."

When she returned to Campton, New Hampshire, she was ready for the battle over the Pemigewasset River and its designation as part of the Wild and Scenic Rivers Act. Earlier that year she had attended a public hearing held to discuss the fate of what the locals call "the Pemi." Two things bothered her about

181

the meeting: the deceptive tactics of those presiding when they concluded the meeting by announcing "overwhelming support" for the proposal; and the push for what Cheryl called "environmental socialism," that is, controlling the property of those along the river in the name of protecting the environment.

Cheryl Johnson concluded that it was not plants and animals that were "threatened," but private property. She saw it as a "national epidemic." Although she saw the situation in many states as "much worse than here in New Hampshire, it's just a matter of time." Cheryl decided to stop it.

Although she had never been politically active, had never voted, never watched the news, was terrified to stand in front of a group and speak, and was almost painfully shy, Cheryl Johnson knew she had to do something. Although the Pemi had been one of the most highly industrialized rivers in New England, although it flows through the center of town after town and is crossed by bridges, power lines and trestles and is paralleled by roads, railroad tracks as well as houses, condos, golf courses and sewage treatment plants, the National Park Service said the Pemi qualified for designation. Why? Because of its "unique and outstanding values." Cheryl knew a land grab when she saw it.

She caught the National Park Service in distortion after distortion, arrogant misrepresentation after arrogant misrepresentation, half truth after half truth, fraudulent denial after fraudulent denial. By networking with her newfound friends around the country, she learned the truth about what happens to private property along wild and scenic rivers and about the heavy hand of the National Park Service and its allies in environmental organizations once designation of a river occurs.

Cheryl Johnson, the quiet wildlife artist, the woman so afraid to speak up in meetings that she got her husband Donald to ask questions from the audience directed to her, started speaking up, started leading. She helped found New Hampshire Landowners Alliance, Inc., (NHLA).

NHLA held forums, meetings and rallies. NHLA protested a National Park Service study committee canoe trip by posting "Go Home NPS" and "No Wild & Scenic" signs up and down the river. NHLA parked a large truck that read, "Say No to Wild & Scenic Rivers" and "If You Like This Truck, Sign It," in prominent locations throughout Plymouth. (A photograph of the

NHLA truck appeared on page one of *The Boston Globe*.) NHLA bought and distributed hundreds of copies of a local paper to ensure that all local residents would find out about and have a chance to vote on the proposed designation.

In the Spring of 1993 Cheryl's NHLA proudly proclaimed "WE WON." Despite massive interference by the National Park Service in the local process, including the funding of so-called "local groups" that supported designation, NHLA won. The reasons why NHLA chalked up this historic victory are instructive.

"We won," says Cheryl Johnson, "because we refused to compromise. We extracted a unanimous statement from our Congressional delegation that they would not introduce a bill if the affected towns did not want the river designated. We learned to use the media. We were not afraid to be controversial."

"Finally we won in spite of being out-spent by at least a ten-to-one margin—maybe fifteen or twenty-to-one." In the end Cheryl Johnson, once and always a conservationist, made up for all the money she sent to environmental groups in Washington, D.C. and New York City and San Francisco. In spades!

C. LARRY MASON
Forks, Washington

At a time when millions of Americans were leaving rural America for the cities and urban life, Larry Mason of Boston, Massachusetts, was heading in the other direction. In 1972 Larry Mason, who had spent his summers growing up along the Maine coast where his grandfather had been a lobsterman, left for the woods of the Olympic Peninsula of Washington State.

Larry Mason left for a variety of reasons, but one of them was that he considered himself an environmentalist and he was disturbed by what he saw taking place around him. "At that time fish were swimming wrong side up in Lake Erie and the Cuyahoga River was catching on fire. I wanted to get away from the polluted world. I wanted to get back to nature."

That's exactly what Larry Mason found in the still rural frontier of the Olympic Peninsula. He settled in Sappho, which was in its last year as a logging camp. It's little more today: a crossroads with a gas station. When Larry arrived, he wanted only one thing: a job that would permit him to work in the woods. He started a reforestation business since it involved putting trees in the ground and required only a minimal capital investment.

Larry Mason thrived. Unlike many of his generation—the counterculture types who made a trip similar to Larry's, to communes, rural homes and isolated mountain cabins—he stayed. While the others were returning to the cities to, in Larry's words, "become yuppies who wax sentimental about rural life from the comfort of their high-rise apartments and glass tower offices," Larry Mason was living the rural life.

Despite the American nostalgia for and love of the frontier, it is an experience foreign to most Americans. "There is an incredible disconnect in this country between consumption and provision. Out here we know that if we don't kill the deer, we don't eat the meat. Most Americans who go into

185

a McDonalds™ haven't given a moment's thought to the blood
and gore that goes into producing beef. If they did they'll
probably choke on their hamburger.

"Out here we understand that nature is not a Bambi
fantasy. We know that nature can be both cruel and benevolent. We also know that it is an undeniable part of our lives.
In fact, rural people chronicle history by natural events. Those
events are the milestones.

"For example, here we talk about 'the 1921 blow' when
8 billion board feet of timber went down in an afternoon. It
was a disaster and would have been even worse if it had caught
on fire. It would have if the entire peninsula hadn't sprung
into action to harvest the blown down wood.

"We also talk about the 1952 fire when 35,000 acres
burned in less than 9 hours. That shocks city people, but it
doesn't shock us. We know that's what happens in the right
conditions: when you have a warm east wind and an
unmanaged forest with a dry fuel load.

"Yet as tough as it is and as brutal as it can be, the
people around here don't want to be anywhere else or to be
doing anything else. We take tremendous pride in the fact
that we are the ones who pull resources from the land and
give them to others to manufacture into usable products. We
are in wealth-creating jobs. All else is wealth-consumption.
Both wealth-creation and service jobs are essential to the quality of life we enjoy. However, if we lose resource extraction
we lose the cornerstone of our economy."

In time Larry Mason—who began in the woods planting seedlings, seedlings that would become trees to be harvested—became a logger working for others. Then he started
his own small logging company. In 1978 he started his own
sawmill. By the mid-1980s he had invested a million dollars
upgrading his sawmill. Ironically, most of the financing for
that upgrade was through the U.S. Small Business Administration, based upon assurances from the U.S. Forest Service
that the mill would have a reliable supply of timber. Such
assurances were crucial since most of the timber on the Olympic Peninsula available to small milling operations is federally owned and managed.

In the timber industry the small operators, unable to
own corporate timber lands, rely upon access to federal lands

for their raw materials. These operators are the businesses that overcome lack of funds with hard work and ingenuity. These are also the businesses that are the backbone of rural communities, the source of industrial innovation with the greatest commitment to sustained yield of the land.

In a very short time Larry Mason's sawmill was recognized as one of the best Douglas fir-cutting mills in the country, cutting for 13 countries internationally, including Japan and countries in Europe and even the Middle East. Larry's company was not exporting raw logs, a favorite bogey man of environmentalists, because federal timber had long been absolutely off limits to export. He was milling it here at home, making value-added products: ladder stock, scaffold, molding grade, door pieces, interior panels, and slicing flitches.

The chief operational tenet of his sawmill was maximum utilization of the natural resources of the Olympic Peninsula. In other words, the mill's profitability depended upon recovery, not upon production. That is, he did not try to produce the fastest and the cheapest, but to get more from less while increasing the value of the product.

"We used very little wood while employing a large number of people. We would do some 50 products out of any one log. In fact, our work at the saw mill was more like dissection than sawing, carefully done to avoid defects in the wood and to produce lumber in both American and metric sizes. I'd give my sawyers a list of all the products we were making, with the values of each, so, when they were looking at the trees and making decisions, they could decide what was the most efficient, most profitable way to go.

"We created a lot of local jobs. Even with more and more automation we were generating more jobs since the new products required more workers. We could afford those workers since our products were much more valuable. We also had a unique product line that was known and respected worldwide. In addition, we used every bit of fiber from the tree. There was no waste. We even used the sawdust for fuel."

In 1988 Larry Mason's mill did $4 million in sales with its 40 employees. It was the second largest employer in the Beaver area just outside Forks. Larry Mason didn't know it, but that was as good as it was ever going to get. In 1989, even before the Northern Spotted Owl was listed under the Endangered Species Act, environmental groups got an injunction against the harvesting of timber from federal lands. The U.S. Forest Service stopped selling timber.

"We struggled along. The first thing to go was our health care program. Ironically, given all the debate about health care now, we had a $100,000 health care program, not because the U.S. Government demanded it or to settle a labor management dispute. We had it because we wanted it for our people. We don't need the government's help to provide health care. We can provide it if the government would let us cut trees."

In 1990 the end came for Larry Mason's grand and glorious dream. He was denied all access to federal timber. He had to close his mill. In 1991 the mill and its equipment was auctioned off. The auction brought in ten cents on the dollar. Larry was broke but not broken.

In 1991 he agreed to become Executive Director of a grassroots organization he had helped create in 1988: The Washington Commercial Forest Action Committee, a spin off from the Forks Chamber of Commerce. WCFAC had membership from all over Washington's western rural communities, representing a broad cross section of people, not just timber workers, but also store owners, business men and women, teachers and others. WCFAC is committed to implementing a responsible and sustained use of the forest to ensure a quality of life and economic foundation for the people of western Washington.

Any other lifestyle is unacceptable to Larry Mason and his neighbors. "We have seen the future the urbanites have in mind for us and it is unacceptable. We didn't come all this way to end up being government employees and service personnel for the pie-in-the-sky tourism industry. Remember that the people who started Forks and other rural natural resource-based communities are the independent people who settled the West, who went over the hill rather than put up with increasing regulation in eastern communities."

In the three years Larry Mason operated WCFAC, he learned a lot about environmentalists and their views and vision, about Bill Clinton and his "Timber Summit" and about Washington and the political process.

On environmentalists: "I've spent a great deal of time searching for reasonable environmentalists to work in partnership with to find a solution. Believe me, there is no such animal, not one. I've been to their offices and I've asked them to come to the forest to see the situation. They don't want to come and they won't come.

"As to their plan, they don't have a plan or a vision. All they have is a strategy, a strategy to lock up more and more land. Furthermore, their views are not grounded in reality. They talk about returning major portions of the forest to 'pre-settlement conditions.' They forget that two hundred years ago forest fires burned from the mountains to the seas and that, by the way, 250 million people did not live in America then.

"Make no mistake, this is a debate about using the forest or not using the forest. It is not a debate about using the forest foolishly or using it wisely. Unfortunately, reaching reasonable solutions based on how we use the forest, not whether we use the forest, has been frustrated by the Clinton Administration. This is an administration full of zealots. The average age in the Clinton Administration is 32 years old. These people are rich, white, from the East Coast, some 3 to 4 years out of law school with little knowledge about politics and no knowledge about real life. These people haven't a clue. They know nothing about the forest. If they had to spend the night in the woods, I think they would surely perish."

On the Clinton "Timber Summit:" "I thought that Clinton could not cut and run from his promise to labor that there would be no net loss of jobs in the Pacific Northwest. I admit that I was taken in personally. Clinton shook my hand, looked me in the eye and said, 'Larry, we won't forget your people.' What I didn't know was that the forest plan was already being written before I spoke with President Clinton. The entire Olympic National Forest is off limits to timber harvesting under Clinton's Option 9.

"Regardless, the Timber Summit, for the first time, did give us the opportunity to speak to the American people in something other than sound bites. For the first time we grassroots timber folks were at the table and were seen as something different from Environmentalists, Inc. and the timber industry. You can see why the environmentalists hate us.

We're the silver bullet. They can't paint us as rich timber barons. What we told Clinton and Gore that day is still true: we are problem solvers by heritage, we can make this work, if given the opportunity. Unfortunately, in the past we have been the first ones hurt and the last ones heard."

On the political process: "I've been to Washington, D.C., 20 times in the last five years. It is terribly important for real people to be involved with their government. You get legislation like the Endangered Species Act passed in 1973 that is just now, 20 years later, hurting people. Somehow we must take the message to Washington with national coalitions like the Alliance for America. Many environmental laws, although well intentioned, need adjusting so they can work for people as well as wildlife.

"Congress, ignorant of rural America, adopts legislation that hurts rural America. It adopts legislation that is naive in concept and vague in structure which in turn creates litigation opportunity for environmental organizations, which takes years to play out. Lobbying Congress has also helped me to see the difference between a citizen's lobby and other more institutionalized lobbying efforts. Citizen lobbyists want resolution so we can go home and back to our lives. The permanent lobby machine in Washington lobbies with the knowledge that it must leave the door open so it can come back to lobby the next day.

"One thing has changed since I started going to Washington. Five years ago, whenever I talked about the need to change the Endangered Species Act, Senators and Congressmen looked at me like I was urinating on the flag. Now nobody looks at me like that. They take the law very seriously. They know that there is a problem and that it will have to be changed."

Yet in the end Larry Mason believes that any solution, whether before the President of the United States or before Congress, must start where he lives, at the grassroots level. What has to happen in Larry's view is for all of the institutions, and particularly the American people, to become aware that there is a problem. Hence, Larry Mason's participation in an act of civil disobedience in the Cold Creek area of the Olympic National Forest.

The Olympic Peninsula is the first land mass encountered by gale force winds traveling across 8,000 miles of open Pacific Ocean. It is not unusual for such winter winds to reach 120 miles an hour as they hit the peninsula. In 1990 and 1991 several storms created patches of "blow down" up to 100 acres in size at numerous locations on the Olympic Peninsula. In the past the U.S. Forest Service would set about to ensure the harvesting of such logs to prevent an outbreak of bark beetle and the fires that would follow. Not this time. The position of the biologist in charge of Northern Spotted Owl recovery—and now in charge of all national forests—Jack Ward Thomas, declared that no timber could be harvested unless it could be proven that the action would benefit the Northern Spotted Owl.

It would have been hard enough to demonstrate that timbering would definitely not harm the owl, since proving a negative is always tough. However, it seemed rudimentary that a massive beetle infestation and subsequent fire would not be a positive for the owl. Jack Ward Thomas wanted more than that: he wanted proof that there would be a long-term benefit. Faced with such an unattainable standard, the U.S. Forest Service sat on its hands.

The salvaging of fallen timber is not just an economic issue for residents of forest lands. It is a crucial matter of forest health. For the bug infestations that often begin in such fallen and decaying timber and the fires that begin from such fuel will soon sweep the healthy forest and even infect adjacent private timberlands. When the fire that these conditions cause roars across the landscape, the environmentalists who demanded attainment of "nature's way," will have long since left. Remaining behind to fight the fires and to attempt to save their homes, their jobs and the land they love are the loggers.

"We need the public to understand that the forest is not a picture post card to be hung on the wall and saved forever. Good forestry and common sense indicate that the removal of blowdown timber can provide for the needs of people, while maintaining the health of the forest. We thought that no one in America could argue with getting these logs out of the woods. We started with that blowdown.

"In January 1992 we had a congressional tour with the press, with entomologists and with other experts to focus upon the problems with blow down timber, with the outbreak of bark beetle, with the loss of revenues, and with the fact that after the salvage, rodents would come in to provide more food for the owls.

"We got supportive resolutions passed in 7 western counties in Washington State, but even with that, nothing happened. We decided to engage in civil disobedience. Twenty one of us went out to a 60-acre patch of blowdown to cut the downed trees into merchantable lengths. We completely blind-sided the U.S. Forest Service. It didn't know what to do.

"Finally, after two days and after we had cut trees on 5 acres, we were arrested for cutting without a permit rather than violation of the Endangered Species Act. That was enough to get Congress moving on the issue. Despite the fact that the League of Conservation Voters called it the ancient forest issue of the year, Congress directed the U.S. Forest Service to harvest those trees. Even with that the trees are still on the ground. The Forest Service is still studying the issue."

Some 22 years after Larry Mason came to Forks, Washington, he considers himself a practicing environmentalist. "I came here to work in the woods and to be an environmentalist. It is a bitter irony to me that I find myself across the table from so-called environmentalists. These misguided people are actually preservationists.

"There is a rage in rural America today. But it is not, as the environmentalists like to say, a rage about job loss. It is a rage about inappropriate job loss, job loss not because of depression or disaster—things we have understood for decades—but job loss because environmentalists have a different view as to how the forests should be used. The government, at the behest of the environmental groups, has cast a dark shadow across our lives. It is wrong. We have a worsened economy, a worsened environment and disastrous social conditions. Most outrageous to us is the fact that some urban environmentalist is sitting in stalled traffic calling a talk radio show on his cellular phone to berate us for defiling nature.

"At the Timber Summit, Clinton was right about one thing: that the nation is changing as more and more Americans go from rural to urban communities. However, he was wrong in his solution, that the nation should work to help us emerge into a modern service economy. He is not just wrong because we don't want to do that. He is wrong because if that happens, where do we get the natural resources essential for the economy he says he wants us to have? William Jennings Bryan said it nearly 100 years ago: '[T]he great cities rest upon our broad and fertile prairies. Burn down your cities and leave our farms, and your cities will spring up again as if by magic; but destroy our farms, and the grass will grow in the streets of every city in the country.'

"The great irony for a politically-correct type like Clinton, with his commitment to diversity and respect for other people, is that while Clinton thinks any kind of discrimination based on race, gender, physical handicap, or sexual orientation is shameful, he apparently thinks nothing about discriminating against rural people simply because they are a political minority."

At a time when millions of Americans were going the other way, Larry Mason became a part of rural America. He is still doing the unconventional, helping to lead the fight for the rural America of which he is now so crucial a part. "I guess the greatest tribute the people of Forks and the Olympic Peninsula have ever paid me is that of permitting me to speak for them." Today, Larry Mason doesn't just speak for Forks. His new position with WCFAC—Associate Director - Federal Affairs—takes his message nationwide, calling upon his talents as a writer and lecturer. He speaks for millions of Americans.

TOM AND KATHY STOCKLEN
Honor, Michigan

Along the Lake Michigan shore west and north of Traverse City in the State of Michigan lies the Sleeping Bear Dunes National Lakeshore. Sleeping Bear Dunes, managed by the National Park Service, winds more than 35 miles along the Michigan coast, from just north of Point Betsie through Empire, Glen Arbor, past Pyramid Point and nearly to Lake Leelanau. As befits a beautiful lakefront area, only four hours drive from Chicago and Detroit, Sleeping Bear Dunes is a popular resort.

However, it is hardly idyllic wilderness. People come, not to disappear into wooded or mountainous isolation, but to canoe and fish and boat and swim and water ski and do all those things that are associated with people, warm weather and water. Thus it was that Riverside Canoes, Inc., located along the Platte River near the town of Honor in the southern portion of Sleeping Bear Dunes, had always done a thriving business. Each year from May 1 through mid-October, people from all over Michigan, the Upper Midwest and elsewhere came to canoe down the Platte River to Platte Lake and from Riverside down to Lake Michigan.

In 1971 Tom and Kathy Stocklen were considering the purchase of Riverside Canoes, Inc., from its longtime owner. Tom and Kathy Stocklen knew that with the passage into law of the Sleeping Bear Dunes National Lakeshore Act in 1970 (retroactive to 1964), the National Park Service had been given virtual control over the vast area encompassed by the Act. In fact, more than 79,000 acres were included within the Sleeping Bear Dunes National Lakeshore.

Tom and Kathy Stocklen learned that there were three categories of property within the boundaries of Sleeping Bear Dunes. Two of the categories, that is, those considered "environmental conservation areas" or "private use and development areas," were subject to restrictions by the National Park Service to ensure that their use was "compatible with the purpose for which the lakeshore was established." If the owners failed to abide by the restrictions or the National Park Service decided the land was needed for public use, the National Park Service could condemn the property.

However, the property owned by Riverside Canoes, Inc. fell into the third category, that is, "public use and development areas," upon which no restrictions could be imposed and regarding which no condemnation was allowed, unless the National Park Service purchased it "immediately." In addition, businesses in existence when the Sleeping Bear Dunes law was enacted were "grandfathered," that is, exempt from condemnation, so long as the "use does not impair the usefulness and attractiveness of the area designated for inclusion in the lakeshore." Congress listed various commercial uses of property that it considered "compatible" with the purposes of the Act. The list included "marinas," such as Riverside Canoes, Inc.

Despite the rather clear provisions of an Act of Congress, Tom and Kathy Stocklen still weren't satisfied. They asked for and obtained, from the National Park Service, a "Certificate Prohibiting Condemnation." Only then did Tom and Kathy Stocklen purchase Riverside Canoes, Inc.

Not more than ten years later the National Park Service was at Tom and Kathy Stocklen's door demanding that they sign a restrictive easement that would have destroyed their business. When Tom and Kathy Stocklen refused, the National Park Service, in clear violation of federal law, initiated condemnation proceedings.

What about the "Certificate Prohibiting Condemnation" that the National Park Service signed? asked Tom and Kathy Stocklen. Responded one National Park Service official, "It's not worth the paper it was printed on, just like the treaties we made with the Indians a hundred years ago."

The remark reminded Tom and Kathy Stocklen of something they had read years before, attributed to the great Sioux Chief Red Cloud: "They made us many promises. More than I can remember. They only kept but one. They promised to take our land and they took it."

Tom and Kathy Stocklen resolved to fight back, resolved not to be victims, resolved to force the U.S. Government to comply with the law, if not keep its promises. When the U.S. Government named Tom and Kathy Stocklen as defendants in a lawsuit, they were ready.

Tom and Kathy Stocklen stood toe-to-toe with the National Park Service. They refused to give an inch. They had the law on their side and they had a signed document. They intended to fight and to win. In the end, Tom and Kathy Stocklen did just that. They kept their land.

TEE JOHN MIALJEVICH
Marrero, Louisiana

Johnﾠ Joseph Mialjevich, Jr. (Mee-AL-uh-vitch) was born in
New Orleans in 1942. Nobody calls him John, Joseph or Joe.
Instead, he is Tee John (Tee is Cajun for "little"). Tee John
Mialjevich was raised in Empire, a tiny town along the Mississippi River more than 50 miles southeast of New Orleans. His
mother ran a "mom and pop" grocery store. His father was a
shrimper and oyster fisherman in Plaquemines Parish.

"I've been on the boats since I can remember. I was seven
years old when I was going out with my father in the Gulf in his
56-foot shrimp boat. I went out every summer with him when I
was growing up."

Tee John Mialjevich played football in high school and
in the summers ran a snowball stand (selling snow cones) to
make money for college. For two and a half years he studied
chemistry at the University of Southern Louisiana at Lafayette.
Then life intervened. Tee John Mialjevich got married and
dropped out of school.

In 1965 Hurricane Betsy passed through. "It wiped out
everything in Plaquemines Parish. My parents lost our shrimp
boat, our home, a rental house, and a service station. That put
the family on its heels. My parents moved to Delcambre and
then my dad got sick. I went back to shrimping and took over
the family's business."

It was when he was shrimping with his father that Tee
John first met the U.S. Fish and Wildlife Service. "About 1968
the Fish and Wildlife Service enforcement people started to bother
the hell out of the shrimpers with their unjustified rules and
regulations. These people had never been out on the boats, and
had no idea what shrimping was all about. They didn't care
about us and whether or not we were able to make ends meet.
After all, they would always have their government paychecks."

Tee John Mialjevich joined a shrimping organization, the
Delcambre Shrimp Association, and soon became one of its leaders. The men respected him and asked him to travel to the state

capitol to argue their case. "So I'd go up to Baton Rouge for them, talk to the legislators and administrators about the shrimp season, convince them not to start it too soon so the shrimp would be too small to harvest and make a living with." Tee John soon became a skilled lobbyist for his friends and colleagues, enjoying a reputation for his knowledge and for his straight-talking truthfulness.

Eventually, the difference in operations between the large shrimpers and the family-owned boats caused Tee John Mialjevich and his friends to form their own organization. "We little shrimpers wanted to catch shrimp with the heads on, make faster trips, catch the sea-bobs, the smaller and medium shrimp. The bigger outfits wanted to bring in the headless shrimp."

One day, after a hard day of shrimping, while tied up together, eating the rice, beans, fried fish and salad that each boat had brought to his deck, Tee John and his friends decided to create their own organization. "We formed up what we called the Concerned Shrimpers of Louisiana. Later I went up to Baton Rouge and asked for something on behalf of our little group. Then after awhile people fishing over in Bayou LaFourche said, 'We like what you're doing. We want to join up.'

"You see the boats migrate. Certain boats go to certain areas for the kind of shrimp that they harvest. The ones that would fish with us—that would talk to us on the radio all the time, if you'd be sinking, or hit something with your boat, tear up your net—would be there to help you. They'd haul you in, tow you in, that kind of friendship. Before we knew it, we had not only the folks at Delcambre, but the guys in Cameron, in Lake Arthur, and down around Morgan City and Houma, people in Bayou LaFourche and Lafitte, Barataria and St. Bernard. They'd all be saying, 'Hey, that's Tee John doing this. Let's get in with him.'

"Soon we had people from Texas to the Mississippi coast in our little group. We ran it for a while fighting things controlled by the states, like the opening of the season, shrimp count, webbing size, stuff like that. Then in 1980 the federal government got involved in managing the shrimp fisheries off the coast of Louisiana—off all the coasts. Then in 1985 the federal government came in with the stuff where they wanted to start saving fish.

"The government started doing experiments with fin fish devices, larger webbing, 'shooter' devices. We were already using a device we called a 'cannonball shooter.' If you took a rack out of your stove oven and cut every other bar out of it, it would be like you were looking out a jail house door, and that's a cannon ball shooter. We put them on an angle in the net to solve the problem of these big jellyfish we call cannonballs that come in the net and fill it up. If we put this bar thing in the net, the cannonballs come shooting up out the hole and out of the way so the shrimp could get through the bar openings and into the trawl. The Government wanted to use the device to exclude fin fish."

Unfortunately for Tee John Mialjevich and his colleagues, environmentalists had yet another idea. Expand the "shooters" so as to exclude 300 pound loggerhead turtles. Soon environmentalists were threatening that if the Government didn't require the use of these vastly enlarged shooters, now called Turtle Excluder Devices (TEDs), the environmentalists would sue.

Tee John was named to The Gulf of Mexico Fishery Management Council and soon discovered that all the noise he had been hearing about TEDs, about putting observers on each boat (to be paid and fed by the shrimpers), about more rules, regulations and restrictions, was for real. He knew he needed to get people organized.

"We had a big meeting in Thibodeaux and over 5,000 people came. The Governor of Louisiana was our main speaker as well as our Congressman. Later, after we started Concerned Shrimpers of America, we met in the Landmark Hotel in New Orleans and got people from Texas, Mississippi, Alabama, Florida and Georgia. We even had interest from North and South Carolina.

"We set up an office in New Orleans. We rented a two-story house. I lived upstairs, offices was downstairs—you don't want to be called in the middle of the night and have to drive five miles to some office. We had a fax machine, three phone lines and a word processor. We spent an awful lot of money on lawsuits, lawyers and lobbyists. We tried, and almost won by about 20 votes in Congress, to get the shrimp industry excluded from the regulations. As hard as we tried, its tough as hell for us common fishermen to beat those environmentalists and their lawyers.

"Of course the big lie is the federal government's statement that we wouldn't lose any shrimp with the TEDs. The government said that when you don't catch the shrimp this drag, you'll catch them the next. But when the shrimp go out with that TED, you don't catch them the next string.

"The National Academy of Sciences did a study with Fish and Wildlife Service people and environmentalists on their panel but not one commercial fisherman. They were just trying to justify the TEDs. I heard two biologists on a test ship once and one said to the other, 'We'll get it to show less than one percent shrimp loss.' And they did. It was lies, nothing but lies."

In July 1989 frustration and anger among the hard working men who put out on the shrimp boats led to what the shrimpers called the Texas Closure. Hundreds of shrimp boats blockaded Galveston Bay demanding an end to any requirement to pull TEDs. Soon there were similar blockades off Aransas Pass, Texas, and then Belfast, near Golden Meadow, Louisiana. Some of the shrimpers were members of Tee John Mialjevich's Concerned Shrimpers of America, but most weren't. Nonetheless, the Government asked Tee John to go to Galveston to end the protest.

The blockade ended when the government made what Tee John calls a series of "false promises:" to make the TEDs work, to help the shrimpers and to lift the TED requirement during the height of the season when it was excluding so many shrimp. A month after the blockade ended, the TED requirements were reimposed and the government started fining shrimpers $8,000 to $12,000 for not pulling TEDs.

Tee John, who asked his people to come in from the blockade, who had believed the government's representations, was furious. "With the Endangered Species Act, folks could go out and kill a loggerhead turtle, cut it up, bring back the meat and get a $500 fine. They could go out and pick up a sack of eggs and get a $500 fine. No criminal charges. But our guys out there without a TED, without a turtle in the net, never had a turtle in the net, never caught a turtle in their life, and get a $8,000 to $12,000 fine and get threatened with 20 year prison sentences. The government's intimidation is incredible. They handcuff you, bring you to the jail house and threaten you.

"It's not just the government. Senators and Congressmen are terrified of the environmentalists. They say, 'Hey, I'll help you with anything but something against the environmentalists.' You're in trouble when your congressman gets chicken legs, afraid he won't get re-elected because the environmental groups will send in electioneering forces, because they got the money."

When his friends were forced, on pain of tens of thousands of dollars in fines and jail time, to pull the TEDs, Tee John's group broke up. Despite the setback, in January 1992 Governor Edwards appointed Tee John to the Louisiana Wildlife and Fisheries Commission.

More recently his friends have been calling him. "So you lost the TED fight. You can't win them all. Nobody ever fought for us like you did. We need you." As a result, Tee John, who thought he was out of the business, has started all over with a new organization to fight for all fishermen, to network with Alliance for America and to build support for commercial fisheries.

"When we first started to get organized, we used to sit on the back deck, eating our fish, rice and beans, and shoot the bull about what needed to be done. We all laughed about how we ought to call our group a 'bulwark' since what we were doing was 'bull work.' Yet despite our defeats, we did a lot more than shoot the bull."

Despite the joke Tee John Mialjevich's friends enjoyed about the work he was being asked to undertake on their behalf, there is not a family among them who does not see "Little John" as the bulwark he has become.

PEGGY A. WAGNER
Hungry Horse, Montana

Hungry Horse, Montana, population 940, is a blue-collar town created when the Hungry Horse Dam was being built to the south to form Hungry Horse Reservoir. Although it has a strip of shops and businesses that cater to tourists on their way to or from nearby Glacier National Park, it is primarily a logging town. It is also the home of Peggy Wagner.

Peggy Wagner was born in Ronan, just south of Flathead Lake, but lived in Charlo—west of Kicking Horse Reservoir—until she was six years old. When she was in the second grade, her family moved to Hungry Horse. She has been there ever since.

As a little girl, Peggy dreamed of "marrying someone tall, dark and handsome, having two children, a boy and a girl, and being a housewife and mother." Her American Dream came true. She married Doug Wagner—she met him the year her family moved to Hungry Horse—who is "still tall, dark and handsome," had Jonathan and Jennilee and busied herself being a housewife and mother.

Doug and Peggy Wagner are avid hunters, fishermen, and lovers of the out of doors. On weekends they would go camping whenever they could. However, she admits that on weekdays, after Doug was off to work, the children were at school, and she had cleaned up the house "a little," she spent the rest of the day watching her favorite soap operas. "I was dedicated, especially when it came to the soap operas. I wouldn't even make a doctor's appointment if it interfered with *General Hospital*."

Peggy also admits she wasn't much interested in local or state issues. She hardly ever read the newspaper or watched the television news. That changed the day she and Doug were urged to attend a meeting on the future of the timber industry—Doug's employer since he graduated from high school. "Good thing the meeting wasn't during *General Hospital*," she acknowledges.

205

She left the meeting, after two hours of listening to representatives of the U.S. Forest Service, the timber industry, preservationists and recreationists, with her "eyes wide open. For the first time I realized that my husband's job was not as secure as I had thought."

A couple of days later, Peggy and several friends were discussing that meeting over coffee. "It just didn't seem to us that the people there that night knew how important the timber industry was to our families and our community. We decided to tell them."

Peggy Wagner and her friends made signs reading, "This Family Supported By Timber Dollars," and placed them in their yards. Their husbands went to work and told their co-workers about the signs. Their co-workers wanted signs too. Peggy and her friends set up a production line in her father's garage.

Local businesses wanted signs reading, "This Business Supported By Timber Dollars." Peggy made signs for them. People who didn't work for the timber industry wanted signs reading, "We Support The Timber Industry." Peggy made those signs too.

She worked on. But elk season was fast approaching and she knew she would have to quit making signs to go hunting with her husband. She set a goal: 10,000 signs or hunting season, which ever comes first. A week before Peggy and Doug Wagner bagged their elk, she had finished her 10,000th sign.

After she returned from hunting, Peggy Wagner contacted people throughout the country to urge them to make signs to educate the public on the importance of the timber industry to local and state economies. When last she counted, in December 1991, some 55 communities were following her example, making signs and spreading the word.

On the hunting trip with which Peggy and Doug celebrated her 10,000th sign, they discovered something unusual in the forest. Roads through the forest that they had traveled only the previous year were now closed. They soon learned that cryptic and indecipherable announcements by the U.S. Forest Service in the local paper had been their only notice. Peggy joined forces with others to oppose the road closures and soon helped form and became one of the leaders of Montanans for Multiple Use.

In the process Peggy discovered that the threats were not just to timber jobs and access to the forest for hunting and camping. Her fellow Montanans who depend on mining, oil and gas exploration or access to federal lands for off-highway vehicle recreation, berry picking, firewood cutting, and other activities were also at risk.

Soon Peggy was helping to organize those willing to fight back throughout Montana. She wasn't alone in her willingness to stand up and be counted. Her example inspired Doug. He gave up his position as president of the multiple use group to run for the Montana State Legislature. With minimal financial backing, but with solid grassroots support he defeated a ten-year incumbent.

Why has Peggy Wagner done all this? "Doug and I want our children to have the choice we had when we grew up: the chance to stay in Montana. When they ask us what we did to make it possible for them to stay, we want to be able to hold our heads high and say we did all that we could."

DENNIS AND NILE GERBAZ
Carbondale, Colorado

For nearly seventy years Dennis and Nile Gerbaz have lived in harmony with the land along the Roaring Fork River in western Colorado, just outside Carbondale.

In the early 1900s their father came to America from Italy. For years he worked as a miner near Leadville and later near Butte, Montana. In 1919 he returned to Italy, married his childhood sweetheart, and brought her back to his new home. Later he purchased the land that is now the Gerbaz ranch.

In 1923 Nile was born. Three years later Dennis was born. From the time they were old enough to walk they worked with their father, learned from him, and when, in 1961 he died, they took over the ranch that he loved. There they have raised their cattle, grown their potatoes, oats and barley, and lived in peace.

Every spring since before either man was born, the Roaring Fork River has flowed high with the melting snows of the Rocky Mountains. As the Roaring Fork plunges past the Gerbaz Ranch, the force of the flowing water sets the boulders—which make up the river bed—to tumbling, emitting the dull roar that gives the river its name.

In 1984 a neighbor requested a permit from the Corps of Engineers to perform some work on the Roaring Fork River. Unfortunately, because of that work the river flooded the Gerbaz ranch—about five acres. Dennis and Nile asked for a permit from the Corps to correct the problem. The government not only denied the permit, it also refused to visit the Gerbaz ranch to see what was happening to the Roaring Fork River.

The following spring rocks, trees and debris created a dam that prevented the river from flowing in its historic channel. Instead, the river flowed onto the land of Dennis and Nile Gerbaz, flooding some 15 acres and washing away 5 feet of precious topsoil over a two acre area. They went to a lawyer and learned that the law permitted them to take action without a permit to protect their land. So they did.

They took the obstruction out of the river, rebuilt the levee that had been washed away, and returned the river to the channel in which it had flowed for decades. Then one day the U.S. government came to their ranch and ordered them to report to federal court to pay a fine of $45 million—each.

The government's exact position was unclear since it refused to tell the Brothers Gerbaz why it sued them. Sometimes the government asserted that when the Roaring Fork River flooded the Gerbaz ranch it created an artificial "wetland" that could not be dewatered without a permit. Sometimes the government asserted that by rebuilding the 50-year old levee the Brothers Gerbaz limited the so-called "reach of the river." Sometimes the government just said that the Brothers Gerbaz were supposed to get a permit and didn't.

One thing is clear. The government intended to make a national example out of Dennis and Nile Gerbaz.

There is one other matter that is less clear. The law allows people like Dennis and Nile Gerbaz to do what they did. It is a well-crafted exception under the Clean Water Act that ranchers and farmers have used carefully for years. Bureaucrats don't like the exemption because it permits people to use their property without a permit. The bureaucrats want to get rid of the exemption without going to Congress. So they are trying to frighten every property owner in America by declaring war on the Gerbaz brothers.

But they can't frighten Dennis and Nile Gerbaz. They are fighting back.

Unable to afford the hundreds of thousands of dollars it would cost to fight the U.S. Government in court, Dennis and Nile Gerbaz turned to Denver, Colorado-based Mountain States Legal Foundation (MSLF). MSLF, a nonprofit public interest legal center, agreed to represent the Gerbaz brothers.

For nearly five years Dennis and Nile, through MSLF, have fought back. They defended against the government's charges. They countersued the government for illegally "taking" their property by allowing flood waters to cover their land and wash away their topsoil. They stopped the government's attempts to mandate a federal "solution" for the Roaring Fork River, a solution that ignored the land owners.

Dennis and Nile Gerbaz know they could lose everything. Yet they are unwilling to lose what they would have to give up to give in: their belief in America and their knowledge that they have done nothing wrong.

DALE AND JERIS FRENCH
Crown Point, New York

"**M**y family moved from Scotland to what is now Vermont in 1735. Around 1800 the family came to the Adirondacks. We've been here ever since," says Dale French of Crown Point, New York, a tiny hamlet of fewer than two thousand people on the southern end of Lake Champlain.

"There's a lot of important history here at Crown Point. Fort Crown Point was erected by the British after they had defeated the French in the French and Indian War. The French Fort that was destroyed by the British had been built in 1735 and was called Fort St. Frederick. During the Revolutionary War, this was a key site. It's ironic that today it's the site of yet another revolution."

On a map, the vast area encompassed in green and labeled "Adirondack Park," isn't really a park made up of land belonging to some federal, state or local agency, but is, instead, a "park" created from the backyards of 130,000 people. All or major portions of 8 counties (Essex, Warren, Hamilton, Herkimer, St. Lawrence, Franklin, Fulton and Clinton) and portions of 4 others (Lewis, Oneida, Saratoga and Washington) comprise the 6-million-acre "park," of which 3 million acres are privately owned.

The Adirondack Park has a long history, but was created in its present form in 1973 by then-Governor Nelson Rockefeller and was placed under the jurisdiction and control of the Adirondack Park Agency. From the beginning, the "Park Agency," as it is called, sought to puff itself up and to intrude into the affairs of ordinary citizens who were attempting to make use of their property.

Dale French remembers the way it was in the early 1960s before he left for college at Clarkston University in Potsdam, New York, and a career as a nuclear engineer at power plants throughout the country. "We were certainly beginning to feel the pinch of regulatory control. The park people were already intruding into our lives."

213

However, when Dale French returned to Crown Point in 1982 to relax in an untroubled rural environment with his wife and his daughters, he was shocked by what he found. "Suddenly the region was under the gun. It was a regulatory nightmare! It got worse.

"In 1990 Governor Mario Cuomo created a new commission to oversee the Adirondack Park. Cuomo and the commission adopted 2,000-acre zoning—meaning that no home could be built on less than 2,000 acres—and 600-foot setbacks from roads and rivers. It was nothing short of a bald-faced attempt to depopulate the entire region."

Dale French could no longer sit back in silence. Although there was an organization already established to watch over and to respond to the regulatory excesses of the Adirondack Park Agency, it was not seen as a true grassroots effort. More importantly, it operated under the philosophy that its members would send in their money and the leadership would keep them advised. Dale French saw a need for the people of the region to do something.

In May 1990 Dale French, his wife and a few other associates sitting at French's kitchen table decided to establish the Adirondack Solidarity Alliance. Before formally organizing, they enlisted the help of local businessman Calvin Carr, who became Executive Director of the Adirondack Solidarity Alliance with Dale French serving as Chairman.

Within a matter of months more than 2,100 citizens joined with the French family. As its first project the Alliance shut down Interstate 87, an expressway linking Albany, New York, and Montreal, Canada. As if to say, "This isn't your park, this is our home—we live here," in order to demonstrate that they existed and were no longer invisible, the people of the Adirondacks created a 50-mile traffic jam. Some fifty Alliance members were arrested including Dale French's wife.

"Suddenly, the powers that be realized for the first time that their regulatory regime wasn't such a good idea. The regulations are still on the books, but the Adirondack Park Agency is not trying to enforce them. The Agency says it will fine violators $500 a day, to which property owners respond, 'make our day.' Right now what we have is an uneasy truce.

"Governor Cuomo has said some pretty outrageous things about us. He said 'we cannot leave the management of the Adirondacks up to those who are less intelligent.' Back in 1987 he said the oppressive regulations being imposed upon us were the 'price they pay for living there.' But what do you expect from a second generation American who spent his entire life in Queens? That's one of our problems today: most people have no contact with life in rural America.

"This isn't just about the abusive powers of the Park Agency and its arrogant disregard for the property rights of the people who live here. This is an assault on our children and our way of life. We chose to live in rural America because we like it and we hope that our children will be able to make the same choice. Now the folks from Albany come in here and tell us we have to leave. Why? So we or our children can live in some nice city like New York where they have to get back to their apartment before dark so they don't get shot?

"Since the 1800s the Adirondacks have had trapping, logging, mining and farming. In fact, the iron ore for the *Monitor*, the Civil War vessel, came from Crown Point. Over time various industrial activities, like farming, became uneconomic, but each time that happened something else took its place. There always was an opportunity for an entrepreneur.

"However, since 1973 when the Adirondack Park Agency came into being, when the regulatory agencies became more powerful, they made it impossible for economic activity to take place here. The regulatory authorities shut down our ability to find economic opportunity. Firms won't come here any more.

"You see the same thing happening all across the country. The radicals, those who believe in bigger and more powerful government, are driving the people off of the land to achieve their own elitist objectives. Look what Secretary of the Interior Babbitt is saying about the people on the Mississippi River and California coast, that they shouldn't be living in such 'high risk areas.' 'High risk?' Those are some of the prime areas of the country!

"The same thing is happening here on a variety of fronts. For example, there is the Northern Forest Lands Council and its attempt to achieve federal control over 26 million acres of privately owned lands in New York, Vermont, New Hampshire and

Maine. They justify that land grab by pointing to the fact that during the boom days of the 1980s, 39,000 acres out of 26 million acres were sold for development. That's .15%. Because of that they want to shut us down. They now say, because of the insignificant amount of land being developed, that it is not the quantity but the quality of the land 'threatened.'"

When the Northern Forest Lands Council attempted to hold one of its meetings in the Adirondacks, Dale French's Adirondack Solidarity Alliance shut the meeting down. When the Council members arrived, they found themselves facing more than 100 angry Alliance members. Despite the presence of 40 New York State Troopers, the Council members abandoned their plans.

"We refused to let them meet in our territory. We saw what they had done in Maine. They opened the meeting with great fanfare, with Senators, Congressmen, Governors and the media out in force. Then they paraded all of their friends and supporters to the microphone for their glowing endorsements of federal takeover. After lunch, when the time finally came for the land owners and the opponents of federal control to speak, there were no more Senators or Congressmen or Governors and the media had long since turned off their cameras, shut down their microphones, closed up their note pads, and gone home. We vowed they wouldn't do that to us."

As the citizen of a rural area who once lived in the big city, Dale French is also offended by the tone of condescension that he hears from officials at Congressional and regulatory hearings. "There is a tremendous amount of intellectual intimidation that goes on at these hearings. Our people are not used to these forums and tend to be excruciatingly polite and cordial. In exchange, they are treated shabbily and made to feel ignorant and unsophisticated to such a degree that they are afraid to speak for fear of appearing a fool."

Dale French has long since lost that fear. From the bully pulpit of a weekly radio talk show conceived by colleague Calvin Carr and hosted by Calvin and Dale, the word goes out through the region on three radio stations. In addition, by means of a weekly television show and a quarterly newsletter, the Adirondack Solidarity Alliance takes on the issues facing lovers of freedom and property rights. Currently, Dale French is embroiled in a fight to remove a United Nations designation of the Adirondack region as a UNESCO "biosphere reserve," one of 75 in the country.

"Ironically, we were designated in 1987, three years after the U.S. pulled out of UNESCO because it was too left wing. We have already had some early success in our efforts. There was to be a major biosphere reserve meeting in Vermont recently. When we found out, we asked for invitations. When they denied us invitations, we announced that we would be there anyway to hold press conferences to inform the public on the nature of these UN zones of occupation within our country. They cancelled the meeting."

Dale and his wife Jeris have gone national with their efforts. One reason was their attendance at the September 1991 Fly-In for Freedom in Washington, D.C., where Dale was shocked to discover that the assault he had witnessed first-hand in upstate New York was a broad-based national attack on the people who feed, cloth and house the nation. The next year Jeris French was in St. Louis to help establish the Alliance for America.

Dale returned to Crown Point, New York, in 1982 to build log homes with his brother and "to sit on a stump and reflect." He has not been able to do that. He has been too busy defending freedom. The nest egg he had set aside for retirement is gone, devoted to fighting "the revolution." He doesn't fear burnout. "Each time you think you're about to burn out, something else happens and you see how important all of this is.

"Before May 25, 1990, when my wife and I formed up the Adirondack Solidarity Alliance, I was the shyest person in the world. I had never spoken before any group or been on the radio and here I was speaking to 600 people. I just looked out over the audience and pretended that no one was there. I just created a new personality. I had to do it. I had to go forward. How could I live with myself if I had the chance to make a difference and turned it down?

"Without the individuals who make up the Adirondack Solidarity Alliance there would be no effective opposition to the agenda of the enviro-extremists and their allies in government. The Alliance is made up of people who are recognized for what they can contribute, what their strengths are. They are ordinary people, farmers, teachers, welders, mechanics—Americans who have decided to fight back."

Robert Burns, who died about the time Dale French's family left for the Adirondacks, put it this way:

> From scenes like these, old Scotia's grandeur springs,
> That makes her loved at home, revered abroad;
> Princes and lords are but the breath of kings,
> 'An honest man's the noblest work of God.'

JOHN E. SHULER
Dupuyer, Montana

John E. Shuler of Ukiah, California, who drove a bakery delivery truck, wanted a better life. He wanted a better life for himself, for his wife, Carmen, and for his two young children. He had been raised on a ranch and he dreamed of the day he could return to that life. In 1976 he did.

The Shulers bought the general store in tiny Dupuyer, a ranching community far out on the seemingly endless plains of western Montana. Three years later John Shuler bought some cattle and leased some land. The next year he bought some sheep. Then in 1986 he bought a ranch and set about to raise his cattle and sheep and a little bit of grain.

John Shuler, who wanted only to ranch, to provide a better life for his wife and his children, and to be left alone, miles from nowhere, never thought of himself as being in the forefront of anything. Yet he is. For John Shuler has become the nation's most troubling confirmation that in the Alice-in-Wonderland world that is the Endangered Species Act, mankind takes second place to nature.

Late on a snowy September night in 1989, John Shuler sat watching television. Earlier in the evening, when his wife stepped outside, her tiny dog, Katie, had refused to leave the porch. At the time, John didn't think too much about it. But later, when he saw three dark shapes speed past the window and when he heard the unmistakable sounds of bones being snapped, he ran into the night.

Clad only in shorts and socks, John Shuler grabbed his rifle from the front porch and dashed into his sheep pen. The sheep were highly agitated, in obvious panic and distress. John Shuler saw three grizzly bears just outside the sheep pen. He stepped forward and fired into the air. Suddenly, the bears were gone.

However, when John turned to go to back to his ranch house he found himself face-to-face with the mother of the three he had just frightened away. She roared, rose up onto her hind

219

legs, towering above him, and spread her huge forepaws. Fearing for his life, John Shuler shot the grizzly bear.

The bear went down with a roar. Immediately it was back up, over the gate and into the field beyond. John Shuler woke his wife and attempted to follow the bear's bloody trail. By then it was snowing very hard. John Shuler abandoned his search.

But he didn't abandon his vigil over his sheep. He sat awake all night, his rifle across his lap. The next day he and his dog, Boone, went into the yard to find the carcass of the bear he had shot. Instead he found the bear, still very much alive. When it charged him, John Shuler defended himself once again, shooting and killing it.

The U.S. Fish and Wildlife Service charged John Shuler with the illegal "taking" (killing) of a grizzly bear and fined him $7,000. John Shuler objected and asked for a hearing to make his case that he killed the bear while defending his property and himself. At the conclusion of the hearing, the Administrative Law Judge (ALJ) ruled that the Endangered Species Act required the ALJ to use the test that is applied when self defense is claimed in the death of a human being. For the first time in legal history, the criminal law self-defense standard was applied to an animal.

The ALJ held that, in considering John Shuler's claim of self defense, he had to apply two principles from criminal law. These well-established legal maxims provide that self-defense cannot be claimed by a person "who was blameworthy to some degree in bringing about the occasion for the need to use deadly force," or "who provokes an encounter as a result of which he finds it necessary to use deadly force to defend himself."

Applying those rules, the ALJ ruled that John Shuler could not claim self defense. The reason: when John Shuler left his front porch and entered his sheep pens to protect his sheep, he "purposefully place[d] himself in the zone of imminent danger of a bear attack." The ALJ ruled that John Shuler must pay a civil penalty of $4,000.

The legal implication of the ALJ's ruling—that a grizzly bear is entitled to the same legal protection as a human being—is not the only aspect that is troublesome. So, too, are the practical consequences. According to the ALJ's ruling, whenever anyone has reason to believe that a grizzly bear may be present in an area—whether open country or one's own property—that person has two choices: either decline to go where the grizzly bear is, or proceed without a deadly weapon.

For John Shuler and others living or working in grizzly bear country, the ALJ's decision makes them prisoners in their own homes. The decision also poses grave consequences for anyone who encounters a grizzly bear. If John Shuler cannot protect his own life on his property, what possible right does someone have to use lethal force when attacked by a grizzly bear in open country?

Yet there is more. The position taken by the U.S. Fish and Wildlife Service and the decision reached by the ALJ is the first evidence of a willingness by the U.S. government to adopt the view of many animal rights fanatics and environmental zealots that human beings are only co-equal inhabiters of the planet, no better than any other creature. It is one thing for fanatics and zealots to espouse such nonsense. It is something else again when a government "of the people, by the people and for the people" does so.

In a debate with Steven Douglas, Abraham Lincoln declared that when we seek to treat men more like beasts, it is not to elevate beasts but to denigrate men. Better than anyone in American, John Shuler, who stood face-to-face with one such wild beast, knows what Lincoln meant.

VALERIE JOHNSON
Salem, Oregon

Valerie Johnson's maternal great-great grandfather was one of Oregon's original white settlers. In 1848, without telling the woman who would become his wife and without even so much as a goodbye to anyone, he left Independence, Missouri, to homestead in Oregon. It wasn't long, however, before he began feeling guilty about his abrupt departure. He wrote a letter of apology to his intended which began with the salutation: "Dear Girl."

In 1851 he sailed from Oregon to the east coast and then returned to Independence from whence he took his bride and her parents to his new home in Oregon. As a result of his earlier experience, and despite his youth, he was made wagonmaster for the 1852 trip west. Forever thereafter he was referred to as "Captain Hale." The first year the family wintered in Cottage Grove, finally settling in Noti, Oregon, some fifteen miles west of Eugene.

Valerie Johnson's grandmother still lives on the family's homestead in a turn of the century house that was in its day the stage house on the route from Eugene to the coast. The rooms upstairs still bear the metal numbers from its days as a way station.

Some five generations later Valerie was born, second child of a man whose first "child" was the timber mill he built in Riddle, Oregon. His father had owned a small mill in Veneta, outside Eugene, but Valerie's dad wanted to strike out on his own after some time in the merchant marines. Striking out meant a few years logging and finally the purchase of land in Douglas County—named after the man whose name was also given the Douglas fir tree—where he put a trailer in which he and his wife lived while he built the mill. The first boards went through the mill in 1951. Six months later Valerie Johnson was born.

Valerie's early memories of her father were of a man who put in long, long hours to make his mill a success. "He was gone long before we were awake in the morning and often back only after we had gone to bed in the evening," remembers Valerie.

223

"But by sheer force of will, hard work and determination he became a success."

The family lived in Myrtle Creek, where Valerie was a cheer leader at South Umpqua High School, from which she was graduated in 1970. That fall she enrolled in Lewis and Clark College in downtown Portland. It was a difficult time for America and a very difficult time for Valerie. A small town girl in the big city, surrounded by liberal college professors, at the height of the national uproar over the Vietnam War, she felt like a fish out of water.

An unabashed hawk, she began to rethink her views a week before the 1972 presidential election. That was the day Valerie Johnson's little brother turned 18 years old and became eligible for the draft. Her concern with the Vietnam War and the very personal stake her brother had in that conflict led her to the voting booth for the first time—to vote for George McGovern. Valerie believes that week was a defining moment for her. "I learned one thing. If you care about something, if you believe in something, you can't stay neutral."

For a time after graduation Valerie worked around Portland. Then in 1974 her father offered her the opportunity to start on the ground floor learning the business in his mill. She returned to Douglas County to become her father's receptionist. For the first time in all the years she had worked around her father's mill—she had spent several summers there growing up— the entire operation began to make sense. She went on into sales and was sales manager for five years. During that time she had gotten married and then divorced and was looking for a change.

In 1983 she took a job in Portland as a lumber salesman. She lived in nearby Tigard, where in 1986 she was elected to the City Council. By 1989 she had grown frustrated with being tied to a desk selling lumber. She concluded that the real action was on the supply side. The year 1988 was also a time when the grassroots were beginning to be heard regarding timber supply issues, as U.S. Senator Mark Hatfield and Governor Neil Goldschmidt conducted timber conferences throughout the state.

In the winter of 1988-89 Valerie was working for Stimson Lumber Company on the top floor of its Portland offices when her fellow employees began asking each other questions about what was happening to the timber industry. She was familiar with some of the problems the industry was experiencing since during her years in Douglas County she had been involved somewhat in the wilderness studies and designation issues—the so-called RARE II studies (Roadless Area Review and Evaluation).

However, what was happening now seemed a lot more serious. Valerie's fellow employees had begun to hear rumors from their friends in other companies that the supply situation could get worse. "Are we in trouble?" they wanted to know. They wanted Valerie to help find the answers.

Ironically, it was these hourly employees who prodded management in search of the answers to their questions. Valerie called in the company's timber manager to make a noon-time presentation. The company provided everyone a sack lunch and Valerie joined with her fellow employees as the timber manager told what was happening on the front lines of the environmental battle. Valerie and the others listened in horror as the seriousness of the situation became abundantly clear.

When the lunch was over everyone was even more anxious than before. However, Valerie and the others were unwilling to exchange their wonder regarding the situation for worry. They wanted to do something. They decided to sponsor a gathering of their colleagues in the Portland area. They got a speaker (noted timber expert Dan Goldy), found a place to meet (The World Forestry Center in Portland) and in May 1989 hosted the first gathering of timber employees to find out what was going on and what it all meant.

Valerie Johnson, the cheer leader, the timber mill owner's daughter, the fifth generation Oregonian, the vivacious, gregarious people-person, was asked to introduce Dr. Goldy. As she remembers the aftermath of the first incredible meeting, "if you're the one who introduces the speaker, then you're the one asked to do the follow up, you're the one toward whom the questions start gravitating."

Valerie then learned of others who were actively involved, not in Portland, but in Oregon's tiny timber-producing communities, those who had been on the receiving end of the push by environmentalists for total shutdown of the timber industry. She learned of Rita Kaley of Hood River, of Charlie Jantz of Springfield, of Dixie Reisch of Mollala. Valerie learned of their truck rallies, their gatherings, and their grassroots groups—the Yellow Ribbon Coalition, the Oregon Project groups and Bruce Vincent's Communities for Great Oregon in Sweet Home and Mill City. Valerie Johnson knew she had to do more than she was able to working full time. Four months after that first brown bag lunch in the company offices she quit her job to devote herself to grassroots.

In early August 1989 Valerie and a group of strangers gathered in Springfield, Oregon to bring all of their efforts together. At the time, Senator Hatfield was pushing compromise legislation—what became known as the Great Northwest Timber Compromise, or Section 318—to balance increased protection for the Northern Spotted Owl with mandated timber harvests. That effort became an issue about which the various groups saw a need to coalesce. On August 31, 1989, the group met again to cement their coalition and to select a name. Although all around the table that day were concerned about the timber issue, they knew they needed an all inclusive name that would serve as a rallying point for all Oregonians threatened by environmental policy gone wild. They called the organization the Oregon Lands Coalition and named Valerie Johnson and John Kunzman co-chairs.

Within two weeks, timber advocates from throughout the Pacific Northwest were desperately needed in Washington, D.C. to walk the Halls of Congress in support of Section 318, the Hatfield-Adams timber compromise. For Valerie and her colleagues in the newly-formed Oregon Lands Coalition, it was their first time on Capitol Hill. It was also the beginning of what became known as the Fly-In for Freedom.

Three weeks later Valerie and the Oregon Lands Coalition helped to coordinate its first major public relations event—a truck caravan to Joann Etienne's mill and a massive timber rally she was hosting in St. Croix, Indiana. OLC members Greg Miller and Jim Peterson drove trucks across the country to Joann Etienne's rally. Bruce Vincent of Libby, Montana, delivered the emotional keynote address, followed by Ron Arnold of Bellevue, Washington, speaking on movement solidarity.

The event was a watershed for Valerie Johnson and the Oregon Lands Coalition. "For the first time we realized we were not alone. For the first time we realized that this was not just an Oregon, or even a Pacific Northwest issue, but a national issue involving truckers, mill workers, lumber dealers and millions of others.

That fall Hurricane Hugo swept ashore in South Carolina, devastating the countryside and rendering hundreds of South Carolinians homeless. The people of South Carolina needed lumber. The people of the Pacific Northwest had it. All that separated the two was three thousand miles. With the help of the Oregon Lands Coalition, tens of thousands of dollars in lumber and freight was donated and then railed cross-country to the victims of the natural disaster.

"The convoy to South Carolina taught us something else—the difficulty of getting media attention if you're on the wrong side of the dominant liberal media culture. The media barely gave us a glance for what we did. If we had been some bleeding-heart liberal group we probably would have been on all three networks. We were learning huge lessons every day."

Obviously, for it wasn't long before Valerie Johnson and Oregon Lands Coalition were in the national spotlight. Thanks in large part to the hard work of OLC's inimitable Jackie Lang, *The Christian Science Monitor* covered OLC's work. Then in June 1990 Valerie appeared on CNN's *Crossfire* with Pat Buchanan, opposite Oregon environmentalist Andy Kerr. The Oregon Lands Coalition reached its stride when Valerie demanded of Andy Kerr before millions of viewers: "Why are you lying to the American people?" Her question signalled the end of the environmental movement's free ride in the media.

When Valerie chaired the first meeting of what was to become the Oregon Lands Coalition, there were 11 organizations at the table, all involved in timber harvesting, with a total membership of 4,000 to 5,000 people. Today, the Oregon Lands Coalition has 62 organizations with a total membership of 81,000 Oregonians, representing a diverse mixture of natural resource-related activities.

The impact of the presence in the timber debate of the Oregon Lands Coalition and its allied grassroots groups cannot be overstated. At a time when Oregon's largest newspaper, *The Oregonian* was attacking the timber industry almost daily, both editorially and in the tone and content of its news articles, the work of grassroots groups was convincing Oregon's citizens that their economic lifeblood was being drained away.

All across the state "Timber Dollars" signs sprouted up and thousands of Oregon families stuffed slips marked, "This bill paid with timber dollars" into the envelopes when they paid their monthly bills. In a little more than two years the number of Oregonians opposing job loss to "protect" the Northern Spotted Owl shot up from 48% to 64%.

In January 1992 Oregon Lands Coalition was permitted to intervene in what became known as the "God Squad Hear-

ings." Under the Endangered Species Act, relief from the Act's
Draconian requirements may be granted only by a cabinet-level
entity called the Endangered Species Committee. Since it appears to have the power of life and death over species—more
likely over communities and even regions—it is most often called
"the God Squad." The God Squad was convened by the Secretary of the Interior to consider the request by Cy Jameson, Director of the Bureau of Land Management, to conduct 44 timber
sales in Oregon counties.

Immediately, a number of environment groups sought to
intervene in the process, as did a regional timber association
and the affected counties. Oregon Lands Coalition, represented
by Mountain States Legal Foundation, demanded a place at the
table. For years, the people of the timber producing communities had been told that their views, their needs, their problems
were irrelevant. For the first time those unique perspectives were
relevant.

"Until the God Squad convened, there was no role for
the people. The rallies we held in Portland during the hearings
made national news and helped people to understand that the
battle did not just involve environmental organizations and the
timber industry, but also included the men, women and children of tiny communities all over Oregon.

"Today more than ever before industry knows how important grassroots is to its eventual success. Industry understands
that it cannot win this battle alone. This is not just a battle that
is being fought on Capital Hill with legislation, or in the federal
bureaucracy with regulation, or before the courts with litigation.
It is a battle for the hearts and minds of the American people.
Industry can not win that battle alone, but together with
grassroots we will. We intend to win."

Valerie Johnson—who helped found the organization that
is the national template for grassroots groups all over the country, that initiated what is now the Alliance for America's Fly-In
for Freedom, that obtained public interest legal counsel and
stepped confidently into the fray, that went national and began
beating the environmentalists at their own public relations
game—has stepped down as Oregon Land Coalition chair. However, she continues to serve on its Board of Directors and to be
active in its work.

Valerie Johnson—like her ancestors who plodded the
Oregon Trail from Independence, Missouri, to Eugene—contin-

ues to break new ground. Today, she hosts her own weekly radio talk show in Portland, a program that is heard just before the tape-delayed broadcast of a man who worked for years in timber country, Rush Limbaugh. Each week tens of thousands of Oregonians are not only enlightened regarding the natural resources and property rights issues facing Oregon, but are enlivened by Valerie Johnson's unique brand of hope, optimism and leadership. Captain Hale would be proud.

PATRICK FRANCIS O'TOOLE
Savery, Wyoming

Across the Hudson River from New York City and south of Newark, New Jersey, in one of the most densely-populated areas of the nation, lies New Brunswick. New Brunswick, New Jersey, is a metropolitan area virtually indistinguishable from the rest of the teeming megalopolis that stretches from Boston, Massachusetts, to Washington, D.C.—except for the fact that it is the home of Rutgers University.

It was at Rutgers University that two professors, a husband and wife team named Deborah E. and Frank J. Popper, reflected during the course of a drive on the Garden State Parkway on the sad shape of their environment. The story goes that during that and subsequent trips into New York City where Deborah Popper teaches environmental studies, the Poppers concluded that they must help to ensure that other areas of the country did not become like northern New Jersey and New York City.

That's when they began to study the Great Plains—a vast area stretching from the 98th Meridian (which intersects San Antonio, Texas) to the curving spine of the Rocky Mountains. In the course of their research they reached a startling conclusion: God never meant for people to live on the Great Plains.

Sooner or later, concluded the Poppers from the comfort of their couches, all those people will be gone. The Poppers thought it should be sooner. They opined that the government should "deprivatize" 100 counties in ten states in which 400,000 people live so that the buffalo could roam again, free and uninhibited. They called their dreamland the Buffalo Commons.

The problem was that the 400,000 people who live there didn't want their property "deprivatized" and they didn't want to leave. Despite the outcry from the people who live in the vast land with which the Poppers want to experiment, the Poppers have refused to back down. Their objective of locking up the land remains.

The Poppers assert that the Great Plains "offers the nation's most advanced region-scale test of the practicality of the preservation-can-pay impulse," to determine the "social value [of] less intense, more restorative land uses." The Poppers are nothing if not ambitious: "The Great Plains' experience has implications for much of the rest of the Western and rural United States."

If not by outright purchase, how do the Poppers propose to depopulate and lock up the Great Plains? They have an assortment of weapons in their arsenal: designation of vast areas for single use (like the Big Open in Montana); purchases by the federal government's land purchasing agents such as The Nature Conservancy; regulating cattle and sheep off federal lands; outright purchases by the government in select areas; and use of the Endangered Species Act to prohibit economic activity. In fact, despite their assertion that the free market itself is helping to achieve the Buffalo Commons, the Poppers admit that of the "potential building blocks for the Buffalo Commons, most of them are federal."

Needless to say, residents of the Great Plains are livid. In tiny communities from North Dakota to Texas, the men and women whose forefathers settled the land are fighting back. When the Poppers travel to the Great Plains, they are greeted not with hostility alone, but also with an intelligent factual rebuttal of their entire thesis.

Nowhere was the reaction more hostile or the intellectual level higher than when the Poppers journeyed to the University of Wyoming campus in Laramie. That night no one was more outspoken than Pat O'Toole of Savery, Wyoming.

Born and raised in Hialeah, Florida, just north of Miami, Pat O'Toole came to Wyoming in 1974 and fell in love, not just with the state and its people, but also with the woman he would marry, Sharon Salisbury. In 1976 Pat and Sharon O'Toole were on the verge of entering the University of Wyoming College of Law to study water law. On the day classes began they called the law school. They would not be coming. Instead, they bought "a band of old ewes," leased some land and formed the Banjo Sheep Company.

From the first they approached their centuries-old occupation with an eye toward innovation. Pat, the philosophy major, and Sharon, the writer and daughter of Wyoming pioneers, were the first wool growers in the state to use guard dogs. Just starting out, they didn't believe that predator losses should be a cost of doing business. When Sharon read about the European guard dogs being used in Texas and New Jersey, she wrote to learn more.

"Although," as Pat O'Toole says, "everyone thought it was crazy because anything new could very possibly be bad," since 1979, "whatever sheep outfits are left have guard dogs." The O'Toole's guard dogs have become somewhat famous through Sharon O'Toole's two books, *Noodles* and *Blizzard*. "I wanted school kids to read about rural people, just to let them know there are people living out here. So far 186,000 kids have read about our dogs and us." Says Pat O'Toole, "It was our effort to help all those who had overdosed on Bambi."

Pat O'Toole—like his father-in-law George Salisbury, who introduced the Wyoming law that defines wolves as dangerous predators to be shot on sight—was elected to the Wyoming State House of Representatives. When the Poppers came to town, he was a member of the State House. That's one reason he went to Laramie. "I couldn't believe Wyoming was spending our tax dollars to pay for these folks who want to eliminate us to come to town.

"The Poppers are the craziest people I've ever met," says Pat O'Toole. They're also the "biggest phonies, once you start tracking back on how much they've made traveling around the West giving speeches about their theory. It's a phony issue. It's just a way to take their western vacations. Besides that they're awful speakers."

During the Poppers' question-and-answer period in Laramie, Sharon O'Toole led the attack with a barrage of questions challenging the facts and figures upon which the Poppers relied. She came away unsatisfied. In Pat O'Toole's words, "the theory doesn't stand up under any statistical criteria. It's just not a valid scientific theory. You don't have to scratch very deep to find out it has no substance."

It was late in the evening when Pat O'Toole stood up. He had heard enough to conclude that the Poppers were all wet, that they didn't know what they were talking about, that there wasn't a shred of evidence to support their theory. Nonetheless, he was worried and he told the Poppers why.

"You are providing the same kind of intellectual framework for environmental zealots that Hitler enjoyed from the university professors who sought to provide an intellectual justification for what he was doing." Although the Poppers were

visibly shaken, Pat O'Toole wasn't done. "Every negative movement against people has to have some intellectual framework.
Whether it's valid or not is irrelevant. It gives credibility to a
nonsensical idea. From now on, any crazy writer or environmental nut case who wants to justify his attack on westerners
need only quote you."

The Buffalo Commons is but one example of the threat
to westerners and other Americans who live in a rural, sparsely
populated area. The Big Open in eastern Montana and the Tall
Grass Prairie in Oklahoma are just two examples of the plans of
environmental elitists for turning other people's homes into rural folk-museums. In fact, the Poppers have drawn delight and
no small pride from what they see as the effort of others to "apply the Buffalo Commons approach to much of the rest of the
rural West. But they mostly do not use the term Buffalo Commons, for there never were buffalo in places like Arizona or Oregon."

However, such land lockup efforts are not only a western
phenomenon. Farmers living anywhere near one of the 365
components of the National Park Service know of the covetousness of bureaucrats and the willingness of the nonprofit land
purchasing agents of the U.S. government to expand the parks
to include peoples' property.

Pat O'Toole, the western rancher, the man selected by
Democratic Governor Mike Sullivan to represent Wyoming during the Clinton Administration transition, knows what this is
all about. "This is a mean spirited, vicious, close minded, negative assault, first upon those who live upon the land and then
upon the very concept of private property. That may be okay
for professors from New Jersey, but it is not okay for us."

NADINE BAILEY
Hayfork, California

Nadine Bailey is unforgettable. More than six feet tall, she stands proud and erect. She speaks with intensity, knowledge, courage and commitment. People look up to Nadine but not just because she towers over most people. She has earned the respect of millions of Americans as a result of her outspoken advocacy of her tiny timber community of Hayfork in northern California.

On a map, Hayfork appears as a speck some 250 miles north of Sacramento. Approaching Hayfork from Sacramento, the first 163 miles is all interstate highway, I-5. Then at Redding the route winds westward onto two-lane California 299, weaving past Shasta, Whiskeytown, and the turnoff to French Gulch. At Douglas City the route veers south onto narrow California 3. The last 23 miles are the most challenging as the mountain road twists deep into Trinity County and the Trinity National Forest. The arduous trip to Hayfork brings to mind the expression, "you can't get there from here."

Hayfork might as well be a million miles from Sacramento, or anywhere else in the United States for that matter. Lying in the heart of one of the nation's most sparsely populated counties—a county that depends upon natural resource activity, mostly logging and ranching, and far from major media outlets—Hayfork has little that seems to interest the outside world. It could easily have become one of those obscure little towns destroyed without even so much as a whimper, let alone a bang, by environmental policy gone wild.

Nadine Bailey declared that would not happen. She has not yet saved Hayfork, but by sheer force of will she has ensured that the community will not "go quietly into that good night" of the post-industrial age envisioned by environment zealots who oppose timbering. Nadine has seen to it that anyone who reads the newspaper or watches television know what is happening to the people of Hayfork, California and why.

Nadine Bailey is the daughter of a third-generation logger. Her husband, Wally, is a timber faller, one of America's brave and hardy souls who goes deep into the woods to do the dangerous work of harvesting timber so that the nation might have the wood products it requires.

When the U.S. Fish and Wildlife Service listed the Northern Spotted Owl as "threatened" under the Endangered Species Act, it wasn't just timber activity in Washington and Oregon that was affected. Suddenly the timberland around Hayfork, California, which had been managed for decades to ensure sustained yield, was off limits to logging. Hayfork's economy plummeted. Nadine Bailey and her husband were forced to close their timber falling business.

When the people of Hayfork held a town meeting Nadine stood up and cried out, "Somebody has to do something." After she sat down she remembered a saying she'd once heard: "It was a job anyone could do, but everyone thought someone else would do it, so no one did it." Nadine Bailey realized the somebody she was talking about was herself.

She started Concerned Citizens of Trinity County, which includes shopkeepers, loggers, bus drivers—a true cross section of the community. The group did more than talk. It filed a lawsuit against the U.S. Fish and Wildlife Service on behalf of several small businesses. Nadine is also a member of Hayfork Women in Timber and a former president of California Women in Timber.

Nadine Bailey became a national grassroots leader, with annual trips to Washington, D.C., for the Fly-In for Freedom and with her vital participation in the 1991 meeting in St. Louis where the Alliance for America was born. Soon Nadine was recognized as a national spokesperson for the plight of northwest timber producing communities, for its men, women and children.

In November 1992, Nadine was there when Vice President Quayle traveled to northern California to learn more about the impact of the designation of the Northern Spotted Owl and to promise relief. In April 1993, she was the most eloquent advocate on behalf of the grassroots during President Clinton's highly publicized "Timber Summit" in Portland, Oregon. Early in 1993, when ABC's Peter Jennings hosted a "Kids Town Meeting" with President Clinton, Nadine's 12-year old daughter, Elizabeth, was there.

During the ABC program Elizabeth showed President Clinton her school yearbook in which the name of every child whose father works in the woods is highlighted in yellow. Having shown what she refers to as her "yellow pages" to hundreds of members of the media and public policy makers throughout the country, she was not hesitant about showing them to President Clinton. Moreover, Elizabeth was not the least bit shy about asking the program's most penetratingly direct question: "Mr. President, what will you do about people like my dad who are losing their jobs because of the spotted owl?"

Nadine Bailey's daughter Elizabeth comes by her directness and refreshing candor naturally. Her mother is unflinching in her willingness to take her message to anyone in the country. In September of 1993, she met with Vice President Al Gore moments before he was to join President Clinton at the Joint Session of Congress announcing the Clintons' health care program.

"I told Vice President Gore that the U.S. Forest Service must be funded at higher levels if it is to be responsible for ecosystem management." She also protested the Clinton Administration's selection of the highly restrictive Option 9 as the final forest plan. She followed her meeting with Vice President Gore with a meeting with Kathleen McGinty, director of the White House Office on Environmental Policy, when she again denounced Option 9, which reduces timber harvests from 5.5 billion board feet to 1.2 billion board feet.

Nadine Bailey compliments the Clinton Administration on the easy access that she has enjoyed to top policy makers. "I think it's wonderful how you can access this administration very easily. We may not like what they do, but at least you can meet with them and they will listen to you."

She is less complimentary about how well they listen. The results of the much ballyhooed "Timber Summit" are a continuing source of disappointment to her. "The greatest accomplishment of the 'Timber Summit' was that, for the first time, grassroots had national credibility. It was no longer just the timber industry standing toe-to-toe with environmental groups. There was a third party involved—the grassroots organizations representing the people of the timber producing communities."

For all who watched the Clinton "Timber Summit," Nadine Bailey's presentation was the most moving and articulate plea on behalf of those most hurt by the carefully orchestrated campaign by environmental groups against timber harvesting in the Pacific Northwest through the use of the Northern Spotted Owl as a surrogate. "They can't just come in and destroy a whole community! The people here are good, good people, and they are worth saving!" Possibly for the first time the American people began to understand that the battle taking place up and down the main streets of tiny timber towns is not about owls, or habitat or environmental protection, but "cultural cleansing" by environmental elitists against rural America. Nadine's message has been heard, not just by President Clinton, but also by millions of others through the nationally-acclaimed video, *A Cry in the Woods*.

Unfortunately, President Clinton's Option 9 decision was a "slap in the face to the men and women of the Pacific Northwest. It is as if he listened but he did not hear. We feel as if we have been sacrificed to fulfill President Clinton's promises to the environmental extremists. But we're not going to give up. There is too much at stake.

"There is hope for northern California if we don't give up," says Nadine Bailey whose friends and neighbors named her Trinity County Citizen of the Year in 1993. "If a housewife from Hayfork can get involved in politics at this level, then democracy really does work. I'm not anything special. Anyone can do this."

At least now the world knows what makes Nadine Bailey so very special. It's the size of her heart.

MARCUS RUDNICK
San Luis Obispo, California

On November 16, 1991, an article written by noted western reporter Lee Pitts appeared in the *Livestock Market Digest*. The article chronicled how the great shortgrass ranches that used to stretch from San Luis Obispo to Bakersfield, California, had been bought out by The Nature Conservancy with the active assistance of the U.S. Bureau of Land Management. Gone were the Washburn, the KCL, American Ranch, the Goodwin, the Van Meter, the Painted Rock, and the MU. Gone too was the shortgrass, replaced by a proliferation of tumbleweed and other noxious plants upon the 180,000 acres of what is now known as the Carrizo Plains Natural Area. The desirable shortgrass had not vanished because of too much grazing before the BLM takeover, but because of lack of grazing after BLM got control.

Lee Pitts wrote his eye-opening article following a tour of the area with longtime San Luis Obispo County rancher, Marcus Rudnick, as his guide. At one time Marcus Rudnick, 74 years young, owned The MU, which he bought in 1950, culminating a lifelong dream. The MU, upon which Marcus can remember grazing cattle as far back as 1936, was made up of 23,000 deeded acres, 15,000 privately-leased acres and 75,000 acres of BLM land. Marcus often ran as many as 2,500 cows with their calves each year, supplemented by up to 2,500 steers. In one especially productive year, he was able to run 6,000 steers with grass remaining.

All that started to come to an end in 1988 when The Nature Conservancy embarked upon a massive program to deprivatize the area. As part of the BLM plan to buy up 180,000 acres in the Carrizo Plains area, The Nature Conservancy first bought 82,000 acres. What happened next is familiar to millions of rural Americans who have seen The Nature Conservancy and other tax-exempt land-buying environmental groups working hand-in-glove with the U.S. Government to remove thousands of acres a day from productive use and from the tax rolls. One by one, the ranches of the Carrizo Plains disappeared.

One of the last to go was Marcus Rudnick's MU. For a while Marcus hung on, reassured by the words of one of the leaders of The Nature Conservancy: "I don't think we'll squeeze the rancher out. The Conservancy won't put pressure on people to sell their property. If they don't want to sell, we won't buy. Where ranchers do want to hang on to their property, the Conservancy works with them." That was before the BLM began to cut back dramatically on Marcus' grazing allotment, reducing the number of cattle he could graze until he could no longer make a living. In the end, Marcus Rudnick felt compelled to sell.

Although Marcus got his money and now merely manages what he once owned, he remains dedicated to the land. He was shocked by what happened to it, so shocked that he wrote to the BLM to complain.

"I have never seen such a prolific crop of tumbleweeds and noxious weeds. Your grazing practices and land management have retarded that area for many years to come. In years past, we have grazed the tumbleweeds as they are high in protein when they are young. This retarded their growth and their very existence.

"Not only have you ruined the country, you have either killed or driven away the quail, kit fox, elk, antelope and other wildlife by your policy of not grazing."

In short, BLM had allowed tumbleweeds to crowd out the shortgrass by eliminating grazing, which had controlled the undesirable growth.

Marcus Rudnick didn't stop there. He wanted others to see and to understand what was happening to the Carrizo Plains where he grew up, where he spent his life and which he loved. Marcus convinced reporter Lee Pitts to tour the Carrizo Plains Natural Area with him. Reporter Pitts was shocked too, and wrote an article titled "This Dying Land" that exposed the degradation that had befallen the land as a result of a political agenda ("Cattle Free By '93"). Pitts' article explained in detail why cattle grazing had kept down the noxious weeds and allowed the shortgrass to thrive, and how the

BLM's "back to nature" scheme had worked all too well—the nature to which it reverted was the common desert of the Southwest.

The article was reprinted in part in a weekly column that appeared in the *San Luis Obispo Telegram*. That article was too much for a local self-proclaimed environmentalist. He wrote the *Telegram* condemning Marcus.

"When Marcus Rudnick bought the MU Ranch in 1936 it was covered by a shrub grassland that fattened livestock and supported an abundance of wildlife. When I visited the MU and adjoining BLM holdings in December 1990, cattle dung was all that remained to protect the soil and the only wildlife species were those that lived underground. The winds had been and continued to blow tons and tons of soil from this denuded range.

"This windswept land furnished an ideal environment for the alien tumbleweed to germinate and grow. When the miracle rains of March 1991 fell, the tumbleweeds flourished and covered the land like a scar protects a wound.

"Now . . . Mr. Rudnick [blames] 'nature groups' for the blanket of tumbleweeds that covers the MU and thousands of other acres on the Carrizo Plain. [He seems] oblivious to the reality that past land use practices have resulted in this dismal stage of degradation. . . . Hats off to the BLM and Nature Conservancy for their attempts to reverse the decades of land misuse on the Carrizo Plain."

Marcus Rudnick was greatly distressed by the accusations of the environmentalist. Cattle ranching has been Marcus's life and the quality of the range is the gauge by which his life's work is measured. He knew with absolute certainty that grazing was what kept down the tumbleweed and that grazing was what allowed the shortgrass to flourish. However, he believed the man who attacked him was simply misinformed. Marcus invited the man to the ranch to see firsthand what was going on and to see what he had shown Lee Pitts. After the tour, Marcus asked the man to retract his statement in a letter to the *Telegram*. The man refused. Marcus sued for defamation of character.

In the end, Marcus won. He won despite the assertion of the environmentalist that his speech was protected by the

First Amendment allowing environmentalists "to say anything we want." Marcus won because the jury believed the expert testimony that he presented and not the testimony from environmentalists that the land was overgrazed. Also devastating to the other side was the misidentification of kangaroo rat nests and habitat as examples of overgrazing—kangaroo rats are highly efficient at denuding the soil. Most damaging was testimony that The Nature Conservancy itself uses cattle grazing as a management tool to control tumbleweeds on its own land. The truth about tumbleweeds was clear to the jury. Marcus Rudnick's sea of shortgrass was clearly the result of good ranching. The BLM's ocean of tumbleweed was clearly the result of no ranching. Marcus Rudnick was awarded $32,500, a dollar for each subscriber who got the weekday edition that contained the damaging letter.

Each year environmental elitists, through the hype, hyperbole and hysteria that is their tool in trade, slander and libel American citizens and the companies that employ them. In order to justify their demands for new legislation, tighter regulations, and confiscatory policies, only the most outrageous accusations appear sufficient to do the job.

As a result, people suffer. The victims spread the spectrum from A to Z. No one is safe, not the apple growers—who were on the receiving end of Meryl Streep's assertion that there were 4,000 to 5,000 cases of cancer each year from Alar alone—not the property owners accused of "destroying" wetlands or threatening the quality of Zion National Park. Occasionally, as in the case of the apple growers, it will become public knowledge that the charges are untrue. Yet it is too late, for the lie has gotten around the world before truth got its boots on. The retraction, if it ever comes, and it rarely does, appears too late to do any real good.

Environmental issues are too complex, too controversial, too susceptible to being contorted and confused to allow slander to be substituted for certitude, to permit libel to replace the literal truth. If the public policy debate that determines environmental policy is to be intelligent and informed, then the demonizaton of people as "environmental criminals" must end.

However, the cause of action for a defamation lawsuit

is a personal one, one that only the victim may bring. It is also expensive. As Marcus Rudnick's attorney noted, libel cases "are so expensive to litigate [that] people just don't do it." Marcus wasn't thinking about expense when he sued. He was thinking about his good name and about the nearly sixty years he spent running cattle on the shortgrass of the Carrizo Plains. Marcus Rudnick, who was once known only to a handful of cattlemen in California, is now a hero to millions.

RITA CARLSON
Lewiston, Idaho

"**I**f I had it to do all over again," says Rita Carlson, "I would have paid more attention in government class than I did. My son is a senior in high school and I read his history book every chance I get."

When she isn't reading about history from her son's textbooks, Rita Carlson is trying to make history by turning around the environmental debate. She knows the environmental movement has a 20-year head start, but she also remembers what President Reagan once said about an endeavor: "If not us, who? If not now, when?"

Rita Carlson was born and raised in Townsend in Broadwater County, Montana. In the winters she lived on her mother's farm and in the summer she lived in town. When she graduated from high school, she attended Northwest Community College in Powell, Wyoming, and then followed her brother to Lewiston, Idaho. In 1977, after a couple of jobs in retail, she signed on with the Potlatch tissue mill in Lewiston.

It was there she met Stephen Carlson. He had been born and raised in Troy, Idaho, attended college in Denver, Colorado, served in the U.S. Army in Vietnam, worked in the construction industry in Seattle, Washington, and then hired on with Potlatch.

Rita Carlson's emergence as an activist on behalf of the wise utilization of timber resources had an atypical, but not altogether exceptional, origin. An active member of The Church of Jesus Christ of Latter Day Saints, Rita Carlson is a conscientious reader of *The Ensign*, the Mormon Church's monthly publication. "Our prophet said that as citizens of this world we have a responsibility to be involved and active in our communities. I reflected on it and decided that I should get involved in our Union.

"I went to our Union president, Jerry Klemm, and told him that I wanted to become more active. He suggested that I attend one of the Union's COMNET meetings. I did and was

245

shocked by how everyone just sat there. I wanted to say, 'Hey, isn't this our job?' I'm not a person to do things half way. I guess you could say I got involved because no one else was going to do it."

Today, Rita Carlson travels throughout Idaho, Oregon and Washington, teaching in classrooms, speaking to gatherings, large and small, and presiding over booths at fairs and other public events. She didn't start out being a multi-media expert. "I started teaching in the classrooms because I love working with children. But because no one wanted to do the booths at the fairs, I started doing that too. It just kind of snowballed. It's like when I went to Washington, D.C., for the Alliance for America Fly-In for Freedom. I walked into the room and someone shouted, 'Rita's here, let's make her vice president.' I must look like someone who ought to be involved.

"Of all the things I do I absolutely love teaching in the schools. The teachers like to have me come too. I usually go into the fifth grade. The fourth graders are a little fidgety and sometimes the sixth graders have their minds made up, but the fifth graders are pretty open-minded. But I do it all from kindergarten through college.

"I show a film that talks about timber, about how forests are taken care of, about how little food there is for wildlife in old growth, and other issues. Then, after seeing a film about making paper done to a rap beat, we make paper ourselves. The kids really love that. We divide into groups, one is the machine, one does the dipping and squeezing and the other does the ironing of the paper. Since the paper sheet is hot, I pull it off the machine and then let the kids divide it up.

"We talk about the byproducts, talk about recycling, how the tree becomes a log, about how we use everything, even the chips and sawdust, to make paper or wood pellets; about how we no longer put the water in the sewer but use the wood byproducts to make plastics—for radios and telephone casings—and the water to extract the vitamins (just like using the water you boil potatoes in to make bread) to make pet food, imitation vanilla and other useful products."

Rita Carlson travels from fair to fair setting up her timber information booth, talking about the issues and answering questions. "I just try to give people the facts and the information they need to make up their own minds. If you try to push an opinion on them, they'll shut you off. I just want them to have the facts. Most of the questions I get are about the Endangered Species Act since the grizzly bear, sockeye salmon, the Bruneau snail, are all very hot issues affecting all of us. Who would ever have thought that a federal law would do this to people."

Rita Carlson is a leader in Potlatch's communications network (COMNET), which works to keep all employees advised on what is happening on the timber front and to get people concerned and active. "Unfortunately, some people are pretty apathetic. They thought that their jobs would last forever. My own view is that if you are not willing to be actively involved in fighting for your job, you shouldn't be working for the company. That's how serious all of this is."

Rita Carlson's COMNET is part of the Northwest Timber Workers Resource Council, a coalition of timber workers from the Pacific Northwest. With quarterly meetings that rotate around the various mills in Washington, Oregon, and Idaho, NWTWC keeps its members informed as to what each is doing and what the hot issues are. The first day of their two-day meetings is devoted to regional reports and the second day to hearing informative speakers on specific issues. Rita Carlson is enthusiastic about the results of such meetings. "In the past, Lewiston has been seen as being in the lead, especially on our school programs, but now the others are catching on and catching up."

Rita Carlson has seen big changes in the attitude of her colleagues as well as the industry in general. "Compared to three years ago when I started there has been a big change. A lot of people thought this mill would be here forever. Now many people wonder. They are coming in to see me saying, 'What can I do to help?' I'm also seeing the industry starting to take a courageous stand. I only wish more companies would step forward and fight for the survival of this industry and our jobs."

Rita Carlson is also a leader in Idaho Women in Timber and a national leader of the Alliance for America. When she traveled to Washington, D.C. in 1993 for the Fly-In for Freedom she was shocked to discover the legislation being proposed and discussed which could affect her job. "I was appalled. I thought, why didn't anyone tell me about this new law and what it is going to do to me. I was just stunned with all the harmful legislation that was being proposed. I think all of us have an obligation to become more aware of what is happening in Washington,

D.C., and let our senators and members of congress know what we think. I also believe that industry must do a better job of telling their employees about what is going on and what it will mean as far as jobs are concerned.

"Right now my job isn't on the line. But I know people whose jobs are. Right now we don't have an endangered species like the northern spotted owl which is shutting down the forests and taking jobs. But my friends in California, Oregon and Washington do. If there is any way I would describe my role it is one of service. I've got to do all that I can to stop the environmental movement cancer that is hurting my friends. That's what I am trying to do.

"I've read what the Sierra Club magazine said about how the way to defeat people like me is to 'demonstrate the irrelevancy of moral and religious dogma to modern life,' and I think that's wrong. My faith isn't irrelevant to this life. My faith tells me that people are more important than other life forms and that service to mankind is a very special calling. I can think of no more important thing to be doing than this. It's not just a job, it's what I believe."

Rita Carlson doesn't need to read that government textbook anymore. She ought to be teaching the course.

LEON SUMMERVILLE
Cozahome, Arkansas

Leon Summerville, Jr. believes that where the Buffalo River flows slowly and serenely through the Ozark Mountains of northwestern Arkansas is one of the world's most beautiful places. Although he was born and raised in Ohio, since 1963, when his parents bought a place along the Buffalo River near Cozahome, he has considered it home.

According to Leon, the Ozark Mountains are "real rough and rugged country with a soil so rocky and poor it was never suited for farming. The forest is mostly hardwood, oak and hickory. While the land along the river was good for farming, up along the ridges, it wasn't. Today, a lot of folks run cows or raise hay; others work in the sawmills, drive trucks, or do the seasonal work associated with tourism."

It is beautiful country, but it can be dangerous. "We've got three types of rattlesnakes and we've got copperheads and cottonmouths. But the most dangerous thing is the tick. We've got billions and billions of them. If you get out in the woods or the weeds, they'll eat you alive. Tick fever's a real threat to all of us."

Unfortunately for the folks of rural Baxter, Newton, Marion and Searcy counties, an even worse threat comes not from nature, but from their fellow man. Over the years the people of Buffalo River country have come to hate and to fear the "cancer" that is growing among them—the National Park Service.

At one time the thought had been to dam the Buffalo River, but legislation to do just that was twice vetoed, once by Eisenhower, once by Kennedy. In 1966 John Paul Hammerschmidt, who, by the time he retired, would represent northwestern Arkansas in Washington for 26 years, ran for Congress. One of his primary issues was opposition to the damming of the Buffalo River. His solution: establish the Buffalo National River as a unit of the National Park Service.

In 1972 Congressman Hammerschmidt achieved his goal when President Nixon signed the legislation creating the Buffalo National River Act. In 1974 two state parks were turned over to the National Park Service. That acquisition gave the National Park Service the land it needed to obtain condemnation authority over the private lands along the Buffalo River.

According to Leon Summerville, Jr., "from 1974 to 1986 the National Park Service moved everyone off the river. A thousand and eight private property owners were driven out. Then, in 1984, the year George Orwell warned us about, after most of the people had been driven out, the National Park Service came in to close down the park.

"Eventually, the National Park Service closed 70% of all roads to vehicular access, roads to old cemeteries, roads to favorite fishing holes, roads to historic homesteads, roads to scenic areas. The National Park Service came in with big boulders and steel barricades and shut down one of the most popular parks in Arkansas. Of all the places for it to happen, who would have thought it would happen to Buffalo River?"

It wasn't the way things were supposed to be. In the beginning, before the creation of Buffalo National River, the people had been promised a park that they could use and enjoy. They were told there would be millions of tourists and that more than 3,500 new jobs would be created. The people were ready, the infrastructure was already there: the canoe rental outfits, the motels, the restaurants, the vacation cabins and the campgrounds. Thousands of families had been coming to Buffalo River for generations. Now it would be better. There would be more people coming and, with the help of the National Park Service, more for them to see and to do.

"It was supposed to be better for everybody," says Leon. "We were supposed to have a park that we could use. While some of us were being asked to make the tremendous sacrifice of giving up our property, it was to be for the good of all. That was when the National Park Service talked about providing recreational opportunities. Now all the National Park Service talks about is 'protecting' the environment, and every couple of years it has a new plan to restrict recreation in the park even more."

The impact has not just been economic. For a region that stresses the importance of tradition, of heritage, of family, and of a link with the land, the break with the past was devastating. For more than 150 years families had grown up in homesteads along and near the Buffalo River. Now those homesteads were gone. Gone too is the link to the past. "We've got a generation of kids who have never seen where their families grew up, who've never seen the old homestead, the lands their ancestors settled, who've never even been able to visit a family graveyard."

In the summers Leon works as a canoe hauler and guide for those who fish the Buffalo River for smallmouth bass. In the winter he runs survey lines for a company in nearby Harrison, a town of 11,000, the largest in the region. In fact, from 1979 to 1984 he helped survey the National Park Service boundary.

"That was when I found out what the National Park Service was really like. I saw the National Park Service forcing people out, treating them like dirt and lying to them. I talked with the survey crews that had worked with the National Park Service in the past. They told me that the same sort of thing was happening to people all across the country. I found out that the National Park Service will flat-out lie to you, then say, 'I was mistaken,' or 'I was misinformed.'"

As a surveyor, Leon Summerville, Jr. has made it a practice to listen to others. "Since the first people in a region were the surveyors, you can learn a lot if you're willing to sit and listen to them and to the old-timers."

Of course, sitting and listening is a tradition in the South. "All through this part of the country, in all the little country stores, the barbershops, what have you, you'll find what we call 'Spit and Whittle Clubs.' Folks get together, chew and spit, whittle a bit without making much of anything, sit and visit, play dominos or checkers, whatever, and talk about what's going on and especially current events.

"Most of the folks around here sit and complain about the National Park Service, what it's done to the people and the land, and the lies it has told us." But Leon, isn't satisfied with complaining. So he travels around the region to visit the "Spit and Whittle Clubs" in the tiny towns along the Buffalo River, Buffalo City, Harriet, Big Flat, Gilbert, Snowball, St. Joe, Hasty, Ponca, and others.

"I've been trying to inform my neighbors, to get them to defend themselves, get them to call their congressman and write to our senators. I try to get television stations to cover our issues, and every time the National Park Service comes out with something new, I get letters going. We've got a group, I call it The Buffalo River Coalition of Spit and Whittle Clubs. It's just neighbors, no dues, no membership. I don't ask anyone for a dime."

In November 1992 the National Park Service announced its intention to implement a new Wilderness Back Country Management Plan. Under the plan, developed in cooperation with a variety of environmental groups, 80% of the park would be closed to all but backpackers. Although there was to be a 50-day comment period, the National Park Service did not publish the required notice locally until a week before the deadline.

Leon Summerville, Jr. swung into action. "They said the Buffalo River was being overused. They said they had to get the people off the river. They said they had to reduce tourism. It was all nonsense. Hell, tourism's been dropping like a stone since 1984. They just wanted to set the place aside for the backpackers. Since there are none of them here, and for a whole bunch of other reasons, we objected."

In the week that remained in the comment period, Leon's groups delivered more than 1,900 of the total 2,200 responses received by the National Park Service. In the end, the comments ran 10 to 1 against the new management plan. The plan that was to have been announced in the spring never appeared. Nor did it appear in the summer or the fall.

Leon Summerville, Jr. has also been at the forefront of the battle by the region's counties to get back the roads over which the National Park Service has asserted dominion. In fact, he was successful in getting the Marion County Quorum Court to adopt a resolution demanding return of authority over its roads.

"These roads belong to our counties and to the people. The law that created Buffalo National River says that the only way the National Park Service can acquire public property is through donation. While we gave away two state parks, we never gave away our roads. We've been after the National Park Service for the last 6 years to explain how they got our roads. The National Park Service just says they've asked the Solicitor but he's been sick and hasn't gotten back to them."

Leon knows all about the national battle for property rights and keeps abreast of what's happening in other regions. "When I first read about the western battle over R.S. 2477 [a little-known federal statute that gives the public the ability to claim a right of way for a public highway over federal land which was not otherwise reserved or withdrawn] and counties trying to get their roads back from the federal government, I thought it might work for us, but it really doesn't apply."

People also know about Leon Summerville, Jr. "A couple of years ago, some people in Virginia called me up and asked me to come to Washington, D.C., to testify before the Vice President's Council on Competitiveness. I couldn't go. I am dirt poor. Here I am in my old overalls and my nasty old work boots, eating squirrels and fish out of the river. The motor on my truck just blew up, so I'm stranded awhile. The old typewriter that I pound on is all wired up to keep the letters from falling off. I call it 'war on a shoestring.' But I'll keep it going as long as I'm able."

Leon Summerville, Jr. has just two goals. His first goal is to get the National Park Service to open up the roads to all of the cemeteries inside Buffalo National River. Incredibly, for an agency that says it cares about history and heritage, the National Park Service has never done a count of the number of cemeteries inside the park.

Leon's second goal is to make Buffalo National River a park for people, where people can drive in and see it and use it. It used to be that way. Before the road closures, Hemmed in Hallow, a 180-foot waterfall, the highest falls between the Appalachians and the Rocky Mountains, was just a half mile off the road. Today, it is a rugged five mile hike from the highway. Hardly anyone ever sees it.

For Leon the battle is more than just over access to family cemeteries and allowing people into the park. "Buffalo River was a very big part of our lives. Those of us who live here love the out-of-doors, to fish, to hunt and just to be outside. We were told that we had to sacrifice so that more people could enjoy what we had and so that we could have a better life too. All that we had has been taken away and what we were promised has never come to pass. If this park truly was established for the good of all, then it's time to make it happen."

Leon Summerville, Jr. says Buffalo River, Arkansas, is one of the world's most beautiful things. It takes one to know one.

MICKEY STRICKLAND
Mentone, Alabama

At the height of her battle against creation of a 34,000-acre national park on land owned for generations by her neighbors' families, Mickey Strickland was interviewed by a newspaper reporter. During the interview, Mickey Strickland quoted Albert Camus: "In the midst of winter, I finally learned that there was in me an invincible summer."

When the article appeared, the reporter thought he smelled a rat. While Mickey Strickland held herself out as a simple country woman, he wrote that in reality she could quote the writings of a French philosopher. Even today, the reporter's response to her literacy makes her angry.

"Are we in the country not supposed to read? Are we not supposed to think, to connect with great ideas, with greater thoughts? Are we simply to eat our beans and cornbread, feed our hound dogs and go to the mill? What makes them think that only people who live in big cities dream great dreams? They think we're just a bunch of illiterate bumpkins who work in the mill and don't have any sense. This is the kind of attitude we have to deal with here."

"Here" is northeastern Alabama, the tail end of the Appalachian Mountains, 40 miles northeast of Gadsden in a ridge-lined valley with Sand Mountain to the west and Lookout Mountain to the east. It has been home to thousands of proud people since long before the Civil War, people who cherish their land, the land where their forefathers lived and died.

Mickey Strickland was born in the valley where, for the most part, she was raised on a farm. When she met and married her husband, Roy Lee, she moved to Lookout Mountain. Roy Lee Strickland is living testimony as to why the land is important to the people of rural Alabama.

Roy Lee's family purchased 157 acres in the 1930s when many people couldn't afford to eat, and when all that they could afford to pay on their property was but "a dime at a time." His parents were some of those people.

Roy Lee's father, Gordon, was a farmer who often had to supplement the family income with outside work, including labor in an underground coal mine. Tragically, Gordon was left with a lifelong injury when a large piece of slate fell on him. Sometimes his injury would flare up and, unable to walk, he would tend the garden by pulling himself along the rows with his elbows and a short-handled hoe. Roy Lee's mother, Eunice, and his sister, Joyce, sold eggs, butter and milk to pay the mortgage.

Roy Lee and Mickey Strickland's property is located on Lookout Mountain on the banks of the Little River, which runs 80 miles down the center of a 12-mile wide plateau, cutting deep ravines through mountain rock. Little River Canyon, one of the deepest gorges east of the Mississippi, accents the river's route.

As Mickey Strickland puts it, "it's pretty but it's not nationally significant. Even if it were, must the federal government take everything considered significant?" However, the land is important as a source of recreation to the people of northeastern Alabama. Some 10,000 acres is owned by Alabama Power and Light Company and managed for recreational activities by the Alabama Conservation Department. Another 5,000 acres lies within the very popular DeSoto State Park.

Unfortunately for local citizens and landowners, a National Natural Landmarks (NNL) evaluation was conducted here by the National Park Service during the 1960s. It was that evaluation that led the National Park Service to conclude that the entire area was one of its "ladies in waiting," waiting for the National Park Service and Congress to take them over.

The takeover attempt began in 1990 when Congressman Tom Bevill, a 26 year Member of Congress, was poised to introduce legislation to create a 34,000-acre national park in northeastern Alabama. To facilitate park creation, Congressman Bevill obtained $150,000 for yet another National Park Service study of the area and another National Natural Landmarks study. The National Park Service also formed a Committee, allegedly composed of citizens, land owners, politicians and others. Instead, the Committee was, in Mickey Strickland's words, "just a cheerleader for the National Park Service." Worse yet, the Committee's meetings, which sought to build public support for the park, excluded all dissenting or dissident views, and at times even the media.

All the while, Congressman Bevill, National Park Service employees, and other park supporters were operating behind the scenes drawing lines, deciding what property would be excluded and what would be included in the new park. For those whose land was coveted by the National Park Service, failure to sell their land meant only one thing: condemnation of the land by the National Park Service.

Intellectually, Mickey Strickland knew what condemnation meant. She could define it. She could explain it. Yet she hadn't related it to her friends until the night she and Roy Lee went to a National Park Service meeting. One by one her friends stood up, told how their ancestors had come to own the land, told what they had gone through to keep it and vowed with tears welling up in their eyes that they would not part with it. Coldly, the men from the National Park Service informed them that if the property could not be gotten through "negotiation," it would be taken and the people would be forcibly removed from it.

One elderly woman from Cherokee County, Mary Wood, told the story of how her great grandfather had come to own the land she now owned, of his belief that the Cherokee Indians should not have been moved out—down the Trail of Tears—of how he had hid them out in Daniel's Cave until the march was over, and of how the bodies of those Cherokee men and women were buried upon her land alongside her great grandfather, grandfather, her father and her husband. She told, too, of meeting a National Park Service representative and of how, in response to one of her questions as to what lands the Government intended to take and not knowing who she was, he swept his hand across the breadth of her property.

"We intended to take all of this," he said. "It will be one of the finest additions to the National Park Service."

"I have a gun in my purse," she responded. "You might as well take it out and shoot me on this spot, for if you take my land you will have taken my life."

After the National Park Service meeting, Mickey Strickland joined with Mary Wood and Miriam Hellreich—whose land runs deep into the canyon—to form Save Our Land. Later, Mary Lou Hopkins came on board and together their group began the battle. Save Our Land became a 5,000 member grassroots organization funded by 500 dues-paying supporters, dedicated to only one thing: denying the National Park Service the authority to condemn people's property. "We wrote letters," said Mickey Strickland, "did research, called people, made contacts, met with the media and spent lots of time on the telephone and the fax machine. I was nearly full time on the fax machine myself."

Mickey Strickland and the others did something else, they reached out to others like them throughout the country. "Someone in radio called us and told us to call Chuck Cushman. Thank God we did. It was the best thing we could have done. Without Chuck Cushman we would all be packing our belongings now. We also met up with Erich Veyhl, Myron Ebell, Joanna Waugh, Ann Corcoran, John Wall and others. They were terrific."

When the rich and famous supporters of the national park traveled to northeastern Alabama to view the area proposed for federal takeover and to party at the home of Randy Owen of the country band, *Alabama*, Mickey Strickland and her friends were not invited. Instead, with the gates locked and guards posted, they watched from the outside as the military helicopters flew the distinguished guests in for their affair.

The disgruntled land owners hastily made signs and marched in protest, demanding no condemnation authority, demanding no park. When Congressmen Bevill and Vento (D-Minnesota) came outside to face the crowd, Vento was intractable: the national park bill would not leave his committee without condemnation authority. It was Mickey Strickland's first, but not her last, encounter with Congressman Vento.

When Congressional hearings were held on the park proposal, Mickey Strickland, Miriam Hellreich and Mary Lou Hopkins traveled to Washington, D.C. to testify against the bill and against condemnation authority. Mickey Strickland had been warned that Congressman Vento would try to intimidate her, to shut her up. She vowed not to be silenced. She wasn't. She was similarly vocal before the U.S. Senate Energy and Natural Resources Committee when hearings were held there.

Congressman Vento had to eat his words about condemnation since the bill left his committee without condemnation authority as a result of intense pressure from Save Our Land and its supporters. Save Our Land's greatest victory was that no private land was included in the bill and that a clause was included providing that no private land could be purchased. Although Save Our Land fought day and night for a presidential pocket veto, at the last minute, then-President George Bush signed the bill into law.

After all was said and done, the Little River Canyon National Preserve as it was now called—a downgrade from the original "park" or even "recreation area" designations—was to be made up only of the 10,000 acres of Alabama Power Company land and the 5,000-acre state park. For Mickey Strickland and others with Save Our Land, it was an incredible victory.

Mickey learned that one person—combined with others of like mind—can make a difference. She learned something else. "At the very least you must have a good relationship with the press. Otherwise, your enemies will chew you up and spit you out. Early on, try to get some members of the press to see that there is another side. Help to take the green scales from their eyes. Let them know that the battle is not about the environment, but about property rights. Then, at least you will be treated with some respect."

Mickey Strickland was successful in getting that respect. Her work was featured on the front page of Georgia's biggest newspaper, *The Atlanta Constitution*, as well as Alabama's largest paper, *The Birmingham News*. CNN also gave favorable coverage to the property battle underway in northeastern Alabama.

Mickey adds a cautionary note in dealing with members of the media. "Just remember they are not your buddy. They are there to get a story. That's their job. If they have a mind to, they'll stick you to the wall. Some did it to me. But most were fair. Just decide what you want to tell them, what you want the story to say, then say it and shut up. Remember, we're going to win or lose this battle in the newspaper, on television and on radio. Politicians fear the media more than anything else, as well they should."

When the battle was over Mickey had mixed feelings.

She realized that the battle was not really over—the National Park Service had its toehold on northeastern Alabama, it would be back—and it would never be over until fundamental changes take place. One of those changes was in the elected official who represented her and her friends and neighbors in Washington. She decided to run for Congress.

"I decided to take a stand. The principal issue is what's happening to us and to our land, what's happening to others throughout the country and to their land and what is happening to the people and their needs: needs like decent schools, justice system reform, and lower taxes. We aren't going to stop the attack on our lands and the wasting of hundreds of millions of dollars until we stop the abuses of the National Park Service and Congress' use of our land as a form of 'park barrel.' Most of these national parks are something we don't need and we don't want. They are not the icing on the cake. They are a candy bar in some congressman's pocket."

Her run for Congress went "surprisingly well for an unknown housewife. After all, nobody knows me from Adam's house cat. All I did was raise my children and serve as the editor of a small monthly newspaper," she said. Friends from Save Our Land put up the $2,500 qualifying fee, and on April 14, 1992, Mickey Strickland began her shoestring grassroots run for Congress.

"We raised $22,000 mostly in small contributions. My daughter, Lisa, and a fellow Save Our Lander, Mary Lou Hopkins, drove me from place to place—a gas station here, a barbecue there—while we ate a lot of peanut butter and raspberry Zingers.™My daughter, Michelle, served as my treasurer. Often, we would sleep at a rest stop or drive all the way home to catch a few hours of sleep before hitting the road again. People always asked if I thought I could win, and I would say 'Yes, I did, but it wasn't about winning, it was about taking a stand.'"

In the end, Mickey Strickland, spent $22,000, got 29% of the vote and held Congressman Bevill, who spent $540,000, to his lowest percentage of victory in nearly three decades. "I know Bevill didn't take me seriously until the radio polls on these tiny stations around here showed me beating him. Then the big money and the expensive advertisements began in earnest. However, for a little housewife from Lookout Mountain to get almost a third of the vote against one of the most powerful men in Congress says a lot." It says a lot about Mickey Strickland.

In the "winter of our discontent" over Congressional disregard for the will of the people, over oppressive federal policies, over the abusive practices of the National Park Service and other agencies, over the blatant disregard for the Constitutional protection accorded property rights, the "invincible summer" within Mickey Strickland gives millions of Americans hope of a coming spring.

MICHAEL MARTIN MURPHEY
Taos, New Mexico

At a National Review Institute "Conservative Summit," Rob Long, scriptwriter for the long-running television comedy *Cheers,* complained about the life of a Hollywood conservative. In the end, however, he admitted he was comforted by the fact that "Statistics show that 1 in 3 Hollywood conservatives goes on to become President of the United States."

We all know that movie-making is done with smoke and mirrors, and that any relationship between the "reality" portrayed by tinsel town and real life is purely coincidental. However, for millions of Americans, particularly for young Americans—the nation's most avid movie-goers and television-watchers—much of the information they receive regarding the "real" world comes from the "reel" world of Hollywood.

What a world it is. From the glass bubble-like isolation of the studios and sound stages of Los Angeles a few hundred executives, producers and writers create video versions of their vision of the world, or the world as they would have it. What America sees at the theaters and at home during prime time is affected not simply by the fact that we are looking through the lenses of one of the most liberal elements of our society, but by the fact that these powerful elitists use their medium to reshape attitudes and thus change the world.

For example, what *Time* magazine calls the "almost complete absence of religious content on prime time" and the political correctness of Hollywood-style environmentalism found fertile ground in *The Simpsons.* The popular cartoon series not only conducted an assault upon timber harvesting in America—depicting the bribery of a Congressman who shouts "Timber"—but ridiculed religious faith by scripting this "prayer" for Bart Simpson: "Dear God, we paid for all this stuff ourselves, so thanks for nothing."

As *The Simpsons* timber episode illustrates, Hollywood's approach to environmental issues reflects its bias and its effort to influence public opinion. While Ted Turner's *Captain Planet* is the worst of the cartoon genre—with its mysticism, factual inaccuracies and demonic portrayal of entrepreneurs—many other animated features also pass out environmental misinformation.

During prime time, either the hero embraces the latest trendy environmental cause or the archvillain is discovered to be a "wealthy developer" bent on environmental destruction.

Meanwhile, at the movies, an environmental subtext is often added to the most innocuous of films. For example, the only subject given serious treatment in *Naked Gun 2½* was the film's characterization of the nation's energy producers as plotting criminals, a portrayal for which the film credits several environmental groups.

Not surprisingly, the same is true with many top recording artists. As a result of their personal guilt over the fortunes they are amassing, their mindless embrace of the latest politically-correct fad, or simply their airy-headed ignorance of the facts of the issues being addressed (and hence their susceptibility to left-wing anti-human propaganda), singers and songwriters are advocates for environmental causes.

Yesterday's anti-war advocacy by Peter, Paul and Mary has evolved into today's anti-free enterprise, anti-timber, anti-mining, anti-rancher, anti-fisheries, anti-property rhetoric advanced by Hall, Oates and King, to name but a few. Daryl Hall and John Oates conducted a tour of Montana to condemn timber harvesting while Carole King railed against timber harvesting on morning talk shows. In addition, Paul McCartney's world tour was little more than an elaborate platform for his two pet causes, environmentalism and vegetarianism.

Yet not all have succumbed to Hollywood's siren song and the go-along-get-along mentality of politically-correct leftist conformity. One refreshing example is country music's Michael Martin Murphey.

Although country music singers have, as a result of the very nature of their music and its audience, embraced traditional rural values, few are as outspoken in their advocacy as Michael Martin Murphey.

A ranch owner in Taos, New Mexico, since the 1970s, Michael Martin Murphey calls his recent albums, "the music of my people, my land, my culture and my own life. I don't wear a hat or boots because I sing cowboy songs. I wear them because I'm a rancher."

Michael Martin Murphey's attitude toward the West and its rural lifestyle was shaped by his research into the real stories of the West: "Researching the West has totally changed my life. I would encourage everyone that, if they ever got a chance to look into their roots or their history, do it. You'll walk away with a changed view of the society you live in today."

Michael Martin Murphey's first hit was the 1972 "Geronimo's Cadillac," followed, three albums and three years later, with two top-ten sensations: "Wildfire" and "Carolina in the Pines." In 1982 he had his first number one country song, "What's Forever For."

Yet Michael Martin Murphey seeks listeners looking for something more. "There is a hunger out there for history and roots and analysis of who we are and what we are all about. There are hundreds of thousands of people out there who seek out music that strikes them on a deep level. Those are the people who I want to connect with."

That desire to connect may have been what prompted Michael Martin Murphey to play a benefit for Stewards of the Range and later took him to Washington, D.C., where he joined with Alliance for America's Fly-In for Freedom in the fall of 1993. "I'm here to sing the praises of my own culture," Michael Martin Murphey said as he stood with hundreds of ranchers, loggers, miners and others. "For too long we've heard only one side of the environmental story at the expense of men and women who work and live off the land."

Michael Martin Murphey may be one of only three conservatives associated with Hollywood's recording industry. He may not become President of the United States but he will help ensure that future presidents sing a different tune on environmental issues.

RON ARNOLD
Bellevue, Washington

Ron Arnold is the white-haired, bearded, bespectacled gentle man whom many regard as the leading philosopher and sage of the movement against the radical agenda of environmental elitists. Yet more than three decades ago, as an avid hiker and lover of the out of doors, he joined the Sierra Club, eventually becoming one of its Pacific Northwest leaders.

Ron was inspired to join the Sierra Club after moving from his native Texas to Washington State because of his belief that the Sierra Club was committed to the wise use of natural resources and that it understood the need for balance between environmental goals and economic growth.

He believed that the Sierra Club was committed to these things because of the writings of Bestor Robinson, Club President in the late 1940s. Wrote Robinson: "Never let your love of nature blind you to the needs of your fellow man. I want wilderness to enhance the American way of life."

Says Ron Arnold, "I agreed with him then. I agree with him now." Yet as Ronald Reagan once said regarding the Democratic Party, "I didn't leave it. It left me."

During the turbulent 1960s Ron began to hear his Sierra Club colleagues assert, "We can never save nature until we eliminate private property," and, "I don't see how we can accomplish our goals if we allow the continued use of resources." Ron wrote it off to the temper of the times, to radical chic, to the elitist tendencies of the highly educated, mostly academic types who made up the Sierra Club leadership. "Harmless thunderbolts," he thought.

How wrong he was. The pressure to eliminate private property rights, to stop the use of natural resources, to preservation as opposed to conservation, to "lock 'em up and kick 'em out," continued. Ron began to have second thoughts.

One day it all came to a head during a meeting of the Sierra Club Conservation Committee. A visitor from Oregon had brought photographs of logs heaped in Molalla Creek not far from the base of Mount Hood on a Weyerhaeuser logging operation. "Let's get the *Seattle Post-Intelligencer* to run these photographs and demand legislation," asserted the visitor. Legislation by headline, it is called.

Yet Ron Arnold, who knew something about logging because he had spent years worth of precious Saturdays on "show me" tours for the Sierra Club's Conservation Committee instead of hiking, recognized that the logs had not been put in Molalla Creek on purpose. Skid marks on the creek bank showed they had slid down from far above the stream. Ron doubted that Weyerhaeuser logging managers even knew their logs had escaped.

Since he had observed a successful creek clean-up program by Weyerhaeuser just a month earlier, Ron offered to contact Weyerhaeuser to ask that it remove the logs and clean up the site.

Brock Evans, then the Sierra Club's Northwest Representative and now a lobbyist for the Audubon Society, objected. Ron recalls Evans claiming that the Sierra Club's demographers had concluded that they only had two or three more years before a backlash occurred. "We need all the victories we can get while the getting is good."

The Sierra Club Conservation Committee voted to send the photographs to the newspaper. A huge stink ensued. Weyerhaeuser eventually sold off its Molalla holdings. Says Ron, "a lot of innocent people got hurt."

Most troubling to him was that the organization to which he belonged, and to which he had committed years of energy and intellect, "had sold out its original vision. I felt alone and betrayed. The Sierra Club didn't give a damn about the creek or the salmon run. All it cared about was politics."

In 1971 Ron Arnold resigned from the Board of Directors of the Sierra Club's Pacific Northwest Chapter and began a consulting firm to help those who had been injured by these new environmentalists. He found plenty of customers.

In 1979 Ron was asked to write a series of articles for *Logging Management* magazine. He titled the series, "The Environmental Battle." In it he put forth a novel idea, something that had not appeared before: "Industry cannot save itself. It and our civilization will be destroyed by environmentalism. Only an activist movement can defeat the environmental movement and stop all the harm it is doing." The series won the 1980 American Business Press award for the year's best magazine series and became the basis of his book, *Ecology Wars,* published after his 1981 debut as an author with *James Watt and the Environmentalists.*

In 1984 Ron became Executive Vice President of the Center for the Defense of Free Enterprise. For nearly a decade, he has sought to foster the movement of which he first dreamed in 1979. He does it by writing articles (he has written hundreds of them), by giving speeches and making public appearances, including television and radio (he has done thousands of them), by publishing the books of many authors through The Free Enterprise Press that he founded in 1986—including his thoroughly researched, highly acclaimed cult best seller, *Trashing the Economy: How Runaway Environmentalism Is Wrecking America.*

The Free Enterprise Press has been recognized for the quality of its original research. For example, the U.S. Forest Service invited Ron to its 1991 Centennial symposium to present his findings on the origin of the forest reserves in 1891—exactly who wrote the national forest legislation and why—a hundred-year-old mystery he solved while editing Wayne Hage's *Storm Over Rangelands.*

Yet Ron Arnold is more. He is an inspirational and selfless leader to thousands of Americans who find themselves besieged by the heavy hand of government and the endless demands of environmental extremists.

He calls the movement that he sees sweeping across the country "wise use." "I call it wise use because the term 'conservation,' which I prefer, has been coopted by environmentalists to mean 'preservation only'—that is, *no* use." Says Ron, "Frankly, 'wise use' is the most concise definition of conservation, which in any dictionary means the wise utilization of resources."

To Ron Arnold the movement is made up of many parts: "the private property movement, the pro-growth and jobs movement, the federal lands multiple use movement and others. Obviously we all don't agree on everything, we're too disparate for that. But we're learning to work together and we will win in the end. Ours is the voice of hope."

One thing most do agree on is the conclusion that Ron Arnold reached after seeing the environmental movement from the inside. "It's not good for man and it's not good for nature."

A Special Note of Appreciation

Alan M. Gottlieb is a friend to all who know him. Generous and giving of his time, magnanimous and supportive with his advice and counsel, direct, yet deferential, Alan Gottlieb is committed to the cause of freedom.

Millions of Americans know and respect him for his spirited defense of the right to own and bear arms. Chairman of the Citizens Committee for the Right to Keep and Bear Arms, author of four nationwide bestselling books on the rights of gun owners, Alan Gottlieb founded the Second Amendment Foundation—the nation's largest foundation committed to the legal defense of gun owners.

Alan has received favorable notice for his work in the *New York Times, Washington Post, Time, People, Rolling Stone, National Review,* and *Outside* magazines. He has appeared on over 2,000 television and radio talk shows, including *McNeil-Lehrer News Hour,* ABC's *20/20,* PBS's *Late Night,* CNN's *Crossfire* and ABC's *Good Morning America.* He is President of KBNP, a Portland, Oregon radio station and President of Chancellor Broadcasting Company, owners of a national talk radio network with more than 70 affiliates coast-to-coast. As a journalist, his articles have appeared in the *Seattle Times, San Francisco Examiner, Washington Post, Cincinnati Inquirer, Chicago Tribune* and *USA Today.*

Alan Gottlieb is also a friend to advocates of multiple use of federal lands and defenders of property rights and other Constitutional liberties. Co-author of the ground-breaking myth-destroying fact-filled *Trashing the Economy,* Alan Gottlieb has done much to advance the cause of putting people back into the environmental equation. Those who love freedom are in his debt.

THE HERO NETWORK

This section lists 1,000 organization and individual contacts who are involved in the fight for private property, individual liberties and free enterprise against environmentalist oppression. The movement against environmentalist oppression is extraordinarily diverse. There are many constituencies and many groups and no one can speak for them all.

The fact that a group or individual is listed here is not a representation of agreement with or connection to any other group or individual listed. We did not ask permission of any group or contact for inclusion in this list. Groups and contacts were selected for inclusion on the basis of public records such as newspaper clippings, legal filings and testimony before legislative bodies, or because they were part of an existing list of a specific aggregation of groups. For example, this directory includes organizations affiliated with Alliance for America, the Blue Ribbon Coalition and many other federations.

Listings are arranged alphabetically by a) state, and b) organization. However, each listing is laid out as follows: 1) Contact's name; 2) Organization name; 3) Mailing address; 4) City, State and Postal Code; 5) Telephone number; 6) FAX number. Item 4 is printed like a mailing label, *i.e.*, no comma between city and state or between state and postal code. Names of groups—and the individuals profiled in the text—are shown in **bold face**. We have done our best to ensure accuracy at press time, but make no claim that names and addresses are current.

Everyone on this list is a hero. Use this directory to find a congenial group to join and become a hero yourself.

We are everywhere.

Alabama (6)
Alabama Association of Conservation Districts, 71 Bowden, Eufala AL 36027.
Helen Crow Mills, **Alabama Forest Owners' Association, Inc.**, PO Box 104, Helena AL 35080, 205-663-1131, FAX 205-663-1131.
John McMillan, **Alabama Forestry Association**, 555 Alabama St., Montgomery AL 36104, 205-265-8733.
Austin L. Rainwater, **Mobile County Landowners Association**, 15100 Airport Blvd., Mobile AL 36608, 205-633-0701 FAX 205-633-0653.
Mickey Strickland, Save Our Lands, Route 1, Box 243, Mentone AL 35984, 205-634-4346 or 205-845-5924, FAX 205-845-2617.
Mike Moody, **Stewards of Family Farms, Ranches and Forests**, PO Box 70482, Montgomery AL 36107, 205-264-4237, 205-264-1878.

Alaska (20)
Troy Reinhart, **Alaska Forest Association**, 111 Stedman Street, Suite 200, Ketchikan AK 99901, 907-225-6114, FAX 907-225-5920.
Terry T. Brady, **Alaska Husky Wood** 2900 Boniface Parkway #672 Anchorage AK 99504 907-333-9462 907-333-9462.
June Christle, Alaska Loggers Legal Defense Fund, PO Box 389, Hoonah AK 99829, 907-945-3628, FAX 907-945-3533.
Steven C. Borell, **Alaska Miners Association**, 501 W. Northern Lights Blvd. #203, Anchorage AK 99503, 907-276-0347, FAX 907-278-7997.
Ric Davidge, **Alaska Public Policy Consulting Corp.**, 3501 Admiralty Bay, Anchorage AK 99515, 907-349-7329.
Ron Godden, **Alaska State Snowmobile Association**, PO Box 210427, Anchorage AK 99521-0427, 907-344-1928, FAX 561-5802.
Jennifer Johnston, **Alaska Support Industry Alliance**, 4220 B St. #200, Anchorage AK 99503-5911.
Tracy Larsen, **Alaska Women In Mining**, PO Box 34238, Juneau AK 99803, 907-463-4636, FAX 907-463-5060.
Sandy Meske, **Alaska Women In Timber**, 111 Stedman Suite 200, Ketchikan AK 99901, 907-225-6114, FAX 907-225-8260.
John Rishel, **Alliance for America**, 1505 Atikinson Dr., Anchorage AK 99504, 907-276-0347.
Chuck Achberger, **Alliance for Juneau's Future**, PO Box 21143, Juneau AK 99802, 907-586-2495, FAX 907-789-3062.
Jim von Bose, **Anchorage Snowmobile Club, Inc.**, PO Box 232196, Anchorage AK 99523, 907-346-1595.
Debbie Reinwand, **Arctic Power**, PO Box 240828, Anchorage AK 99524-0828, 907-563-2697, FAX 907-562-6782.
Fairbanks Snow Travelers Association, PO Box 80053, Fairbanks AK 99708-0053, 907-474-8711.
Glenda Smith, **Mat-Su Motor Mushers Club**, PO Box 876135, Wasilla AK 99687, 907-376-4726.
John Korobko, **Miners Advocacy Council**, PO Box 73824, Fairbanks AK 99707, 907-479-0471.
Paula Easley, Municipality of Anchorage, Box 196650, Anchorage AK 99519, 907-343-4431 or 907-274-6800; FAX 907-343-1991.

Marla Jean Adkins, **Reclaimers for Alaska**, PO Box 461, Cordova AK 99574, 907-424-7311, FAX 907-424-5861.

Becky Gay, **Resource Development Council for Alaska, Inc.**, 121 W. Firewood Lane, Suite 250, Anchorage AK 99503-2035, 907-276-0700, FAX 907-276-3887.

Oscar H. Bailey, **Western Mining Council - Kenai Chapter**, Old Nash Rd., Seward AK 99664, 907-224-5963.

Arizona (17)

Dan Miller, **Amigos**, (Mining Suppliers Trade Association), PO Box 25187, Phoenix AZ 85004, 602-279-3199, FAX 602-230-1287.

Arizona Cattlemens Association, 1401 N. 24th Street, Suite 4, Phoenix AZ 85008, 602-267-1129.

R. Bruce Whiting, **Arizona Citizen's Coalition On Resource Decisions**, PO Box 63542, Phoenix AZ 85082, 602-840-5555 FAX 602-952-6972.

David C. Ridinger, **Arizona Mining Association**, 2702 N. Third Street, Suite 2015, Phoenix AZ 85004, 602-266-4416, FAX 602-266-4418.

Don Drake, **Arizona Motorcycle Dealers Association**, 6717 E. McDowell, Scottsdale AZ 85257, 602-899-9088.

Charlie Connell, **Arizona Prospectors Association**, Litchfield Park AZ 85340, 602-935-2007.

Gene Mrotek, **Arizona Road Runners**, 464 E. 7th Place, Mesa AZ 85203, 602-969-4942.

Howard Giemsoe, **Arizona Trail Riders**, PO Box 31877, Phoenix AZ 85046, 602-437-2394.

Bea Wiser, **Arizona Trappers' Association Inc.**, HC 30, Box 746, Prescott AZ 86301, Home: 602-445-2790, Work: 602-776-3724.

Joe Melton, **Arizonans for Wildlife Conservation**, PO Box 82773, Phoenix AZ 85071, 602-783-0747, FAX 602-343-4853.

Al Bruner, **Bullhead 4 Wheelers Inc.**, PO Box 2403, Bullhead City AZ 86430, 602-758-1396.

Jeannie Hunt, **CORE**, Box 466, Fredonia AZ 86022, 602-643-7029, FAX 602-643-7529.

Ronnie Smith, **Northern Arizona Riding & Recreation Club**, PO Box 2454, Cottonwood AZ 86326, 602-634-4411.

Gary Davidson, **Our Land Society**, 3911 E. Dover, Mesa AZ 85205, 602-985-0212, FAX 602-924-4636.

Russ Corn, **Southwestern Mineral Exploration Association**, PO Box 40938, Tucson AZ 85725, 602-622-6257.

Chuck Diaz, **Speak Up America**, 9121 East Tanque Verde, Suite 105-162, Tucson AZ 85749, 602-749-8425, FAX 602-749-8425.

Dr. Peter A. Strittmatter, Steward Observatory, University of Arizona, Tucson AZ 85721, 602-621-6524, FAX 602-621-7852.

Arkansas (7)

Frank Davis, **Alliance for America**, PO Box 95, Cove AR 71937, 501-387-2884, FAX 501-387-2244.

Chris Barneycastle, **Arkansas Forestry Association**, 410 S. Cross Street, Suite C, Little Rock AR 72201-3014, 501-374-2441.

Leon Somerville, Buffalo River Coalition of Spit and Whittle Clubs, HC80, Box 750, Cozahome AR 72639, 501-448-5920.

Donna Ryals, **Concerned Citizens Coalition**, PO Box 95, Cove AR 71937, 501-394-3427, FAX 501-387-2244.

Bonnie Blackburn, **Farm Bureau - Polk County**, PO Box 1139, Mena AR 71953, 501-394-3650.

M S R, Box 130, Clarksville AR 72830, 501-754-6993.

Ozark Trail Vehicle Association, PO Box 264, Avoca AR 72711, 501-756-1923.

British Columbia (Canada)

Patrick Armstrong, **Moresby Consulting,** 6573 Southampton Road, Nanaimo BC V9V 1A5, 604-390-2020.

Lou Lepine, **North Island Citizens for Shared Resources**, 9550 Scott, Port Hardy BC V0N 2P0, 604-949-9879.

Ray Deschambeau, **Share the Stine**, Box 246, Boston Bar BC V0K 1C0, 604-867-9696.

Liza Furney, **Truck Loggers Association**, Box 333, Port McNeill BC V0N 2R0, 604-956-3333.

California (116)

Roberta Rawlings, **88 Spurs Riders Snowmobile Club**, PO Box 1272, Jackson CA 95642-1272, 209-295-7852, FAX 209-296-7834.

Nadine Bailey, Alliance for Environmental Resources, PO Box 849, Hayfork CA 96041, 916-628-5304.

John Ponce, **Alta California Alliance**, 418 5th Street, Eureka CA 95501, 707-444-2473.

John Barthel, **American Trappers Association**, 6239 Marlborough, Goleta CA 93117, 805-964-5097.

Ed Ehlers, **Associated California Loggers**, 555 Capitol Mall, #745, Sacramento CA 95814, 916-441-7940, FAX 916-441-7942.

Janette Frazier, **Bear River Trail Riders, Inc.**, 40800 Hwy 88, Pioneer CA 95666, 209-727-5726.

Norm Sovereign, **Bucks Lake Snow Drifters**, 6637 Myrtle Way, Paradise CA 95969, 916-877-7025.

William Hazeltine, **Butte County Mosquito Abatement District**, 5117 Larkin Road, Oroville CA 95965, 916-533-6038.

Jim Bramham, **California Association of 4WD Clubs**, 3104 'O' Street #313, Sacramento CA 95816.

Patrice Davison, **California Association of 4WD Clubs**, PO Box 2151, Riverside CA 92516, 714-369-8960.

Todd Juvinall, **California Association of Business Property & Resource Owners**, PO Box 902, Grass Valley CA 95945, 916-478-1331, FAX 916-478-9528.

Toni Forni, **California Cattlewomen's Association**, PO Box 1173, El Dorado CA 95623, 916-622-3797, FAX 916-622-3797.

Mike Ahrens, **California Desert Coalition**, 6192 Magnolia Ave., Suite D, Riverside CA 92506, 714-684-6509, FAX 909-684-2043.

Grover Roberts, **California Farm Bureau**, 1601 Exposition Blvd., Sacramento CA 95815.

R. Brad Shinn, **California Farm Water Coalition**, 717 K Street, Suite 510, Sacramento CA 95814-3406, 916-441-7723, FAX 916-441-7842.

Kathy Kvarda, **California Forestry Association**, 1311 I Street, Suite 100, Sacramento CA 95814, 916-444-6592, FAX 916-444-0170.

Carol Crow, **California Forestry Products Commission**, 2150 River Plaza Drive, Suite #325, Sacramento CA 95833.

Mary-Lou Smith, **California Mining Association**, One Capitol Mall, Suite 220, Sacramento CA 95814, 916-447-1977, FAX 916-447-0348.

Ken Harn, **California Mining Journal**, PO Box 2260, Aptos CA 95001, 408-662-2899, 408-663-3014.

Charles Beesley, **California Mosquito & Vector Control Association**, 197 Otto Circle, Sacramento CA 95822, 916-393-7216.

Ken Nelson, **California-Nevada Snowmobile Association**, PO Box 236, Quincy CA 95971, 916-587-7802, FAX 619-934-9289.

Dave Swoger, **California Off-Road Vehicle Association**, 7821 Jellico Avenue, Northridge CA 91325, 818-345-1138.

Hildamae Voght, **California Outdoor Recreation League**, 35205 Johil Rd., Newberry Springs CA 92365, 619-257-3350.

Jeff Buck, **California Wildlife Federation**, 23041 Alcalda, Laguna Hills CA 92653, 714-951-9201, FAX 714-472-0457.

Marsha Rogers, **California Women for Agriculture Greater Westside Chapter**, 23719 Avenue 14, Madera CA 93637.

Loretta Stringfellow, **California Women In Timber - Quincy Chapter**, 2219 Mansell, Quincy CA 95971, 916-283-1205, FAX 916-283-4447.

Doris McCutcheon, **California Women In Timber - Sacramento Chapter**, PO Box 7070, Eureka CA 95502, 707-444-2937, FAX 916-842-1665.

California Women In Timber - Shasta / Tehama Chapter, PO Box 1546, Anderson CA 96007, 916-365-2865.

Barbara D. Hill, **California Women In Timber - Trinity Chapter**, PO Box 453, Hayfork CA 96041, 916-628-5169.

James Zuchelli, **Californians for Constitutional Government**, PO Box 1107, Pleasanton CA 94566, 510-426-8756.

Audrey Bozarth, **CARE - Sierra**, 4640 Abbey Rd., Placerville CA 95667, 916-644-1248.

Shirley Tresidder, **Central Sierra Alliance for Resources and Environment**, PO Box 1349, North Fork CA 93643, 209-683-1818.

Checkers Off Road, 13237 Sierra Hwy, Saugus CA 91350.

Kathie Cooke, **Citizens Alliance for Resource & Environment**, PO Box 1391, Ukiah CA 95482, 707-937-5590, FAX 707-485-7918.

Lou Sciochetti, **Community Solidarity Coalition**, PO Box 1646, Fort Bragg CA 95437, 707-961-0609.

Margaret Stafford, **Concerned Citizens of Arcata**, 3411 Martha Court, Arcata CA 95521.

Barbara Keating-Edh, **Consumer Alert**, 913 Wycliffe Court, Modesto CA 95355, 209-522-6572, FAX 209-522-6963.

Tom Mattingly, **C.O.R.E.**, PO Box 1278, Arleta CA 91334-9278.

Margaret Allender, **Desert Conservation Institute**, 427 Broadway, Jackson CA 95642.

John Brown, **East Mojave Property Owners Association**, PO Box 103, Cima CA 92323, 818-956-0008, FAX 818-353-4583.

Henry Alden, **Eldorado Alliance for Environment & Resources**, PO Box 486, Camino CA 95709, 916-644-2311, FAX 916-644-6205.

Joy Andrews, **Eldorado Property Owners to Protect the Fifth Amendment**, 3031 Alhambra, Suite 101, Cameron Park CA 95682, 916-677-1747, FAX 916-626-4205.

Billie Redemeyer, **Facilitator**, Rt. 4, Box 507A, Chico CA 95926, 916-895-0226, FAX 916-895-1848.

Sue Sutton, Family Water Alliance, PO Box 365, Maxwell CA 95955, 916-438-2026, FAX 916-438-2920.

Farwest Motorcycle Club, PO Box 3198, Eureka CA 95502, 707-445-9747.

Terry Logan, **Feather River Alliance for Resources & Environment**, PO Box 3953, Quincy CA 95971, 916-283-2519, FAX 916-283-4868.

Walter and Sue Shultz, **Fifth Or Fight**, PO Box 114, Cool CA 95614, 916-823-2886, FAX 916-823-3377.

Hector Eribez, **Fishermen's Coalition**, 2405 East Harbor Drive, San Diego CA 92113, 619-233-1633.

Teresa Platt, Fishermen's Coalition/Fishermen's Education Foundation, 826 Orange Avenue, Suite 504, Coronado CA 92118, 619-575-4664, FAX 619-575-5578.

Judy D. Hodge, **The Forest Scene**, 633 Brighton Street, Grass Valley CA 95945, 916-273-5044.

Allen Henninger, **Forests Forever**, 10828 Crothers Rd., San Jose CA 95127.

Frank Linnenkohl, **Four Wheel Drive Club of Fresno**, 42447 Juniper, Auberry CA 93602, 209-855-2060.

George Massie, **Gold Prospectors Association of America**, PO Box 507, Borsall CA 92003, 619-728-6620, FAX 619-728-4815.

Golden State Sno-Blazers, 2488 Coloma Rd., Placerville CA 95667-3312, 916-622-1117.

Jim Waddell, **Happy Camp Citizens**, PO Box 527, Happy Camp CA 96039, 916-493-2231, FAX 916-493-2742.

Ron Schiller, **High Desert Multiple-Use Coalition**, 1163 S. Garth, Ridgecrest CA 93555.

Joyce Benton, **I CARE**, PO Box 1700, Burney CA 96013, 916-335-3681.

Inland Empire Four Wheelers, PO Box 5153, San Bernardino CA 92412-5153, 714-874-7446.

Mark A. Smith, **Jeepers Jamboree & Jeep Jamboree, Inc.**, PO Box 1660, 6180 Hwy 193, Georgetown CA 95634, 916-333-4771.

Joan Smith, **KARE**, PO Box 1234, Yreka CA 96097, 916-842-9030, FAX 916-842-5041.

Mark Pollot, Attorney At Law, **Keck, Mahin & Cate**, 1 Maritime Plaza, 23rd Floor, San Francisco CA 94111, 415-392-7077, FAX 415-392-3969.

Jim Ostrowski, **Klamath Alliance for Resources & Environment**, 427 Alder, Mt. Shasta CA 96067.

Lake Tahoe Hi-Lo's Four Wheel Drive Club, PO Box 8248, South Lake Tahoe CA 96158.

Richard J. Scriven, **La Porte Snowmobile Club**, PO Box 261, La Porte CA 95981.

Susan Baremore, **Lassen CARES**, 84 N. Lassen St., Susanville CA 96130, 916-257-5898, FAX 916-257-8266.

Los Altos Dirt Bikers Motorcycle Club, PO Box 390370, Mountain View CA 94039.

Susan Small, **Los Aventureros**, 16822 Lahey Street, Granada Hills CA 91344.

Lost Angels Motorcycle Club, 8648 Lehigh Avenue, Sun Valley CA 91352, 818-767-7813.

Mike Gherardi, **Liberty Express**, PO Box 400, Georgetown CA 95634, 916-333-1776, FAX 916-333-0536.

Lee Pitts, **Livestock Digest**, PO Box 616, Morro Bay CA 93442, 805-528-5836.

Maier Manufacturing, 416 Crown Point Circle, Grass Valley CA 95945, 916-272-9036.

Toni Clark, **Mendocino Community Solidarity Coalition**, PO Box 1646, Fort Bragg CA 95437.

Julie Mann, **Minerals Producers of California**, 30984 Soap Mine Road, Barstow CA 92311, 619-256-2520, FAX 619-256-0127.

Dave McCracken, **Modern Gold Miner & Treasure Hunters Association**, PO Box 47, Happy Camp CA 96039, 916-493-2062, FAX 916-493-2095.

Bruce Main, **Modoc CARES**, PO Box 617, Bieber CA 96009, 916-294-5221, FAX 916-294-5876.

Modoc County Farm Bureau, PO Box 1692, Alturas CA 96101, 916-233-3276.

Jim Williams, **Motorcycle Industry Council**, 2 Jenner St. Ste 150, Irvine CA 92718, 714-727-4211.

Mt. Shasta Snowmobile Club, Inc., PO Box 341, Mt. Shasta CA 96067, 916-926-2824.

Robert Sanregret, **National Association of Mining Districts**, 17461 Irvine Blvd., Suite A, Tustin CA 92680, 714-731-1335, FAX 714-544-8406.

National Federation of Independent Business, 150 W. 20th Avenue, San Mateo CA 94403, 415-341-7641, FAX 415-378-1685.

Orange County ATV Association, 1809 Glenview Avenue, Anaheim CA 92807, 310-970-1944.

James Burling, **Pacific Legal Foundation**, 2700 Gateway Oaks, #200, Sacramento CA 95833, 916-641-8888, FAX 916-920-3444.

Greg Ouellette, **Pacific Mining Association**, 2051 Pacific Avenue, Norco CA 91760, 909-371-6493, FAX 909-737-2508.

Don Williams, **Plonkers Trails Club**, 613 Fremont Avenue, South Pasadena CA 91030, 714-735-5602.

Dan Smith, **Plumas Sierra Citizens**, PO Box 989, Quincy CA 95971, 916-283-3292.

Gary Gundlach, **Redwood Region Communications**, 512 Nob Hill Rd., Fortuna CA 95540, 707-764-5007.

Marcus Rudnick, San Juan Ranch, Route 1, Box 76A, Santa Margarita CA 93453, 805-438-3440

Salinas Ramblers Motorcycle Club, PO Box 541, Salinas CA 93902-0541.

Nanette Martin, **San Joaquin County Citizens Land Alliance**, 12067 W. Lammers Road, Tracy CA 95376, 209-835-6467, FAX 209-835-7380.

Victor Everett, **Santa Clara Miners Association**, PO Box 1208, Alviso CA 95002, 408-287-0414, FAX 408-254-3088.

Dick Kelly, **Shasta Alliance for Resources & Environment**, 1357 A Hartnell, Redding CA 96002, 916-223-2562, FAX 916-223-2571.

Bob Doelker, **Shasta Miners and Prospectors Association**, PO Box 720084, Redding CA 96099, 916-241-8777.

Sierra Buttes SnowBusters, PO Box 287, Sierra City CA 96125, 916-862-1128.

Joyce Corbett, **Sierra C.A.R.E.** 8981 Wentworth Springs Rd., Georgetown CA 95634, 916-338-4288.

Mark E. Smith, **Sierra Nevada Mining & Industry Council**, PO Box 1567, Grass Valley CA 95945, 916-272-2448, FAX 916-272-8533.

Marcia H. Armstrong, **Siskiyou County Farm Bureau**, 809 South Fourth St., Yreka CA 96097, 916-842-2364, FAX 916-842-5041.

Sonora Pass Sno-Goers, PO Box 3231, Sonora CA 95370, 209-532-9580.

Stephen Braun, **Southern California Building Industry Association**, Paragon Homes, 1448 15th Street, Santa Monica CA 90404, 310-393-1431, FAX 310-394-6871.

R. Peter Ingram, **Tahoe Area Citizens Alliance for Resources & Environment - TACARE**, PO Box 787, Nevada City CA 95959, 916-273-9282, FAX 916-272-7514.

Dave Cruzan, **Taxpayers for Environment and its Management (T.E.A.M.)**, PO Box 651, Fortuna CA 95540-0651, 707-764-5158.

Team Dual Dogs of Southern California, 8535 Amestoy Avenue, Northridge CA 91325, 818-701-1913.

Burt Bundy, **Tehama Alliance for Resources & Environment**, PO Box 1224, Red Bluff CA 96080, 916-527-4655, FAX 916-529-0980.

Stephen Braun, **The Valley Group**, 1448 15th St., Santa Monica CA 90404, 310-393-1431, FAX 310-394-6871.

James Craine, **Timber Association of California**, 1311 I Street, Suite 100, Sacramento CA 95814, 916-444-6592.

Timekeepers Motorcycle Club, 238 Pinehurst Avenue, Los Gatos CA 95030.

Toyota Land Cruiser Association Inc., PO Box 607, Placerville CA 95667-0607, 916-622-4428.

Trailbike Sportsman Association, PO Box 60772, Sacramento CA 95860.

Tom Walz, **Trinity Resource Action Council**, PO Box 1626, Weaverville CA 96093, 916-623-4301, FAX 916-623-5876.

Kathy Smith, **Trinity Women In Timber**, 2284 Saturn Skyway, Redding CA 96002, 916-223-2740.

Nancy Rosasco, **Tuolumne County Alliance for Resources and Environment - TUCARE**, PO Box 3361, Sonora CA 95370, 209-533-1662, FAX 209-533-0210.

Nancy Bailey, **Tulelake Growers Association**, PO Box 338, Tulelake CA 96134, 503-798-5605, FAX 916-667-3919.

Larry Duysen, **TACARE**, PO Box 10060, Terra Bella CA 93270, 209-535-4893, FAX 209-535-4515.

Tom Lealos, **United Forest Families**, PO Box 11, Standard CA 95373.

Gregory P. Ouellette, **Western Mining Council**, 2051 Pacific Avenue, Norco CA 91760, 714-371-6493.

Jay Koehler, **Western Mining Council, Inc. - Rand-El Paso Mountain Chapter**, PO Box 127, Randsburg CA 93554.

Western States Petroleum Association, 505 N Brand Blvd, Ste 1400, Glendale CA 91203.

Colorado (54)

Mike Haynes, **Alliance for America**, PO Box 1800, Pagosa Springs CO 81147, 303-731-4111, FAX 303-731-4455.

Tom McDonnell, **American Sheep Industry Association, Inc.**, 6911 S. Yosemite Street, Englewood CO 80112, 303-771-3500, FAX 303-771-8200.

Marianna Raftopoulos, **Children of the West**, 2991 Pineridge Rd., Craig CO 81625, 303-824-9411, FAX 303-824-6010.

Colorado 500, 2561 Frying Pan Road, Basalt CO 81621, 303-927-4010.

Colorado Association of 4 Wheel Drive Clubs, Inc., PO Box 1413, Wheatridge CO 80034.

Colorado Blizzards of Greeley, PO Box 1049, Greely CO 80632.

Reeves Brown, **Colorado Cattleman's Association**, Livestock Exchange Bldg., Suite 220, Denver CO 80216, 303-296-1112, FAX 303-296-1115.

Ray Christensen, **Colorado Farm Bureau**, 2211 W. 27th Avenue, PO Box 5647, Denver CO 80211, 303-455-4553.

David R. Cole, **Colorado Mining Association**, 1340 Co. St. Bank Blvd., 1600 Broadway, Denver CO 80202, 303-894-0536, FAX 303-894-8416.

Glenn Graham, **Colorado Off Highway Vehicle Coalition**, PO Box 620523, Littleton CO 80121-0523, 303-866-3581.

Lynn Toedte, **Colorado Property Rights Association**, PO Box 7031, Golden CO 80403, 303-985-0427.

Shirley Walker, **Colorado Snowmobile Association, Inc.**, Box 468, South Fork CO 81154, 719-873-5923.

J. Don Berry, **Colorado Timber Industry Association**, PO Box 95, Lake City CO 81235, 303-944-2742.

Marcie Hervey, **Colorado Wool Growers Association**, 211 Livestock Exchange Bldg., Denver CO 80216, 303-294-0854, FAX 303-297-1031.

Susan Albertson, **Cowboys Conservation Coalition**, PO Box 26, Burns CO 80426, 303-653-4449.

Constance E. Brooks, Attorney At Law, **Davis Wright Tremaine**, Suite 1245, Mellon Financial Center, 1775 Sherman Street, Denver CO 80202, 303-863-0836, FAX 303-863-0309.

Dee Cockcroft, **Delta Sno-Krusers Snowmobile Club**, 1468 G Road, Delta CO 81416.

Heinz W. Siegel, **Denver Mining Club, Ltd.**, 8520 N. Franklin, Denver CO 80229, 303-288-5438.

Nicholas Brown, **Earth Vision Institute**, PO Box 420, Gypsum CO 81637, 303-524-9770, FAX 303-524-9708.

Flattoppers, PO Box 1681, Glenwood Springs CO 81602, 303-945-2084.

Dennis and Nile Gerbaz, 1265-100 Road, Carbondale CO 81623, 303-963-2345.

Dave Carriker, **Harry's Roamers, Inc.**, 31 E. Easter Ave, Littleton CO 80122-1118.

Heart of the Rockies, PO Box 241, Poncha Springs CO 81242.

High Country Connection, 404 E. Rainbow Blvd., Salida CO 81201, 719-539-6168.

Bill Hornung, **K.C.C. Wise Use**, 2262 Rural Delivery 34, Stratton CO 80836, 719-348-5454.

Loring Ranches & Rangeland Users Association, PO Box 147, Whitewater CO 81527, 303-245-8729.

Jerry Cronk, **Mile-Hi Jeep Club**, PO Box 8293, Denver CO 80202.

William Shepard, **Minerals Exploration Coalition**, 2700 Youngfield, Suite 250, Lakewood CO 80215, 303-232-4310, FAX 303-233-3347.

John C. Martin, **Motorcycle Trail Riding Association**, PO Box 3204, Grand Junction CO 81502, 303-242-2211.

Susan Hussemann, **Mt. Sopris Snow Riders**, PO Box 1035, Carbondale CO 81623.

William Perry Pendley, **Mountain States Legal Foundation**, 1660 Lincoln St., Suite 2300, Denver CO 80264, 303-861-0244, FAX 303-831-7379.

Robert Tonsing, **Nationwide Public Projects Coalition**, Littleton CO 80122, 303-798-6772, FAX 303-347-0018.

Bruce Taylor, **Pikes Peak Enduro Club**, 351 Sunnywood Lane, Woodland Park CO 80863.

Terri Greer, **Pro Rodeo Cowboy Association**, 101 Pro Rodeo Dr., Colorado Springs CO 80919, 719-593-8804.

Dave Foss, **Public Lands Access Coalition**, 7146 S. Dexter Ct., Littleton CO 80122, 303-290-0164.

Doug Alford, **Rampart Range Management Committee**, 1540 Billings D-12, Aurora CO 80011, 303-399-4250.

Rocky Mountain Enduro Circuit, 1555 Clover Place, Loveland CO 80537, 303-667-6153.

Carla Wilson, **Rocky Mountain Oil & Gas Association**, 1860 Lincoln Street, Denver CO 80295, 303-860-0099, FAX 303-860-0310.

Mike Haynes, **San Juan Wise Use Alliance**, PO Box 1800, Pagosa Springs CO 81147, 303-731-4111, FAX 303-731-4455.

Snowskippers-Western Slope SM Association, PO Box 4964, Grand Junction CO 81502, 303-242-2172.

Carl Haywood, **Society for Mining Metallurgy & Exploration**, 8307 Snaffer Parkway, Littleton CO 80127, 303-973-9550.

Peter Jackson, **Society for Range Management**, 1839 York Street, Denver CO 80206.

Ed Toner, **Southwestern Water Conservation District**, PO Box 479, Pagosa Springs CO 81147, 303-731-5565.

Roger Brown, **Summit Films**, PO Box 420, Gypsum CO 81637, 303-524-9769, FAX 303-524-9708.

Thunder Mountain Wheelers, 1210 A Street, Delta CO 81416, 303-874-8343.

Timberline TrailRiders, Inc., PO Box 1794, Steamboat Springs CO 80477-1794, 303-879-0167.

P. Miklos, **United Four Wheel Drive Association**, 15290 West 77th Drive, Golden CO 80403, 1-800-448-3932.

John Stecher, **Upper Yampa Water Conservancy District**, Steamboat Springs CO 80448, 303-879-2424.

Jack Sheets, **Western Chapter - International Snowmobile Association**, 2350 Stoneridge Drive, Colorado Springs CO 80919, 382-8319.

Nadine Stoneburner, **Western Slope ATV Association**, PO Box 4964, Grand Junction CO 81505, 303-242-2172.

Bill and Barbara Grannell, **Western States Public Lands Coalition ("People for the West")**, PO Box 4345, Pueblo CO 81003, 719-543-8421, FAX 719-543-9473.

Laurie Baker, **Women In Timber - Colorado**, 680 E. Bridge St., Hotchkiss CO 81419.

Connecticut (3)

Scott Gardiner, **Alliance for America**, PO Box 736, Waterford CT 06385, 203-444-0434.

Steve Varno, **Nipmuck Trail Riders**, 9 Orcuttville Rd., Stafford Springs, CT, 06076-3614.

Art Noyes, **United Mobile Sportsfishermen, Inc.**, 300 South St. Apt. R-4, Vernon, CT, 06066.

Delaware (2)

G. Wallace Caulk, Jr., **Delaware Farm Bureau Federation**, 233 S. DuPont Highway, Camden DE 19934, 302-697-3183, FAX 302-697-1428.

High Dust ATV Club, RR 3, Box 145 O, Laurel, DE, 19956.

District of Columbia (28)

Reed Irvine, **Accuracy In Media**, 1275 K St. N.W., Suite 1150, Washington DC 20005, 202-371-6710.

David Senter, **American Agriculture Movement**, 100 Maryland Ave. NE, Washington DC 20002.

American Association of Nurserymen, 1250 I Street NW, Suite 500, Washington DC 20005, 202-789-2900.

Rosemarie Watkins, **American Forest & Paper Association**, 1250 Connecticut Ave. NW, #200, Washington DC 20036, 202-463-2770, FAX 202-463-2708.

Larry Wiseman, **American Forest Council**, 1250 Connecticut Avenue NW, #200, Washington DC 20036.

Tracey Herdrich, **American Legislative Exchange Council**, 214 Massachusetts Ave., NE, Washington DC 20002, 202-547-4646.

Keith Knoblock, **American Mining Congress**, 1920 N Street NW, Suite 300, Washington DC 20036, 202-861-2800, FAX 202-861-7535.

American Petroleum Institute, 1220 L Street NW, Washington DC 20005, 202-682-8176.

American Property Rights Alliance, 1212 New York Avenue NW, Suite1210, Washington DC 20005, 202-371-5566.

Associated Builders and Contractors, 729 15th Street NW, Washington DC 20005, 202-637-8800.

Jerry Taylor, Director, Natural Resource Studies, **Cato Institute,** Washington DC 2000 202-842-0200.

Willa Johnson, **Capital Research Center**, 1612 K Street N.W., Suite 704, Washington DC 20006, 202-822-8666.

Steven Gold, **Citizens for A Sound Economy**, 1250 H Street NW, Suite 700, Washington DC.

Craig Rucker, **Committee for a Constructive Tomorrow**, PO Box 65722, Washington DC 20035, 202-319-0104.

Fred Smith, **Competitive Enterprise Institute**, 233 Pennsylvania Ave. S.E., Suite 200, Washington DC 20003, 202-547-1010, FAX 202-546-7757.

Stephen V. Gold, **Citizens for the Environment**, 470 L'Enfant Plaza, S.W., Suite 7401, Washington DC 20024, 202-488-7255, FAX 202-488-8282.

Nancie G. Marzulla, **Defenders of Property Rights**, 6235 33rd Street NW, Washington DC 20015, 202-686-4197, FAX 202-686-0240.

Ben Hart, **Freedom Alliance**, PO Box 96700, Washington DC 20090, 703-709-6618.

Michael J. Bennett, **Investigative Journalism Project,** 907 6th S.W., Waterside Towers, Apt. 313C, Washington DC 20024, 202-488-7692.

Richard Minard, **Mineral Resource Alliance**, 1301 Connecticut Ave. N.W., Washington DC 20036, 202-659-0330, FAX 202-296-1775.

Tom Cooke, **National Cattlemen's Association**, 1301 Pennsylvania Ave. NW, Suite 300, Washington DC 20004, 202-347-5355, FAX 202-638-0607.

General Richard V. Lawson, **National Coal Association**, 1130 17th Street NW, Washington DC 20036, 202-463-2625, FAX 202-463-6152.

Laurence Jahn, **National Fish & Wildlife Coalition,** 1101 14th St. NW, #725, Washington DC 20005.

Leroy Watson, **National Grange**, 1616 H Street NW, Washington DC 20006, 202-628-3507.

Rob Gordon and Ben Patton, National Wilderness Institute, 25766 Georgetown Station, Washington DC 20007, 703-836-7404, FAX 703-549-6889.

Myron Ebell, **American Land Rights Association**
  (National Inholders Association,
  Multiple Use Land Alliance and
  League of Private Property Voters)
  233 Pennsylvania Ave. SE, Suite 301, Washington DC 20003, 202-544-6156, FAX 202-544-6774.

National Wetlands Coalition, 1050 Thomas Jefferson NW, 6th Floor, Washington DC 20007, 202-298-1879.

Florida (18)
O. C. Mills, **American Environmental Foundation**, PO Box 7015, Milton FL 32570, 904-626-1783.
Ralph Ritteman, **American Environmental Foundation**, PO Box 5386, Navarte FL 32566, 904-939-9182, FAX 904-939-6528.
L. M. Buddy Blain, Attorney At Law, **Blain & Cone, P.A.**, 202 Madison Street, Tampa FL 33602, 813-223-3888, FAX 813-228-6422.
David Russell, Citizens for Constitutional Property Rights, PO Box 757, Crestview FL 32536, 904-682-6156, FAX 904-678-3321.
Michelle Wells Usher, **Conch Coalition**, P.O. Box 501785, Marathon FL 33050-1785, 305-743-8637.
Jan Michael Jacobson, **Everglades Institute**, PO Box 653954, Miami FL 33265, 813-695-3143.
Ben Parks, **Florida Farm Bureau**, 150 S. Monroe St., Suite 300, Talla-hassee FL 32301, 904-222-2557.
Carroll Lamb, **Florida Forestry Association**, Box 1696, Tallahassee FL 32302, 904-222-5646.
Bob Jones, **Southeastern Fisheries Association, Inc.**, 312 East Georgia Street, Tallahassee FL 32301, 904-224-0612, FAX 904-222-FOOD.
Florida Lands Council, 202 Madison Street, Tampa FL 33602, 813-223-3888, FAX 813-228-6422.
Florida Trail Riders, Inc., PO Box 5141, Titusville FL 32783-5141, 407-269-1920.
Dr. Felix R. Livingston, **Institution for World Capitalism**, Jackson-ville University, 2800 University Blvd. N., Jacksonville FL 32211-3393, 904-744-9986, FAX 904-744-9987.
Dr. John W. Cooper, **James Madison Institute for Public Policy Studies**, PO Box 13894, Tallahasse FL 32317, 904-386-3131, 904-386-3131, FAX 904-386-1807.
Woodrow A. Kantner, **Kantner Investment Corporation**, PO Box 2353, Stuart FL 34995, 407-283-3280.
Kenneth Wilkinson, **Save Our Homes**, PO Box 1114, Fort Myers FL 33902.
Bill Nettles, **Southeastern Wood Producers Association**, Box 9, Hillard FL 32046, 904-845-7133, FAX 904-845-7345.
Dennis Henderson, **Southwest Florida Shrimp Association**, PO Box 3098, Fort Myers Beach FL 33931, 813-463-3341, FAX 813-765-1828.
P. T. Rampy, **Treasure Coast Coalition, Inc.**, 1322 U.S. 1, Sebastian FL 32958, 407-589-4944, FAX 407-589-6141.

Georgia (12)
Deborah Baker, **Alliance for America**, 2900 Chamblee, Trucker Bldg 5, Atlanta GA 30341, 404-451-3545, FAX 404-451-2976.
Robert W. Pollard, Jr., **Alliance for America**, Rt. 3 Box 1340, Appling GA 30802, 706-541-1343, FAX 706-541-1880.
Gene Doss, **Calhoun County Young Farmers**, Box 383, Edison GA 31746.
Wallis W. Wood, **The Eco-Profiteer** (Soundview Publications, Inc.), 1350 Center Drive, Suite 100, Dunwoody GA 30338, 800-728-2288.

Ray Harbin, **Dendroi Conservation,** 5875 Colonist Drive, Fairburn GA 30213, 404-964-7813, FAX 404-969-9249.

B. Jack Warren, **Forest Farmers Association,** 4 Executive Park East, N.E., Atlanta GA 30329, or Box 95385, Atlanta GA 30347, 404-325-2954.

Robert L. Izlar, **Georgia Forestry Association Inc.,** 500 Pinnacle Court, #505, Norcross GA 30071-3634, 404-840-8961.

Lee Lemke, **Georgia Mining Association,** 900 Circle 75 Parkway, Suite 1740, Atlanta GA 30339, 404-952-7975, FAX 404-952-7986.

Rudy Underwood, **Landowners for Responsible Natural Resource Management,** PO Box 964, Kennesaw GA 30144, 404-419-1916, FAX 404-419-1916.

G. Stephen Parker, **Southeastern Legal Foundation,** 2900 Chamblee-Tucker, Atlanta GA 30341, 404-458-8313.

Mark Barford, **Southeastern Lumber Manufacturer's Association,** Box 1788, Forest Park GA 30051-1788, 404-361-1445.

Deborah Baker, **Southern Timber Purchasers Council,** 2900 Chamblee Tucker Rd., Bldg. 5, Atlanta GA 30341, 404-451-3545, FAX 404-451-2976.

Hawaii (4)

Miriam Hellreich, **Alliance for America,** 40 Aulike St., Suite 311, Kailua HI 96734, 808-261-9120.

Miss June Curtis, **Hawaii Island Geothermal Alliance,** P.O. Box 896, Pepeekeo HI 96783, 808-961-3424.

Daniel Makuakane, Hawaii Island Geothermal Alliance, P. O. Box 2064, Pahoa HI 96778, 808-965-7126.

Sam Slom, **Small Business Hawaii,** 770 Kapiolani Blvd., #111, Honolulu, HI 96813, 808-596-2277, FAX 808-596-0682.

Idaho (57)

Rollie Adams, **Alliance for America,** RR 1, Box 224-50, Salmon ID 83576, 208-756-3611.

Rita Carlson, Alliance for America, 3416 10th St., Lewiston ID 83501, 208-799-1178, FAX 208-799-1810.

Pat Holmberg, **Alliance of Independent Miners,** PO Box 7042, Boise ID 83707-1042, 208-344-8679, FAX 208-764-2927.

Clark Collins, Blue Ribbon Coalition, PO Box 5449, Pocatello ID 83202, 208-237-1557, FAX 208-237-1566.

Boise Basin Trailbreakers Snowmobile Club, PO Box 445, Idaho City ID 83631.

Roger D. Tipton, **Boise Ridge Riders, Inc.,** 3602 Chinden Blvd., Boise ID 83714, 208-362-0653, FAX 208-338-5981.

Boise Snowmobile Club, Inc., 11132 Tioga, Boise ID 83709, 208-362-3687.

Tom Hildesheim, **The Brush Bunch,** W 7225 Hauser Lake Road, Post Falls ID 83854.

D. Allen Dalton, **Center for Study of Market Alternatives,** 2285 University Drive, Boise ID 83706, 208-368-7811.

Mike Rokavina, **Central Idaho Rod & Gun Club**, PO Box 177, Challis ID 83226, 879-4430.

Mike Duggar, **Clearwater Resource Coalition**, PO Box 1846, Orofino ID 83544, 208-476-4597, FAX 208-476-7799.

Steve Wheeler, **Coalition for Responsible Mining Law**, PO Box 469, Wallace ID 83873, 208-752-1131.

Al Beauchene, **Coeur D'Alene Snowmobile Club**, West 3390 Bean Avenue, Coeur d'Alene ID 83814.

Donna Rose, **Concerned Citizens of Triumph**, Box 3730, Ketchum ID 83340, 208-788-9300, FAX 208-788-9337.

Helen Chenoweth, **Consulting Associates, Inc.**, 1843 Broadway, Suite 102, Boise ID 83706, 208-345-2670, FAX 208-345-2676.

Cougar Mountain Snowmobilers, PO Box 7601, Boise ID 83707, 343-0368.

Margaret Gabbard, **Free Enterprise Legal Defense Fund**, P.O. Box 44704, Boise ID 83711, 208-336-5922, FAX 208-336-7054.

Robert W. Johnson, **Garden Valley Snowmobile Club**, HC 76, Box 4219, Garden Valley ID 83622, 208-462-3250.

Phillip Nisbet, **Grassroots for Multiple Use - Salmon Chapter,** 307 State Street, Salmon ID 83467, 208-756-4578, FAX 208-756-2573.

High Mountain Trail Machine Association, Box 52, Grangeville ID 83530, 208-983-0312.

George Bennett, **Idaho Cattle Association**, 2120 Airport Way, Boise ID 83701, 208-343-1615.

Suzanne Budge, **Idaho Council on Industry and the Environment,** PO Box 255, Boise ID 83701, 208-336-8508, FAX 208-388-5623.

Bill George, **Idaho Falls Trail Machine Association**, PO Box 3625, Idaho Falls ID 83403-3625, 208-529-3734.

Dave Bivins, **Idaho Farm Bureau,** PO Box 167, Boise ID 83701, 208-342-2688, FAX 208-342-8585.

Jack Lyman, **Idaho Mining Association,** PO Box 1660, Boise ID 83701, 208-342-5003, FAX 208-345-4210.

Carl Struthers, **Idaho Motorcycle Dealers Association**, 5550 West State Street, Boise ID 83703, 208-853-5550.

Trent L. Clark, **Idaho Private Property Coalition**, PO Box 15977, Boise ID 83715-5977, 208-344-2271, FAX 208-336-9447.

Bob James, **Idaho Snow Riders**, HC 87, Box 208, Pine ID 83647.

Irene Atamanczyk, **Idaho State Snowmobile Association**, PO Box 3324, Idaho Falls ID 83403-3324, 208-524-5179.

Ernie Lombard, **Idaho Trail Machine Association**, 3590 Ballentine Lane, Eagle ID 83610-2438, 208-377-1296, Work: 208-383-7028.

Jean Messinger, **Idaho Women for Agriculture - Chapter II**, RT 1, Box 100, Culdesac ID 83524, 208-836-5543.

Roberta P. Witteman, **Idaho Women for Agriculture - Chapter 5,** 9506 Missouri Ave., Nampa ID 83686, 208-466-2998.

Stan Boyd, **Idaho Wool Growers Association,** PO Box 2596, Boise ID 83701, 208-344-2271, FAX 208-336-9447.

Frank Favor, **Intermountain Logging Conference Inc.,** PO Box 1177, Coeur D'Alene ID 83814.

Larry McMillan, **Latah County SnowDrifters**, PO Box 8687, 731 Camas, Moscow ID 83843.

Jack & Naomi Cole, **Lewis and Clark SnowDrifters**, PO Box 1991, Lewiston ID 83501, 743-3864.

Magic Valley Snowmobilers Inc., PO Box 1009, Twin Falls ID 83301.

Magic Valley Trail Machine Association, PO Box 1023, Twin Falls ID 83303.

Mt. Harrison Snowmobile Club, PO Box 301, Burley ID 83318-0301, 208-436-4181.

Mt. River Sno-Riders, PO Box 50903, Idaho Falls ID 83405.

Jennifer Johnson, **North Idaho Trail Blazers**, #2 Forest Lane, Post Falls ID 83854, 208-773-3503.

Jim Gray, **North Idaho Trail Riders Organization**, PO Box 294, Wallace ID 83873-0294, 208-752-5281.

Northwest Powerboaters Association, PO Box 1381, Lewiston ID 83501.

Dale Newberry, **Panhandle Off-Road Vehicle Association**, PO Box 9516, Moscow ID 83843, Home: 208-882-6103, Work: 208-882-0514.

Panhandle Snowmobile Club, PO Box 900, Bonners Ferry ID 83805.

Pocatello Pathfinders, 730 Canal, Chubbuck ID 83202, 208-237-2295.

Pocatello Trail Machine Association, PO Box 4459, Pocatello ID 83205-4459.

Jerry Klemm, **Pulp & Paper Workers Resource Council,** 701 Burrell, Lewiston ID 83501, 208-743-5450, FAX 208-799-1077.

S.I.D.R.A. Inc., 930 Powerline, Nampa ID 83651, 208-467-3593.

Salmon Ridge Runners Snowmobile Club, PO Box 636, Salmon ID 83467.

Sawtooth Snowmobile Club, Box 572, Bellevue ID 83313.

Snake River ATV, 7646 Lemhi Street #1, Boise ID 83709, 208-377-8770.

Ernest Lombard, **Treasure Valley Trail Machine Association**, PO Box 1913, Boise ID 83701, 208-342-5283.

Valley Cats Snowmobile Club, PO Box 487, Kooskai ID 83539.

Darby Helms, **West Mountain Snowmobile Club**, PO Box 959, Cascade ID 83611.

Illinois (27)

Trenna Grabowski, **American Agri-Women,** PO Box 726, Mt. Vernon IL 62864, 618-242-4311, 618-242-4324.

John Hosemann, **American Farm Bureau Federation,** 225 Touhy Ave., Park Ridge IL 60068, 312-399-5746, FAX 312-399-5896.

Bruce Sutchar, **American Freedom Coalition,** 512 Zenith Drive, Glenview IL 60025.

Douglas Fender, **American Sod Producers Association,** 1855-A Hicks Road, Rolling Meadows IL 60008.

Big Blue River Conservancy District, 122 1/2 Broad Street, New Castle IN 47362.

Walter A. (Bud) Houston, **Conference of 14,** PO Box 305, Rushville IL 62681, 217-322-2620.

Charles Daugherty, **Conservation Coalition,** 124 North Rod Lane, Carbondale IL 62901, 618-529-5098.

Ray Morris, **Conservation Coalition,** PO Box C, Golconda IL 62938, 618-949-3869.

John Gepford, **Dirt Riders, Inc.,** RR 1, Box 134, Warrenburg IL 62573.

Eleanor Zimmerlein, **Illinois Agri-Women,** 1518 Baseline Road, LaMoille IL 61330, 815-638-2050.

Bill Schumann, **Illinois Association of Snowmobile Clubs,** 2904 E 24th Road, Marseilles IL 61341, Main Address 815-795-2021.

Tim O'Connor, **Illinois Beef Association,** 993 Clock Tower Dr., Springfield IL 62704.

John Hamm, **Illinois Cattleman's Association,** R.R. 1, Box 15, Adair IL 61411, 309-653-2590.

Lloyd Burling, **Illinois Fertilizer & Chemical Association,** PO Box 186, St. Anne IL 60964, 815-427-6644, FAX 815-427-6573.

Grover Webb, **Illinois Wilderness,** RR 1, Box 271, Simpson IL 62985.

Eugene Huggins, **Illinois Wood Products Association,** 115 W. Indian Trail, Aurora IL 60506, 708-897-5545.

John C. Wilson, **JSD Land Trust,** 22 S. Granger Street, Harrisburg IL 62946, 618-253-7063.

C. Kozel, **McHenry County Snowmobile Association,** 3305 S. Riverdale, McHenry IL 60050, 815-459-3154.

Rod Harder, **National Trappers Association,** PO Box 3667, 216 N. Center, Bloomington IL 61702-3667, 503-925-3022, FAX 503-925-4122.

Tom Koutny, **Neil Association of Snowmobile Clubs, Inc.,** 103 N. Longmeadow, Lindenhurst IL 60046.

Ben Thrall, **North Shore Association,** 4862 Reservation Rd., Oswego IL 60543, 708-554-1252.

Ron Kern, **Ogle County Farm Bureau,** PO Box 195, Oregon IL 61061, 815-732-2231, FAX 815-732-3412.

Jerome Varel, **Okaw River Basin Coalition,** 12517 Pioneer Rd., Bartelso IL 62218.

Southern Illinois ATVers, PO Box 960, Harrisburg IL 62946.

Karen W. Steve, **S.T.O.P. (Stop Think Organize Prevail!),** 6N759 Route 31, St. Charles IL 60175, 708-377-6299.

Nancy Huddleston, **United Motorcyclist of Illinois,** 311 E. Mulberry St, Bloomington IL 61701-3123.

Ken Smalley, **Windy City Trail Riders,** 3903 Grand Avenue, Western Springs IL 60558-1134.

Indiana (10)

ABATE of Indiana, Inc., PO Box 665, Bargersville IN 46106-0665, 317-422-8040.

Bill Theis, **Alliance for America,** PO Box 599, Chesterton IN 46304, 219-926-6315, FAX 219-926-4651.

Joann Etienne, Phil Etienne's Timber Harvest, Inc., St. Route Box 20-A, St. Croix IN 47576, 812-843-5208; 836-2162(H), FAX 812-843-5362.

Diane Selke, **Help Enlighten Laporte,** PO Box 505, Westville IN 46391, 219-785-2675.

Indiana 4 Wheel Drive Association, Inc., 6142 Franklin Road, Hagerstown IN 47346.

James D. Barnett, **Indiana Farm Bureau**, PO Box 1290, Indianapolis IN 46206, 317-692-7819, FAX 317-692-7854.

Deak Thornton, **Indiana Snowmobile Association**, PO Box 15010, 6732 E. State Blvd., Ft. Wayne IN 46885.

Martin and Linda Okos, **Protect Property Rights**, Box 323, Battle Ground IN 47920, 317-567-2750.

Joanna Waugh, **Stop Taking Our Property**, 500 Potowatomi Trail, Chesterton IN 46304, 219-926-7007, FAX 219-926-8879.

Susan Showers, **Stop Taking Our Property**, PO Box 599, Chesterton IN 46304, 219-926-6315, FAX 219-926-4651.

Iowa (11)

Judy Hageman, **Alliance for America**, Rt. 1, Box 89A, Decorah IA 52101, 319-532-9803.

Sandy Greinder, **American Agri-Women**, Rt. 2, Box 193, Keota IA 52248, 515-636-2293.

Joe Zajicek, **Basic Freedoms Inc.**, 3405 Rochester Ave., Iowa City IA 52240.

Iowa ATV Association, PO Box 143, Johnston IA 50131.

Dan Frieberg, **Iowa Fertilizer & Chemical Association**, 1900 Des Moines St., Suite 150, Des Moines IA 50309, 515-262-8323.

Iowa Motorcycle Dealers Association, 4113 Columbia Street, Des Moines IA 50313, 515-280-6596.

Dale Vagts, **Iowa State Snowmobile Association**, PO Box 159, Hwy 9 East, Cresco IA 52136.

Devon Woodland, **National Farmers Organization**, 505 Elwood Drive, Ames IA 50010.

Sno Hawks Snowmobile Club, Inc., 1116 Higby Drive, Cedar Falls IA 50613.

SnowDrifters, Inc., PO Box 531, Solon IA 52333.

Douglas M. Kleine, **Soil & Water Conservation Society,** 7515 NE Ankeny Road, Ankeny IA 50021-9764.

Kansas (7)

Bill Campbell, **The American Oil & Gas Reporter**, PO Box 343, Derby KS 67037-0343, 316-788-5796, FAX 316-788-7568.

Lee Wray Russell, **Associated General Contractors**, Box 535, Eureka KS 67045.

Larry Fischer, **Kansans for Fair Taxation, Inc.**, 1834 N. Kansas Ave., Suite 200, Topeka KS 66608, 913-354-8688, FAX 913-273-0400.

Kansas ATV Association, PO Box 8495, Topeka KS 66608-0495.

Howard Blender, **Kansas Grassroots Association,** Route 5, Box 77, Emporia KS 66801.

Kansas Land Coalition, RR 1, Box 212, Wakefield KS 67487, 913-461-5533.

Bill Hans, **SAKW,** PO Box 726, Newton KS 67164.

Kentucky (3)
James Lee, **Kentucky Forest Industries Association,** 310 Kings Daughters Drive, # 7, Frankfort KY 40601, 502-875-3136.
Paul Sandefur, **Kentucky Landowners Association,** PO Box 425, Beaver Dam KY 42320, 502-274-4044.
Dr. Irwin W. Tucker, **National Council for Environmental Balance,** 4169 Westport Road, PO Box 7732, Louisville KY 40257, 502-896-8731.

Louisiana (20)
Donald Powell, **Alliance for America,** Rt 1, Box 154, Pollock LA 71467, 318-765-3922, FAX 318-765-9331.
Matthew Yates, **American Mosquito Control Association,** 707 E. Prien Lake Rd., Lake Charles LA 70606.
American Shrimp Processors Association, PO Box 50774, New Orleans LA 70150.
Mike Voisin, **Louisiana Seafood Processors Council,** PO Box 3916, Houma LA 70361-3916, 504-868-7191, FAX 504-868-7472.
Tommy Bush, **Louisiana Shrimp Association,** 2401 Manson St., Suite C, Metairie LA 70002, 504-885-7110, FAX 504-885-6806.
C. A. "Buck" Vandersteen, **Louisiana Forestry Association,** PO Box 5067, Alexandria LA 71307-5067, 318-443-2558, FAX 318-443-1713.
Louisiana Landowners Association, PO Box 565, Franklin LA, 818-828-5480.
Michael J. Bourgeois, **Louisiana Landowners Association,** PO Box 44121, Baton Rouge LA 70804-4121, 504-927-5619, FAX 504-928-7339.
Jane Black, **Organization of Louisiana Fishermen,** Rt. 2, Box 328 - L, Cut Off LA 70345, 504-475-6770, FAX 504-396-2749.
P O P % Abbeville Mix Plant, 516 Meyers Street, Abbeville LA 70510.
Peter Vujnovich, Jr., **Plaquemines Oyster Association,** PO Box 253, Port Sulpher LA 70083, 504-564-2966.
Tee John Mialjevich, Political Action League of Shrimpers, 2621 Wyoming Drive, Marrero LA 70072, 504-347-8151.
Southeast Louisiana Commercial Fish Association, Rt. 1, Box 903, St. Bernard LA 70085.
Digges Morgan III, **Southern Forest Products Association,** Box 641700, Kenner LA 70064-1700, 504-443-4464, FAX 504-443-6612.
Dick Davis, **Sportsman Productions,** 1027 Windy Dr., Pineville LA 71360, 318-445-7395.
St. Bernard Oyster Leaseholders Association, 912 Florissant Rd., St. Bernard LA 70085.
Southwest Louisiana Fish Association, 712 Arthur Avenue, Lake Arthur LA 70549.
Southwest Pass Oyster Dealers & Growers Association, HC 71, Box 394, Franklin LA 70538.
Terrebonne Fish Association, 5347 Grand Caillou Rd., Dulac LA 70353.
Terrebonne Parish Oyster Leaseholders Association, Box 39-D, Theriot LA 70397.

Maine (10)
Michael S. Coffman, Ph.D., **Environmental Perspectives, Inc.**, 1229 Broadway, Suite 313, Bangor ME 04401-2503, 207-945-9878.
Maine Alliance, 100 Middle St., PO Box 189, Portland ME 04112, 207-774-1001.
Robert O. Voight, Maine Conservation Rights Institute, PO Box 220, Lubec ME 04652, 207-733-5593, FAX 207-733-5593.
Jon Olsen, **Maine Farm Bureau,** 478 Western Avenue, Augusta ME 043330, 207-622-4111.
Ted Johnston, **Maine Forest Products Council,** 146 State Street, Augusta ME 04330, 207-622-9288.
Mary Adams, **Maine Freedom Fighters,** Box 10, Garland ME 04939, 207-924-3835.
Maine Snowmobile Association, Inc., PO Box 77, Augusta ME 04332, 207-622-6983.
Abbott Ladd, **Small Woodland Owners Association,** PO Box 926, Augusta ME 04332, 207-626-0005.
Tom Nannery, **Sportsmans Alliance of Maine,** PO Box 2783, Augusta ME 04338.
Bo Thott, **Washington County Alliance,** NCR 69, Box 336, Cutler ME 04626, 207-259-3384.

Maryland (9)
Nancy Kefauver, **Alliance for America,** 18140 Mansfield Rd., Keedysville MD 21756, 310-432-5633.
Baltimore County Trail Riders Association, 2918 Manns Avenue, Baltimore MD 21234, 401-661-1838.
Margaret Ann Reigle, Fairness to Land Owners Committee (The FLOC), 1730 Garden of Eden Road, Cambridge MD 21613, 410-228-3822, FAX 410-228-8357.
Ann Corcoran, Land Rights Letter, PO Box 568, Sharpsburg MD 21782, 301-797-7455.
Maryland Landowners Association, 202 High St., Cambridge MD 21613, 301-228-3610.
Suzanne Lushbaugh, **Save Historic Antietam With Responsible Policies,** PO Box 512, Sharpsburg MD 21782.
Society of American Foresters, 5400 Grosvenor Lane, Bethesda MD 20814, 301-897-8720, FAX 301-897-3690.
Dr. Julian L. Simon, **University of Maryland at College Park,** College of Business and Management, Tydings Hall, College Park MD 20742, 301-951-0922.
Wanderers Dirt Machine Riders Club, 701 Wedeman Avenue, Linthicum Heights MD 21090, 410-636-1002.

Massachusetts (10)
Karen Campetti, **Alliance for America,** HC 66, Box 143, Sandisfield MA 01255, 413-258-4500, FAX 413-258-4275.
Peggie Daigle, **Alliance for America,** PO Box 582, Sandisfield MA 01255, 413-258-4007, FAX 413-258-4275.

Ludwik S. Tluszcz, **Friends of the River**, Rt. 8, Box 202, Sandisfield MA 01255, 413-258-4472.
Knox Trail Sno-Riders Club, PO Box 363, East Otis MA 01029.
Douglas P. Gillespie, **Masssachusetts Farm Bureau Federation, Inc.**, PO Box 651, 15 Great Road, Bedford MA 01730, 617-275-4374, FAX 617-275-7420.
Mill Valley Snowmobile Club, PO Box 1373, Belchertown MA 01007.
John Conner, **OURS**, 267 Middlefield Rd., Hinsdale MA 01235, 413-655-2141, FAX 413-499-0911.
Dean Zuppio, **Snowmobile Association of Massachusetts**, 28 Laurelwood Road, Rutland MA 01543, FAX 508-886-2162.
Doug Desroches, **Snowmobilers United, Inc.**, 6 Hazel Avenue, Shrewsbury MA 01545-1212.
Erich Veyhl, Washington County Alliance, 24 Orchard Road, Concord MA 01742, 508-369-9308.

Michigan (17)
American Motorcyclist Association, District #14, 9943 Park Avenue, Allen Park MI 48101.
Larry Lindenberg, **Bent Wheels Cycle Club**, 7624 Emerson, Washington MI 48094.
Jim Hoffman, **CCC - Capitol Chapter**, 14630 Dewitt Road, Lansing MI 48906, 517-321-0096.
Bob Fink, **Citizens Council,** 2579 Woodhill Dr., Okemos MI 48864, 517-332-2929.
Webb Cook, **Citizens Council of the Sleeping Bear Dunes Area,** Glen Arbor MI 49636.
Phil Kropf, **Independent Co-Op Milk Producers Association,** 263 Mart SW, Grand Rapids MI 49508, 616-247-6761.
Peter C. Grieves, **Michigan Association of Timbermen,** PO Box 486, Newberry MI 49868, 906-293-3236, FAX 906-293-5444.
McLain B. Smith, **Michigan Forest Association,** 1558 Barrington, Ann Arbor MI 48103, 313-665-8279.
Mike Thorne, **Michigan Landowners Association,** 10025 Nashville Hwy., Vermontville MI 49096, 517-726-1253.
Michigan Recreation Vehicle Riders Association, PO Box 530, St. Helen MI 48656, 313-686-4320.
Michigan Snowmobile Association, 5181 Plainfield, NE, Grand Rapids MI 49505, 616-361-2285.
Muskegon Motorcycle Club, 2222 Getty Street South, Muskegon MI 49444-1208.
Tom and Kathy Stocklen, Riverside Canoe Trips, 5042 Scenic Highway, Honor MI 49640, 616-325-5622, FAX 616-882-4072.
Lynnwood Stephens, **Total Resources Evaluation,** 22 North Hazel Avenue, Gaylord MI 49735.
Jim Firkis, **T.R.A.L.E. Up**, PO Box 79, Bergland MI 49910, 906-575-3547.
West Shore Snowmobile Council, 2440 Wisconsin Avenue, Muskegon MI 49445.

Minnesota (19)
"Fossil" Bill Kramer, **The Angry Environmentalist**, PO Box 146,
   Silver Bay MN 55614, 218-226-4303.
Eric Mayranen, **Associated Contract Loggers Inc.**, 9066 Peppard
   Road, Britt MN 55710, 218-749-3161, FAX 218-749-1433.
Jerry Barbur, **A T V A M**, 14443 Raven Street NW, Andover MN 55304,
   612-754-6162.
Irvin Anderson, **Citizens' Council on Voyageurs National Park**,
   509 Third Street, International Falls MN 56649-2317, 218-283-3507.
Edward C. Krug, Ph.D., **Committee for a Constructive Tomorrow**,
   513 Kerry Fr., #101, Winona MN 55987.
Mary Tome, **Conservatioinists With Common Sense**, HC1, Box 2673,
   Ely MN 55731, 218-365-3727.
Jerry Schaack, **Dakota County Trail Association**, 8677 295 St E, Can-
   non Falls MN 55009.
Lyle Vogt, **Eagan Valley Rangers/Dakota County Trails**, 1816 Cin-
   nabar Ct., Eagan MN 55122, 612-454-4744.
Ely Igloo Snowmobile Club, PO Box 464, Ely MN 55731.
Lakeville Sno-Trackers, PO Box 10, Lakeville MN 55044.
Cathy Roth, **Midwest Four Wheel Drive Association**, 2410 N.W. 15
   1/2 Street, Faribault MN 55021.
Marion Jones, **Minnesota 4 Wheel Drive Association**, 6688-84th
   Court No., Brooklyn Park MN 55448.
Minnesota United Snowmobilers Association, 4215 Winnetka Ave.
   N. #222, Minneapolis MN 55428.
Don Parmeter, **Northern Resources Alliance of Minnesota,** HC 8,
   Box 456, International Falls MN 56649-9627, 218-286-3579, FAX 218-
   286-5045.
David Buresh, **Prior Lake Snowmobile Association**, 20600 Langford
   Way, Jordan MN 55352.
Range Trail Committee, PO Box 149, Virginia MN 55792.
John F. Wilkinson, **River Warren Research Committee**, P.O. Box
   37, Rockford MN 55373, 612-477-6156.
Barbara J. Pisansky, **RiverWatch**, 24920 Avenue SW., New Brighton MN
   55112, 612-636-1895.
Carol Hahn, **Women In Timber Minnesota,** Hahn Machinery, 124
   2nd Avenue, Two Harbors MN 55616, 218-834-2156, FAX 218-834-
   5640.

Mississippi (8)
Robert Hutson, **Association of Mississippi Agriculture Organiza-
tions**, PO Box 1972, Jackson MS 39215-1972, 601-957-3200.
Ralph Young, **Committee on Wetlands Awareness**, 1418 20th Av-
   enue, Gulfport MS 39501.
Mississippi Farm Bureau, PO Box 1972, Jackson MS 39215, 601-957-
   3200.
Steve A. Corbitt, **Mississippi Forestry Association**, 620 N. State Street,
   #201, Jackson MS 39202-3398, 601-354-4936.
Mississippi Gulf Coast Wetlands Coalition, 600 Convent St.,
   Pascagoula MS 39567, 601-769-3056.

Richard Reeves, **Mississippi Loggers Association,** PO Drawer 620, Quitman MS 39355, 601-776-5754.

H. C. & Jean Williams, **Save America's Seafood,** 1312 Communy Ave., Pasoaquola MS 39567, 601-762-1184, FAX 601-872-4869.

Sonny Weir, **TRVWMD,** PO Box 616, Tupelo MS 38802.

Missouri (9)

Cameron Young Farmers, Cameron High School, 1022 S. Chestnut, Cameron MO 64429, 816-632-7713.

Ray Cunio, **Citizens for Private Property Rights,** Route 1, Box 429, Sullivan MO 63080, 314-627-3328, FAX 314-627-2043.

Jim Moon, **Friends of Chadwick**, 2804 W. Chestnut, Springfield MO 65802, 417-883-3632.

John McBride, **Livestock Marketing Association,** 7509 Tiffany Parkway, Kansas City MO 64153.

Steve Thomas, **Midwest Trail Riders Association**, PO Box 1203, Maryland Heights MO 63043, 314-576-4013.

John Key, **Mining Industry Council of Missouri**, 225 E. Capitol, Jefferson City MO 65102, 314-635-7308, FAX 314-635-6030.

Bernard M. Kertz, **Missouri Landowners Association,** Rt 1, Box 130, Huntsville MO 65259, 816-277-3125.

Norm Schroeder, **Missouri Motorcycle Dealers Association**, 223 E. Capitol, PO Box 592, Jefferson City MO 65102.

Brian S. Unnerstall, East Perry Lumber Company, PO Box 105, Frohna MO 63748, 314-824-5272, FAX 314-824-5275.

Montana (29)

Merle Lloyd, **Alliance for America,** 1035 Hamilton Heights, Corvallis MT 59828, 406-961-3300, FAX 406-961-4770.

Mark M. Chamberlain, **Billings Motorcycle Club, Inc.**, PO Box 20421, Billings MT 59104-0421, 406-259-4433, FAX 406-259-4066.

Wimp & Effie Kimp, **Bitterroot Ridge Runners Snowmobile Club**, PO Box 265, Hamilton MT 59840, 406-363-4689.

Terry Frost, **Bitterroot Stockgrowers Association,** 360 Frost Lane, Corvalis MT 59828.

Capital Trail Vehicle Association, PO Box 4088, Helena MT 59604.

William H. and Gene Covey, **Citizens Equal Rights Alliance**, PO Box 215, Big Arm MT 59910, 406-849-5068.

Bruce Vincent, Communities for a Great Northwest, PO Box 1320, Libby MT 59923, 406-293-8821, FAX 406-293-4739.

Sam Harvey, **Gallatin Valley Snowmobile Association,** 602 South 13th, Bozeman MT 59771, 406-586-6546.

Mike Nickols, **Grassroots for Multiple Use,** PO Box 383, Darby MT 59829, 406-961-3300, FAX 406-961-4770.

Great Falls Snowmobilers Inc., Box 6032, Great Falls MT 59406.

Jim Rathbun, **Kootenai Timber & Land Coalition,** PO Box 1250, Libby MT 59923, 406-293-3995, FAX 406-293-5158.

Don Harden, **Montana 4X4 Association**, 2403 41st St. W., Billings MT 59106, 656-5509.

Kim Enkerud, **Montana Association of State Grazing Districts,** 420 No. California Street, Helena MT 59601, 406-442-3420, FAX 406-449-5105.

Jim Mockler, **Montana Coal Council,** 2301 Colonial Drive, Helena MT 59601, 406-442-6223, FAX 406-449-6628.

Jake Cummins, **Montana Farm Bureau Federation,** 502 S. 19th St., Bozeman MT 59715, 406-587-3153, FAX 406-587-0319.

Gary Langley, **Montana Mining Association,** 2301 Colonial Drive, Helena MT 59601, 406-443-7297, FAX 406-443-7299.

Susan Brooks, **Montana Stock Growers Association,** PO Box 1679, Helena MT 59624, 406-442-3420, FAX 406-442-3420.

Bob Reynolds, **Montana Snowmobile Adventurers,** PO Box 5, Neihart MT 59465.

Montana Trail Riders Association, 3301 W. Babcock, Bozeman MT 59715, 406-587-4505.

Montana Trail Vehicle Riders Association, PO Box 2884, Great Falls MT 59401.

Peggy Wagner, Montanans for Multiple Use, PO Box 190068, Hungry Horse MT 59919, 406-387-5535, FAX 406-387-4262.

Sam Harvey, **Oversnow Access, Inc.,** PO Box 1355, Big Timber MT 59011-1355, 406-586-6546.

Terry Anderson, **Political Economy Research Center,** 502 S. 19th Avenue, Suite 211, Bozeman MT 59715, 406-587-9591, FAX 406-994-5647.

Kathleen Marquardt, Putting People First, 44 North Last Chance Gulch, PO Box 1707, Helena MT 59624-1707, 406-442-5700.

George Vogt, Jr., **Ravalli County Legislative Coalition,** 803 South 4th Street, Hamilton MT 59840.

John Shuler, PO Box 144, Dupuyer MT 59432, 406-472-3222.

Jack L. Demmons, **Timber Heritage Foundation,** PO Box 565, Seeley Lake MT 59868, 406-677-2775.

Michelle LeFurge, **Western Environmental Trade Association Coalition,** 305 W. Mercury St., #303, Butte MT 59701, 406-723-6211.

Lana Sheen, **Women In Timber - Montana,** PO Box 1151, Livingston MT 59047, 406-222-6039, FAX 406-222-0540.

Nebraska (7)

Betty Palmer, **Alliance for America,** HC80 Box 22, Springview NE 68778, 402-497-2656, FAX 402-497-2655.

Eva A. McGill, **Missouri-Niobrara River Association,** RR1, Box 83, Lynch NE 68746, 402-569-2552 or 402-857-3515.

Roger Barnesberger, **Nebraska State Snowmobile Association,** 939 N. 3rd, Box 8, Hampton NE 68843, 402-783-3272.

Irene Graves, **Niobrara Land Owners Conservancy,** RR 2, Box 256, Ainsworth NE 69210, 402-387-2719.

Wesley Rothleutner, **Public Lands Council,** Drawer 88, Kilgore NE 69216.

Earl Martens, **Syracuse Snoflakers,** RR 1, Box 70, Syracuse NE 68446.

TBQ Trikes/Bikes/Quads- Sport Club, Inc., PO Box 663, Grand Island NE 68802.

Nevada (20)

Karen Zimmerman, **Alliance for America,** PO Box 1388, Fallon NV 89406, 702-423-4269, FAX 702-423-1511.

Bill Dart, **American Motorcyclist Association - District 36,** 333 S. Carson Meadow, Suite 41, Carson City NV 89701, 702-885-0650.

Don Smith, **Citizens for Mining,** 2057 Thomas Jefferson, Battle Mountain NV 89820, 702-635-5696, FAX 702-635-2181.

Pinkey Herzog, **Elko Mine Support Group,** 920 Mountain City Highway, Elko NV 89801, 702-738-4061.

Brad Roberts, **Elko Sno-Goers,** PO Box 5185, Elko NV 89801, 702-738-7325.

Wayne Hage, Free Enterprise Legal Defense Fund, P.O. Box 513, 592 Desert Queen Street, Tonopah NV 89049, 702-482-3372, FAX 702-482-5753.

Ed Presley, **Home Rule Coalition,** 1350 E. Flamingo Road, #519, Las Vegas NV 89119, 702-796-8736.

Gene Gustin, **Mining Support Group,** PO Box 894, Elko NV 89803, 702-738-5081, FAX 702-738-1137.

Dorothy Kosich, **Mining World News,** 90 W. Grove St., Suite 200, Reno NV 89509, 702-827-1115, FAX 702-827-1292.

Doug Busselman, **Nevada Farm Bureau,** 1300 Marietta Way, Sparks NV 89431, 702-358-3276.

Dave Parkhurst, **Nevada Miners and Prospectors Association,** PO Box 4179, Carson City NV 89702, 702-829-2148.

Michael J. Doyle, **Nevada Mining Association,** 5250 S. Virginia St., #220, Reno NV 89502-6046, 702-829-2121, FAX 702-829-2148.

Mark Trinko, **Nevada Off-Highway Users Council,** 724 Straight St., Las Vegas NV 89110-3936, 702-453-4958.

Rick Lassen, **Nevada Public Lands Alliance,** 17290 Sunbird, Reno NV 89506, 702-334-2772, FAX 702-334-2770.

Russell A. Fields, **Nevada State Department of Minerals,** 400 W. King St., #106, Carson City NV 89710, 702-687-5050, FAX 702-687-3957.

South Nevada Off Road Enthusiasts, PO Box 4394, Las Vegas NV 89106.

Cliff Gardner, **Stewards of the Range,** HCR 60, Box 700, Ruby Valley NV 89833, 702-779-2234.

John W. Hengen, **Western Mining Council Nevada,** 11715 Chesapeake Dr., Reno NV 89506-9427, 702-972-3883, FAX 702-972-6773.

Grant Gerber, **Wilderness Impact Resource Foundation,** 555 6th Street, Elko NV 89801, 702-738-2009.

Kathleen Benedetto, **Women's Mining Coalition,** 1375 Greg St., Suite 106, Sparks NV 89431, 702-356-0616, FAX 702-356-5982.

New Hampshire (9)

George Lagassa, **Granite State Hydropower Association,** c/o Mainstream Associates, PO Box 947, North Hampton NH 03862, 603-964-7113, FAX 603-964-4077.

Hudson Sno-Men, 45 Chase Street, Londonderry NH 03053.

Denis Laliberté, **Merrimack Valley Trail Riders**, RFD 1, Box 112, Hillsboro NH 03244, 603-529-7629.

Y. Leon Favreau, Multiple Use Association, 332 North Road, Gorham NH 03581, 207-836-2624, FAX 207-836-2200.

Cheryl Johnson, New Hampshire Landowners Alliance, PO Box 221, Campton NH 03223-0101, 603-726-4025, FAX 603-726-4308.

Harold Case, **New Hampshire Snowmobile Association**, PO Box 38, Concord NH 03302-0038, 603-224-8906.

Charles Neibling, **New Hampshire Timberland Owners Association**, 54 Portsmouth St. Concord NH 03301, 603-224-9699, FAX 603-228-0423.

Pat Keller, **Northeast Chapter - International Snowmobile Council**, PO Box 419, Hampton Falls NH 03844, 603-926-1204.

Southern New Hampshire TrailBlazers, PO Box 263, Kingston NH 03848.

New Jersey (3)

Inez Caon, **Alliance for America,** 200 Industrial Parkway, Branchburg NJ 08876, 908-725-4900, FAX 908-725-9086.

Marvin Hatlack, **Pineland Landowners Defense Fund,** PO Box 482, Chatsworth NJ 08019.

Kenny Coughlin, **South Jersey Enduro Riders**, 13 Beebe Road, Southamton NJ 08088.

New Mexico (17)

Louis Oliver, **Alliance for America,** Rt. 15, Box 1025, San Lorenzo NM 88041, 505-536-9511.

Tom Vining, **Carlsbad Sportsman Club,** PO Box 1603, Carlsbad NM 88220.

James and Charlotte Mitchell, **Citizens Equal Rights**, Canyon Route, Box 18A, Jemez Pueblo NM 87024, 505-829-3799.

Ronnie Merritt, **Corona People for the West,** HC66 Box 30, Yeso NM 88136, 505-849-1128, FAX 505-849-1128.

Jackalopes Motorcycle Club, Rt 1, Box 40-B, Taos Canyon, Taos NM 87571.

Las Cruces 4 Wheel Drive Club, 5171 Creek Trail, Las Cruces NM 88001, 505-382-3051.

Lillian K Harris, **Mimbres Farm & Livestock Bureau,** Box 12, Mimbres NM 88049-0012, 505-536-9379.

Al Schneberger, **New Mexico Cattle Growers Association**, 2231 Rio Grande Blvd., NW, Albuquerque NM 87104, or PO Box 7517, Albuquerque NM 87194, 505-247-0584, FAX 505-842-1766.

B. J. Porter, **New Mexico Farm & Livestock Bureau**, 421 North Water, Las Cruces NM 88001, 505-526-5521, FAX 505-525-0858.

Charles E. Roybal, **New Mexico Mining Association**, 4952 T. B. Catron NW, Albuquerque NM 87114, 505-897-0572, FAX 505-842-0734.

New Mexico Motorcycle Dealers, 1476 St. Francis Dr., Santa Fe NM 87501, 505-988-9615.

Bud Eppers, **New Mexico Public Lands Council**, Dunlap Route, Box 1139, Roswell NM 88201, 505-623-6103, FAX 505-625-9608.

Beverly Merritt, **New Mexico Wool Growers Action Committee,** PO Box 220, Roswell NM 88201.

Lewis Derrick, **People for the West - New Mexico,** 1207 Pecan Avenue, Artesia NM 88210, 505-746-4734, FAX 505-365-7671.

Prairie Dawg Motorcycle Club, PO Box 1192, Alamorgordo NM 88310.

Dora G. Davis, **Public Land Users Association,** PO Box 1990, Cuba NM 87013.

Michael Martin Murphey, Wildfire Productions, Box FFF, Taos NM 87571, 505-758-1871.

New York (28)

Donald Curtis, **Adirondack Blueline Confederation,** 399 CoHwy 112, Gloversville NY 12078, 518-725-1090, FAX 518-725-8239.

Donald Sage, **Adirondack Conservation Council,** Letsonville Rd., Paradox NY 12585, 518-585-7250.

Carol LaGrasse, **Adirondack Cultural Foundation,** 136 Main Street, PO Box 705, Warrensburg NY 12885, 518-494-7800, FAX 518-494-7141.

Susan Allen, **Adirondack Fairness Coalition,** PO Box 460, Chestertown NY 12817, 518-576-9861, FAX 518-494-7768.

Joe Rota, **Adirondack Park Local Government Review Board,** HCR 1, Box 137, Loon Lake NY 12968, 518-499-1436.

Judith A. Ford, **Adirondack Solidarity Alliance,** Box 820, RR1, Clintonville NY 12924, 518-834-9812.

David Howard, Alliance for America, PO Box 1111, Gloversville NY 12078, 518-725-1090, FAX 518-725-8239.

Harry MacIntosh, **Alliance for America,** PO Box 450, Jct. Rt. 10 & 29A, Caroga Lake NY 12032, 518-835-6702, FAX 518-835-2527.

Dr. Elizabeth M. Whelan, American Council on Science and Health, 1995 Broadway, 2nd Floor, New York NY 10023-5860, 212-362-7044; FAX 212-362-4919.

Robert Hall, **Central Adirondack Association,** c/o Tourist Information Center, Old Forge NY 13420, 315-369-6983.

Claude LeCours, **Central Adirondack Defense Committee,** Box 883, Old Forge NY 13420, 315-369-6181.

Greg & Cheryl Nelson, **Central New York Quad Riders,** PO Box 160, Freeville NY 13068, 607-898-3214.

Jeris and Dale French, Citizen Aid Fund, Rt. 1, Box 202B, Crown Point NY 12928, 518-597-4131, FAX 518-597-3061.

Clayton Brooks, **Coalition of Watershed Towns,** Sundown Rd., Sundown NY 12782, 914-985-7282, FAX 518-589-9959.

Lee Welch, **Foothills Confederation,** Box 557, Wells NY 12190, 518-924-5152, FAX 518-924-2301.

George Fuge, **Hamilton County Federation of Sportsmen's Clubs Inc.,** Raquette Lake NY 13436, 315-354-4691.

Hudson Highlands ATV Club, 70 Mountain Avenue, Beacon NY 12508, 914-831-0701.

Earl Yousey, **Lewis County Sportsmen,** Box 255, Route 1, Croghan NY 13327, 315-346-1207.

Pieter V. C. Litchfield, **New York Blue Line Council,** 46 Fieldstone Drive, Gansevoort NY 12831, 518-587-2599.

Rick Zimmerman, **New York Farm Bureau**, Route 9W, PO Box 992, Glenmont NY 12077-0992, 518-436-8495, FAX 518-436-5471.

Mary Brusoe, **New York Snowmobile Coordinating Group**, 31 Hughes Street, Whitesboro NY 13492, 315-736-7905.

Harry Probst, **New York State Conservation Council Inc.,** 8 East Street, Ilion NY 13357, 315-894-3302.

Linda Lucksinger, **New York State Timber Producers Association,** PO Box 300, Boonville NY 13309, 315-942-5503.

Jon Greenwood, **North Country Citizens For Responsible Land Use**, RD 3, Box 174A, Canton NY 13617, 315-386-3231.

George Mitchell, **Northeastern Logger's Association Inc.,** PO Box 69, Old Forge NY 13420, 315-369-3078.

Oswego County Vegetable Growers Association, RD 1, Box 513A, Phoenix NY 13135, 315-598-7888.

Donald H. Gerdts, **Property Rights Council of America**, PO Box 705, Warrensburg NY 12885, 518-696-2066, 518-696-5145.

John Courtney, **Tupper Lake Woodsmen's Association,** Box JJ, Tupper Lake NY 12986, 518-359-9444.

North Carolina (8)
Darleene Carawan, **Alliance for America,** Rt 1, Box 314, Aurora NC 27806, 919-322-4572.

James L. Gundy, **Appalachian Hardwood Manufacturers Inc.,** Box 427, High Point NC 27261, 919-885-8315.

Charles Woodard, **Multiple Use Council,** Route 3, Box 167, Sylva NC 28779, 704-586-6353, FAX 704-586-3197.

North Carolina Association of Water Districts, PO Box 1236, Brevard NC 28712.

Jerry Schill, **North Carolina Fisheries Association,** PO Box 2303, New Bern NC 28561, 919-633-2288, FAX 919-633-9616.

Robert Slocum, Jr., **North Carolina Forestry Association,** 1600 Glenwood Avenue, Suite I, Raleigh NC 27608-2355, 919-834-3943, FAX 919-832-6188.

Zachary Taylor, **North Carolina Landowners Association,** PO Box 1088, New Bern NC 28563, 919-633-5106.

Johnny Shields, **Smokey Mountain ORV Club**, 335 B East Main St, Sylva NC 28779, 704-586-5679.

North Dakota (7)
Dennis Gravseth, **Lake Metigoshe Family Snowmobile Club**, PO Box 122, Bottineau ND 58318, 701-228-2890.

Ben & Char Varnson, **Landowners Association of North Dakota,** RR 1, Box 77, Lansford ND 58750, 701-259-2127.

Little Missouri Snowmobile & ATV Riders, PO Box 841, Dickinson ND 58601, 701-227-8729.

Patrick Miller, **Magic City DriftBusters**, Box 1094, Minot ND 58701, 701-852-2653.

Rough Riders Snowmobile Association, 900 N 33rd Street, Bismarck ND 58501.

Snowmobile North Dakota, 1800 Valle Moore Drive, Bismarck ND 58501.

Surrey TrailBlazers, Box 248, Surrey ND 58785.

Ohio (13)

Grace Simic, **Alliance for America,** 9401 Hillside Rd., Independence OH 44131, 216-524-3142.

Eric Lundquist, **American Motorcyclist Association, Inc.,** PO Box 6114, Westerville OH 43081-6114, 614-891-2425, FAX 614-891-5012.

Marty Griffith, **Cuyahoga Valley Homeowners Association,** 3634 Oak Hill, Penninsula OH 44264.

Ben Turley, **East Coast Four Wheel Drive Association,** 545 N. Basil Street, Baltimore OH 43105, 862-4937.

Bill Kaeppner, **Enduro Riders Association,** 898 Bruck Street, Columbus OH 43206, 314-444-9600.

Dane Lavin, **Family & Farm Association of Columbiana County,** Box 174, Columbiana OH 44408, 216-424-3354, FAX 216-792-8102.

Grand River Trail Riders Snowmobile, PO Box 22, Austinburg OH 44010.

Mary Savioli, **Hillside Road Residents,** 8315 Hillside Rd., Independence OH 44131.

Roy Palmer, **Hocking Technical College,** Nelsonville OH 45764, 614-753-3591.

Ron Cornell, **Ohio Forestry Association,** 1335 Dublin Road, Suite 203D, Columbus OH 43215, 614-486-6767, FAX 614-486-6769.

Donald E. Stineman, **Ohio State Snowmobile Association,** 2466 Spore-Brandywine Rd, Bucyrus OH 44820, 419-562-2862.

Ohio Valley Competition Club, 7603 Live Oak Drive, Westchester OH 45069, 513-922-7635.

Marilyn Parkes, LaCroft Elementary School, 2460 Boring Lane, East Liverpool OH 43920, 216-386-8770, FAX 216-386-2160.

Oklahoma (5)

American Land Users, Rt 3 Box 601, Broken Bow OK 74728, 405-420-6474.

Merrill Harkey, **American Land Users Association,** PO Box 1004, Idabel OK 74745, 405-286-7387.

Oklahoma Association of Conservation Districts, Box 208, Kinter OK 74552, 918-768-3542.

Oklahoma Farm Bureau, 2501 N. Stiles, Oklahoma City OK 73105, 405-523-2300.

John T. Alf, **Rocky Mountain Federation of Mineralogical Societies,** 816 Whippoorwill Ct., Bartlesville OK 74006, 918-467-0662.

Ontario (Canada)

Ross Irvine, **Enviro-Scan** (Public Relations Management Ltd.), 16 Westhill Road, Guelph, Ontario N1H 7P6, 519-767-0444, FAX same.

Thom Loree, **The Northern Miner Magazine**, 7 Labatt Avenue, Toronto, Ontario M5A 3P2, 416-378-1265.

Oregon (84)

Steve Martin, **Aerial Forest Management Foundation**, PO Box 95, Canby OR 97013, 503-678-2665.

Agnes Barnes, **Alliance for America,** 1995 Keasey Rd., Roseburg OR 97470, 503-673-1208, FAX 503-673-5506.

Tom Hirons, **Alliance for America,** 51755 Gates Bridge East, Mill City OR 97360, 503-897-3343, FAX 503-897-2467.

Jean Plaisance, **Alsea Valley Alliance,** 750 Hillcrest Drive NW, Salem OR 97304, 503-362-3619.

Loydee Grainger, **American Agri-Women,** 11525 Bursell Rd., Dallas OR 97338, 503-838-3250, FAX 503-838-2301.

Shepard Tucker, **American Forest & Paper Association**, Western Office, 1515 S.W. Fifth Ave., Suite 518, Portland OR 97201, 503-222-7456, FAX 503-248-0160.

Bill Crapser, **American Pulpwood Association,** 2300 Oakmont Way, Suite 206, Eugene OR 97401, 503-683-3950.

Mike Miller, **Associated Oregon Loggers,** PO Box 12339, Salem OR 97309-0339, 503-364-1330.

Bruce Malcoa, **Blue Mountain Forest Products,** PO Box 1559, Pendelton OR 97801.

Central Oregon MC & ATV Club, 23031 Donna Lane, Bend OR 97701, 503-388-3368.

Holly Swanson, **Citizens Information Network,** 1042 Dead Indian Rd., PO Box 1091, Ashland OR 97520, 503-488-2320, FAX 503-488-2321.

Michael Wiedeman, **Citizens Natural Resource Group,** RT 1, Box 179, Enterprise OR 97828.

Columbia Gorge Power Sledders, PO Box 943, The Dalles OR 97058.

Jim Gourley, **Communities First,** C/O Pope & Talbot, Halsey OR 97348.

Sherry Ulin, **Communities for a Great Oregon,** PO Box 997, Mill City OR 97360, 503-897-2864, FAX 503-897-2467.

Don Smith, **Communities for a Great Oregon - Prineville,** 204155 Wain Wright Rd., Prineville OR 97754.

Gert Helvey, **Communities for A Great Oregon - Sweet Home,** 28030 Meridian Heights, Sweet Home OR 97386.

Dallas Ferry, **Counterpoint Foundation**, PO Box 23894, Tigard OR 97223, 503-639-7320.

Troy Reinhart, **Douglas Timber Operators Inc.,** Suite 208, 3000 Stewart Parkway, Roseburg OR 97470, 503-672-0757, FAX 503-672-3833.

Chuck Chase, **Eastern Oregon Mining Association,** 740 Valley Avenue, Baker OR 97814, 503-523-3285, FAX 503-523-7870.

Rita Kaley, **Gorge Resource Coalition**, PO Box 185, Odell OR 97044, 503-354-1297.

Grant County Snowballers, Inc., PO Box 337, John Day OR 97845.

Alme Allen, **Illinois Valley Resource Coalition,** PO Box 1691, Cave

Junction OR 97523.

Klamath Basin SnowDrifters, PO Box 1125, Klamath Falls OR 97601.

Lapine Lodgepole Dodgers, PO Box 70, LaPine OR 97739.

Lobo's Motorcycle Club, 14000 S. Forsythe Road, Oregon City OR 97045, 503-656-5801.

Dixie M. Reisch, **Molalla Timber Action Committee**, PO Box 193, Molalla OR 97038, 503-829-8812, FAX 503-829-7365.

Moon Country Sno-Mobilers, PO Box 5596, Bend OR 97708-5596, 503-389-8072.

Jerry Watkins, **Motorcycle Riders Association**, PO Box 1471, Medford OR 97501-0109.

Mount Baker Motorcycle Club, PO Box 132, Bellingham WA 98227-0132, 206-734-8295.

Mt. Hood Snowmobile Club, PO Box 191, Boring OR 97009.

Mt. Scott Motorcycle Club, 17641 So. Holly Lane, Oregon City OR 97045, 503-655-0419.

Patti Strand, **National Animal Interest Alliance**, PO Box 66579, Portland OR 97290, 503-761-8962.

Tony Grebene, **Nehalem Valley Timber Coalition**, 1161 Rivers St., Vernonia OR 97064.

Northwest Sand Deuces, 7620 SW Cedarcrest, Portland OR 97223.

Allan Beck, **Northwest Steelheaders Association**, 3413 Crawford St. SE, Salem OR 97302.

Geri McCloud, **OFPTA - Linn-Benton**, 42122 Clark Smith Dr., Lebanon OR 97355.

Phil Coblentz, **OFPTA - Statewide**, 27725 Jahn Road, Willamina OR 97396.

Amy Johnson, **Oregon Cattle Women**, RT 1, Box 43, Wallowa OR 97885.

Mike Doverspike, **Oregon Cattlemen's Association**, SR 1, Box 134A, Burns OR 97720.

Jim Krahn, **Oregon Dairy Farmers Association**, 10505 SW Barbur Blvd., Portland OR 97219, 503-229-5033, FAX 503-245-7916.

Doug Breese, **Oregon Farm Bureau**, 1701 Liberty St. SE, Salem OR 97302-5158, 503-399-1701.

Rod Harder, **Oregon Fur Takers**, 93601 Pope Rd., Blachly OR 97412.

Valerie Johnson, Oregon Lands Coalition, 247 Commercial Street, N.E., Salem OR 97301, 503-635-2201 or 503-363-8582, FAX 503-363-6067.

Jackie Lang, **Oregon Lands Coalition**, 280 Court St. NE, Suite 5, Salem OR 97301, 503-363-8582, FAX 503-363-6067.

Oregon Off-Highway Vehicle Association, 34074 E. Peebles Road, Eugene OR 97405, 503-759-3507.

Jake Jacobsen, **Oregon Off-Highway Vehicle Association**, PO Box 190, Lakeside OR 97449.

Robert Gardner, **Oregon Project - Curry County**, PO Box 239, Brookings OR 97415, 503-469-4996, FAX 503-469-0581.

Audrey Barnes, **Oregon Project - Douglas County**, 1995 Keasey, Roseburg OR 97470.

Norm Clark, **Oregon Sheep Growers Association**, Box 162, Drewsey OR 97904.

Fred Vannatta, **Oregon State Home Builders Association,** 565 Union Street NE, Salem OR 97301-2477, 503-378-9066, FAX 503-362-5120.

Howard Geiger, **Oregon State Snowmobile Association,** PO Box 435, LaPine OR 97739.

Donna Fagg, **Oregon Trail Snowmobile Club,** PO Box 565, Pendleton OR 97801.

Loydee Grainger, **Oregon Women for Agriculture,** 11525 Bursell Rd., Dallas OR 97338.

Marilyn Parry, **Oregon Women for Timbe**r, PO Box 2963, LaGrande OR 97850.

Terry Witt and **Paulette Pyle**, **Oregonians for Food and Shelter,** 567 Union St. NE, Salem OR 97301, 503-370-8092, FAX 503-370-8565.

Frank Nims, **Oregonians In Action,** PO Box 230637, Tigard OR 97281, 503-620-0258, FAX 503-639-6891.

Al Wilson, **Pacific Logging Congress,** 2300 SW 6th Ave., Suite 200, Portland OR 97201, 503-224-8406.

Rolf D. Glerum, **Pacific Rim Trade Association**, 1211 S.W. Fifth Ave., Suite 2740, Portland OR 97204, 503-226-6855.

Robert R Legg, **Responsible Environmentalism Foundation,** 14780 SW Osprey Drive, Beaverton OR 97007.

George Wilber, **Save Our Industries & Land,** HCR 30, Box 11, Burns OR 97720, 503-573-6151, FAX 503-573-3056.

Ivel Vickers, **Save Our Sawmills,** 3072 Levi Circle, Medford OR 97504.

Dave Vail, **Sensibly Managing All Resources Together,** PO Box 162, Estacada OR 97023, 503-630-3352, FAX 503-630-5806.

Bill Rice, **Sisters Sno-Go-Fers**, 66885 Fryrair Road, Bend OR 97701.

Robert B. Slagle, **Southern Oregon Resource Alliance - Josephine County,** PO Box 1273, Grants Pass OR 97526.

Michael & Linda Meyer, **Southern Oregon Resource Alliance**, PO Box 1658, Klamath Falls OR 97601, 503-882-1077, FAX 503-882-3405.

Pat Anderes, **Southern Oregon Resources Alliance - Roseburg,** PO Box 2168, Roseburg OR 97470.

James Peterson, **Evergreen Foundation,** PO Box 2220, Roseburg OR 97470, 503-479-1300.

Penny Franklin, **Third Force for Forestry,** 1800 Gilbert Drive, Lebanon OR 97355.

Tom Goodall, **Timber & Wood Products Northeast Oregon Region,** 1917 Jackson St., LaGrande OR 97850, 503-962-2071.

Chris Boschler, **Timber Employees Association for Responsible Solutions,** 1795 Washington St., PO Box 1074, Oregon City OR 97045.

Julie A. Wright, **Timber Resources Equals Economic Stability (T.R.E.E.S.),** PO Box 56, Dillard OR 97432-0056, 503-679-6604, FAX 503-679-9683.

David Rose, **TREES - Coastal Chapter,** PO Box 216, Coquille OR 97423, 503-396-2131, FAX 503-396-4712.

Vicki Shaylor, **Voters for Oregon Timber Resources,** 9400 SW Barnes Rd., 400, Portland OR 97225.

Walker Rim Riders, Box 48, Crescent Lake OR 97425.

Shannon Lathrop, **Wallowa County Cattlewomen's Association,** 66097 Golf Course Road, Enterprise OR 97828, 503-426-3026.

Rod Childers, **Wallowa County Stockgrowers,** HCR 61, Box 20, Enterprise OR 97828.

A. W. McAuliffe, **Water for Life Inc.**, PO Box 456, Fort Klamath OR 97626.

West Oregon Timber Supporters, PO Box 151, Philomath OR 97370, 503-929-3975, FAX 503-929-3980.

Debbie Knudsen, **Western Oregon Timber Supporters,** 23547 Woods Creek, Philomath OR 97370.

Julie Stangell, **Willamette Forestry Council,** PO Box F, Springfield OR 97477, 503-747-6630, FAX 503-747-6669.

Elizabeth Nelson, **Women for Multiple Use of Resources,** 905 N. Bayshore Dr., Coos Bay OR 97420.

Susan Cox, **Workers of Oregon Development,** PO Box 521, Canyonville OR 97417-0521, 503-839-6451, FAX 503-863-7182.

Merrilee Peay, **Yellow Ribbon Coalition,** PO Box 240, Springfield OR 97477, 503-747-5874, FAX 503-747-0612.

Pennsylvania (24)
Allegheny Hardwood Utilization Group, PO Box 845, Bradford PA 16701.

Allegheny Valley Board of Realtors, PO Box 171, Oil City PA 16301.

Lorraine Bucklin, **Alliance for America,** PO Box 391, Waterford PA 16441, 814-796-3578, FAX 814-796-6757.

Carol Ann Gregg, **American Agricultural Women,** 147 Old Mill Road, Grove City PA 16127, 412-458-8181.

Henry Ingram, Attorney At Law, **Buchanan Ingersoll Professional Corporation**, 58th Floor, 600 Grant St., Pittsburgh PA 15219, 412-562-8800.

Jason Makansi, **Common Sense on Energy and Our Environment,** PO Box 215, Morrisville PA 19067, 215-736-1153.

William C. Baer, **Hardwood Lumber Manufacturers Association of Pennsylvania**, Suite A, One Commerce Square, 417 Walnut St., Harrisburg PA 17101, 717-236-9207, FAX 717-238-6341.

Susan M. Regan, **Hardwood Manufacturers Association,** 400 Penn Center Boulevard, # 530, Pittsburgh PA 15235, 412-829-0770.

Holiday Pocono Civic Association, Box 57, Albrightsville PA 18210.

David Yaeck, **ICWP,** 235 W. Market Street, West Chester PA 19382, 215-692-7878.

Arvilla Backlund, **Independent Landholders Association,** PO Box 57, Milanville PA 18443, 717-224-4666.

Kent A. Fox, **Invesco of Pennsylvania, Inc.**, PO Box 694, Mt. Gretna PA 17064, 717-964-3669.

Clifford Strauss, Jr., **Lehigh Valley ATV Association,** 1918 Wehr Avenue, Allentown PA 18104, 215-434-9070, FAX 215-867-8702.

National Landowners Association, Cradle of Freedom, 1427 Broad Street, Philadelphia PA 19147, 215-271-1931.

Mary Wirth, Pennsylvania Forest Industry Association, PO Box 506, Kane PA 16735, 814-837-8944.

Rhonda McAtee, **Pennsylvania Landowners' Association,** 1131 Route 97, PO Box 391, Waterford PA 16441, 814-796-3578, FAX 814-796-6757.

Sean Duffy, **Pennsylvania Leadership Council Inc.,** 223 State Street, Harrisburg PA 17101, 717-232-5919.

Ted Young, **Pennsylvania Snowseekers, Inc.,** RD 2, Box 301A, New Brighton PA 15066, 412-452-8807.

David Weaver, **Pennsylvania State Snowmobile Association,** PO Box 81, Annville PA 17003.

Pennsylvania Trail Riders Association, PO Box 77, Thomasville PA 17364.

Judy L. Obert, **Pike County Sno Runners,** PO Box 600, Greentown PA 18426.

N. Charles Bolgiano, Ph.D., **Unified Sportsmen of Pennsylvania,** 824 Dorsea Road, Lancaster PA 17601, 717-898-8834.

Dave Hook, **United Four Wheel Drive Associations - Pennsylvania,** RD 2, Box 190, Felton PA 17322.

Marck F. Golitz, **Walter H. Weaber Sons, Inc.,** R.D. #4, Box 1255, Lebanon PA 17042, 717-867-2212.

Rhode Island (1)
Jim O'Malley, **East Coast Fisheries Federation,** PO Box 649, Narragansett RI 02882, 401-782-3440, FAX 401-782-3440.

South Carolina (7)
Jim Kuykendall, **Alliance for America,** PO Box 100540, Florence SC 29501, 803-667-6252.

Family Riders Motorcycle Club, 105 Castleway Lane, Goose Creek SC 29445, 553-3473.

David Lucas, 7 Fairway Oaks Lane, Isle of Palms SC 29451, 803-886-4654, FAX 803-884-6257. See also listing under Virginia.

Kelly Smith, **Mining Association of South Carolina,** PO Box 1368, Irmo SC 29063, 803-772-5354.

Robert R. Scott, **South Carolina Forestry Association,** Box 21303, Columbia SC 29221, 803-798-4170.

Maggi Hall, **Wildlife Action Inc.,** PO Box 543, Mullins SC 29574, 803-464-8473.

South Dakota (5)
Interlakes SnowRoamers, Rt 2, Box 177, Madison SD 57042.

Thomas Troxel, **Intermountain Forest Industry Association,** 2040 W. Main St., Suite 315, Rapid City SD 57702, 605-341-0875, FAX 605-341-8651.

Off-Road Riders, 301 Cambell, Rapid City SD 57701, 605-342-2242.

Dianna Miller, **South Dakota Mining Association,** 3801 S. Kiwanis, Suite #5, Sioux Falls SD 57105, 605-332-3803, FAX 605-344-1938.

Allen Dykema, **South Dakota Snowmobile Association,** 2733 W. Melgaard Road, Aberdeen SD 57401, 605-229-1037, FAX 605-642-7103.

Tennessee (8)

Thomas Bennett, **Alliance for America,** 201 Amy Dr., Maryville TN 37801, 615-577-7577, FAX 615-573-9319.

Ray Bryant, **Delta Commission,** 7777 Walnut Grove Rd., Memphis TN 38119.

Henry Lamb, **Environmental Conservation Organization,** PO Box 191, Hollow Rock TN 38342, 901-986-0099.

Memphis Motorcycle Club, PO Box 18395, Memphis TN 38181-0395.

M.T.R.A., 1425 Luverne Street, Memphis TN 38108.

Elizabeth Pease, **National Hardwood Lumber Association,** PO Box 34518, Memphis TN 38184-0518, 1-800-933-0318, FAX 901-382-6419.

Stan Butt, **Tennessee Cattleman's Association,** PO Box 906, Columba TN 38401.

Candice Dinwiddie, **Tennessee Forestry Association,** Box 290693, Nashville TN 37229, 615-883-3832, FAX 615-883-3832.

Texas (20)

Deyaun Boudreaux, **Alliance for America,** PO Box AF, Port Isabel TX 78578, 512-943-2788, FAX 512-943-2788.

Kay Love, **Alliance for America,** PO Box 1209, Alpine TX 79831, 915-364-2230, FAX 915-837-7425.

Melvin Tower, **Alliance for America,** PO Box 625, Port Isabel TX 78578, 512-943-2643, FAX 512-943-6135.

Dr. Margaret Maxey, **Chair of Free Enterprise, University of Texas,** Austin TX 78712, 512-471-7501, FAX 512-471-9605.

Ben Love, Davis Mountains Trans-Pecos Heritage Association, PO Box 1209, Alpine TX 79842, 915-837-3461, FAX 915-837-7425.

Kathryn Heideman, **Hill Country Landowners Coalition,** 1002 Ash Street, Georgetown TX 78626, 512-863-2935, FAX 512-863-2935.

Barry Klein, **Houston Property Rights Association,** 5075 Westheimer, Suite 777, Houston TX 77056-5606, 713-224-4144, FAX 713-227-4131.

Ben Wallis, **Human Rights Institute,** 7550 Interstate Highway 10 West, Suite 245, San antonio TX 78229, 210-525-1500, FAX 210-525-9323.

Floy Lilley, Attorney At Law, 3816 South Lamar, Suite 1122, Austin TX 78704, 512-415-8293.

Ken Bull, **McCulloch County Property Owners Association,** Route 1, Box 57A, Rochelle TX 76872, 915-597-1226.

Arthur R. Nagel, **Riverside & Landowners Protection Coalition Inc.,** Rt. 2, Box 2505, Boerne TX 78006, 512-537-4830, FAX 512-249-9037.

Patrick Henry, **Seafood Producers of Upper Texas,** PO Box 325, Port Bolivar TX 77650, 409-684-1241, FAX 409-684-8992.

South East Texas Off Road Riders, 2224 Ashley, Beaumont TX 77701, Darrell 409-842-2000, 409-833-1903.

Texarkana Dirt Riders, 5710 Pleasant Grove Road, Texarkana TX 75501, 903-832-5323.

Don King, **Texas & Southwestern Cattle Raisers Association,** 1301 W. 7th Street, Fort Worth TX 76102, 817-332-7064, FAX 817-332-5446.

Ronald H. Hufford, **Texas Forestry Association,** Box 1488, Lufkin TX 75902-1488, 409-632-8733.
Glen Duncan, **Texas Mining and Reclamation Association**, 314 Highland Mall Blvd., Suite 251, Austin TX 78752, 512-467-1300, FAX 512-451-9556.
Wilma Anderson, **Texas Shrimp Association,** PO Box 1077, Aransas Pass TX 78336, 512-758-5024, FAX 512-758-5853.
David Langford, **Texas Wildlife Association,** 1635 NE Loop 410, Suite 108, San Antonio TX 78209-1600, 512-826-2904, FAX 512-826-4933.
Richard L. McLaren, **West Texas Agricultural and Wildlife Research Foundation**, HCR-74, Box 101A, Fort Davis TX 79734, 915-426-3402.

Utah (23)
Ed Wright, **Arctic Alliance**, PO Box 461, Payson UT 84651, 801-465-0850.
Karen Alvey, **Coalition of Responsible Environmentalists,** PO Box 704, Kanab UT 84741, 801-644-2937.
Russ Fullmer, **Desert Trackers 4X4 Club**, 1878 N. 775 W. Woods Cross UT 84087-1161, 801-250-1302.
Alice Lemons, **Dinaland Snowmobile Club**, PO Box 178, Vernal UT 84078, 801-789-9451.
Sheldon Steed, **Escalante Chapter—Western Alliance of Land Users,** PO Box 522, Escalante UT 84726, 801-826-4215.
Louise Liston, Commissioner, **Garfield County**, P.O. Box 77, Panguitch UT 84759, 801-676-8826 (O); 801-826-4363 (H); FAX 801-826-4529.
Met Johnson, **Iron County Multiple Land Use Coalition,** PO Box 560, New Harmony UT 84757, 801-586-4239.
Ruth Kaiser, **National Federal Lands Conference,** PO Box 847, Bountiful UT 84011, 801-298-0858.
Mike Ferick, **People for the West,** 380 South 480 West, #13, Wellington UT 84542 801-637-7503.
William D. Howell, **Southeastern Utah Association of Local Governments,** PO Drawer 1106, Price UT 84501-0881, 801-637-5444, FAX 801-637-5448.
Ron Russell, **Utah 4-Wheel Drive Association,** 3621 South 2700 West, Roy UT 84067.
Utah 4 Wheel Drive Association, Inc., PO Box 20310, Salt Lake City UT 84120.
Mark Walsh, **Utah Association of Counties,** 4201 S. 7th E., # 100, Salt Lake City UT 84107-2103.
Valyn Hatch, **Utah ATV Association**, 4933 W. Elaine Drive, West Valley City UT 84120, 801-969-1340.
Brent Tanner, **Utah Cattlemens Association,** 150 South 6th East, #10-B, Salt Lake City UT 84102-1961, 801-355-5748, FAX 801-532-1669.
Victor J. Saunders, **Utah Farm Bureau Federation,** 5300 South 360 West, Salt Lake City UT 84123.

THE HERO NETWORK

Dean Richardson, **Utah Federation of Gem & Mineralogical Societies**, 1223 North 1500 West, Salt Lake City UT 84116, 801-595-6750.

Jack E. Christensen, **Utah Mining Association,** 825 Kearns Building, 136 S. Main Street, Salt Lake City UT 84101, 801-364-1874, FAX 801-359-7561.

Jim Peacock, **Utah Petroleum Association,** 311 South State, Salt Lake City UT 84111.

Rainer Huck, **Utah Trail Machine Association**, 1680 Atkin Avenue, Salt Lake City UT 84106-3727, 801-467-3795.

Ted Lee, **Utah Wool Growers Association,** 150 S. 600 E. #10-B, Salt Lake City UT 84102.

Gordon Parker, **Western Association of Land Users - Carbon County Chapter**, 80 West Main, Price UT 84501, 801-888-3355.

John Keogh, **Western Association of Land Users - Grand County Chapter**, PO Box 783, Moab UT 84532, 801-259-7425.

Vermont (10)

Dave Eddson, **Alliance for America,** PO Box 582, Underhill Center VT 05490, 802-899-3029, 802-878-2605.

Agnes Mitchell, **Citizens for Property Rights,** PO Box 393, Jonesville VT 05466, 802-434-2402.

Rod Clark, **Freedom for the Road,** RD 4 Box 1215, Montpelier VT 05602, 802-223-1556.

James Campbell, **Landowners United,** PO Box 682, Newport VT 05855, 802-334-3400.

Martin S. Harris, Jr., **Small Holders Association of Vermont**, RD 2, Box 2716, Vergenne VT 05441, 802-877-3961.

Nancy Stringer, **Task Force on Families in Crisis,** PO Box 9376, South Burlington VT 05407, 802-862-5286.

Vermont Association of Snow Travelers, PO Box 839, Montpelier, VT, 05602.

Thomas J. Morse, **Vermont Property Rights Center,** RR1 Box 8000, Underhill VT 05489, 802-899-4668.

Barbara Hobbs, **Vermonters for Constitutional Preservation,** 22 Freedom Drive, Montpelier VT 05602, 802-223-3243.

Joy McKenna, **Woodford SnoBusters, Inc.,** Star Route, Woodford VT 05201, 802-442-9341.

Virginia (18)

Ann G. Harrell, **Appalachian Forest Management Group,** Route 2, Box 233, Covington VA 24426, 703-862-7621, FAX 703-862-3375.

Sharon Lane, **Back Bay Citizens Alliance,** 308 Teal Crescent, Virginia Beach VA 23457, 804-721-3658.

Thomas Leri, **Blue Ridge Coalition News,** PO Box 36, Wolftown VA 22748, 703-948-6423, FAX 703-948-5202.

Sue Hansohn, **Citizens for Land Rights,** PO Box 1362, Culpepper VA 22701, 703-825-8275, FAX 703-825-2948.

310 It Takes A Hero

Patricia Bradburn, **Citizens Forum/Truth & Progress,** 12750 Chatter Brook Drive, Catharpin VA 22018, 703-368-9922, FAX 703-368-6573.

Scott Pattison, **Consumer Alert,** 1555 Wilson Blvd., Suite 300, Arlington VA 22209, 703-875-8644, FAX 202-296-1148.

David Henry Lucas, **Council on Property Rights,** 1963 Barton Hill Road, Reston VA 22091, 703-620-5723, or 803-886-4634.

Bonner Cohen, **E.P.A. Watch,** 13130-L Parke-Long Court, Chantilly VA 22021.

Cathy Ahern, **International Snowmobile Council,** 3975 University Drive #310, Fairfax VA 22030.

Roy Muth, **International Snowmobile Industry Association,** 3975 University Dr. Suite 310, Fairfax VA 22030, 703-273-9606.

J. R. Bush, **Lumber Manufacturers' Association of Virginia Inc.,** Box U, Sandston VA 23150-0160, 804-737-5625.

William P. Gimbel, **Madison County Preservation Coalition,** PO Box 745, Madison VA 22727, 703-948-3925, FAX 703-948-3910.

Marc Weiss, **Marc Weiss & Associates,** 831-C South King St., Leesburg VA 22075, 703-777-7985.

Motorcycle Industry Council, 1235 Jefferson Davis, Arlington VA 22202, 703-521-0444.

Howard Phillips, **US Taxpayers Alliance,** 450 Maple Avenue East, Vienna VA 22180, 703-281-9426, FAX 703-281-4108.

John Johnson, **Virginia Farm Bureau,** 200 West Grace Street, Richmond VA 23261, 804-788-1234.

Charles F. Finley Jr., **Virginia Forestry Association,** 1205 E. Main Street, Richmond VA 23219, 804-644-8466.

Alice Menks, Virginians for Property Rights, PO Box 986, Madison VA 22727, 703-948-7165, FAX 703-948-7165.

Ronald W. Thompson, **Virginia Snowmobile Association,** PO Box 1444, Salem VA 24153, 703-389-4823.

Washington (90)
Frank Davis, **Alliance for America,** PO Box 28151, Spokane WA 99228, 509-326-2487, 509-326-2487.

Bob White, **Alliance for America,** 12519 SE 17th Vancouver WA 98684 206-694-3368 206-694-7882.

Jon Spunuagle, **American Lands Access Association Inc.,** 13732 NE 12th St., #201, Bellevue WA 98005-2862, 206-957-1343.

Bill and Vi Iund, **American Timberman and Trucker,** PO Box 1006, Chehalis WA 98532, 206-748-0206, FAX 206-748-0244.

Barbara Mossman, **American Loggers Solidarity,** Box 2141, Forks WA 98331, 206-327-3778, FAX 206-327-3887.

Jack Merry, **American Plywood Association,** PO Box 11700, Tacoma WA 98411-0700, 206-565-6600, FAX 206-565-7265.

Loren McGovern, **Backcountry Horsemen of Washington,** PO Box 1727, Olympia WA 98507, 763-3470.

Tommy A. Thomson, **Bremerton Cruisers Motorcycle Club,** PO Box 4328, Bremerton WA 98312-0328, 206-275-6344.

Robert E. Brittain, **Cascade Driftskippers Snowmobile Club,** 14931 251st Place SE, Issaquah WA 98027-8229.

Cascade SnowDrifters, 181 Fontaine Lane, Naches WA 98937-9418, 509-697-6586.

Ted Cowan, **Cedar County Committee,** 14222 Hobart Road, Issaquah WA 98027, 206-392-6896, FAX 206-392-6896.

Ron Arnold, Center for the Defense of Free Enterprise, 12500 N.E. 10th Place, Bellevue WA 98005, 206-455-5038, FAX 206-451-3959.

Alan Gottlieb, **Center for the Defense of Free Enterprise,** 12500 N.E. 10th Place, Bellevue WA 98005, 206-455-5038, FAX 206-451-3959.

Dick Van De Mark, **Chelan County Chapter Washington Trucking Association,** 3971 Dixie Lane, Malaga WA 98828, 509-663-0234.

Chinook Pass Snowmobile Club, 530 Clover Springs Road, Naches WA 98937, 509-658-2687.

Dan Wood, **Citizens for Responsible Resource Use,** Box 714, Hoquiam WA 98550, 206-533-1644.

Emma H, Smith, **Columbia Gorge United,** PO Box 372, Stevenson WA 98648, 206-837-3711.

Bud Mercer, **Columbia/Snake River Irrigators Association,** PO Box 722, Prosser WA 99350-0722, 509-786-1000, FAX 509-786-7110.

Freda Allen, **Concerned Citizens for Forest Wood Cutting,** PO Box 352, Naches WA 98937, 509-697-6570.

Joe Earley, **Concrete Use,** PO Box 57, Lebam WA 98554, 206-942-3111.

Eastern Washington Dirt Riders Association, PO Box 5681, Kennewick WA 99336-5681, 509-735-1857.

Dena Borg, **The Evergreen Partnership** 3600 Port of Tacoma Rd., East World Trade Center, Ste. 502, Tacoma WA 98424, 206-922-6640, FAX 206-922-2769.

Karen Jensen, **Friends of Lake Crescent,** 6565 East Beach Road, Port Angeles WA 98362.

Kelly Kreps, **Gorge Resource Coalition,** 421 B-Z Glennwood Rd., White Salmon WA 98672, 503-354-2804.

Kellee Haynes, **Grassroots of Washington,** 1325 Oak St., Kettle Falls WA 99141, 509-738-2318, FAX 509-738-2117.

Edwin Davis, **Great Northwest Coalition,** PO Box 28151, Spokane WA 99228-8151, 509-326-2487, FAX 509-326-2487.

Kay Lloyd, **International Snowmobile Council - Western Chapter,** 13208 136th N.E., Kirkland WA 98034, 206-882-5110, FAX 206-821-4756.

William S. Marlow, **Jefferson County Property Rights Alliance,** PO Box 618, Port Hadlock WA 98339, 206-385-3469.

John Sawyer, **Lake Roosevelt Property Owners Association Inc.,** PO Box 459, Davenport WA 99122, 509-725-1241.

Bob Lloyd, **Methow Alliance for Nature,** PO Box 318, Twisp WA 98856, 509-997-2441.

Charles Cushman, American Land Rights Association (National Inholders Association, Multiple Use Land Alliance and League of Private Property Voters), PO Box 400, Battle Ground WA 98604, 206-687-3087, FAX 206-687-2973.

Richard Welsh, **National Association of Reversionary Property Owners**, 2311 E. Lake Sammamish Place, S.E., Issaquah WA 98027.

Dave Waisman, **Northeast Mining Geological Society**, Box 658, Republic WA 99166.

Renea Martin, **Northeast Washington Women In Timber,** PO Box 224, Colville WA 99114, 509-684-5688, FAX 509-684-8447.

Tonya Dowse, **North Olympic Timber Action Committee,** PO Box 1057, Port Angeles WA 98362, 206-452-6645, FAX 206-452-0718.

George Christian, **North Shore Association,** 904 North Shore Rd., Amanda Park WA 98526-9702, 206-288-2751.

Jim Gold, **Northwest Coalition,** 196 Dekay Rd., Hoquiam WA 98550-9316, 206-533-7995.

Northwest Independent Forest Manufacturers, PO Box 11346, Tacoma WA 98411, 206-564-0452, FAX 206-565-7265.

Jeanette Burrage, **Northwest Legal Foundation,** 557 Roy St., #100, Seattle WA 98109-4219, 206-283-0503.

Karl W. "Bill" Mote, **Northwest Mining Association,** 10 N. Post, Suite 414, Spokane WA 99201-0772, 509-624-1158, FAX 509-623-1241.

Rick Dahl, **Northwest Motorcycle Association,** 1276 Lincoln Creek Road, Rochester WA 98579, 206-330-0607.

Ron Morgenthaler, **Northwest Motorcycle Association,** 19937 Woodinville-Duvall Road, Woodinville WA 98072, 206-788-0162.

Northwest TrailRiders Association, PO Box 118, Maple Valley WA 98038, 206-432-7825.

Scott Redmond, **Northwesterners for Balance,** 16610 21st Ave. SW, Seattle WA 98166-3308, 206-443-8846.

Pacific Northwest Four Wheel Drive Association, 21520 SE 346th St., Auburn WA 98002, 206-278-3514.

Richard & Carol Walker, **Polar Bears Snowmobile Club**, 23406 112th Ave. SE, Kent WA 98031.

Jeanne Ring, **People for the West,** PO Box 582, Snohomish WA 98920, 206-338-3675.

Maxine Keesling, **Property Rights Alliance**, PO Box 985, Redmond WA 98073, 206-242-9569.

John Welch, Sr., **Property Rights Alliance,** 12421 Pacific Highway South, Seattle WA 98168, 206-242-9569, FAX 206-246-2234.

Candi Parr, **Public Land Users Coalition,** c/o Boise Cascade Corp., South 110 Boise Road, Kettle Falls WA 99141-9412, 509-738-6421, FAX 509-738-2723.

Ron Morganthaler, **Public Land Users Society,** 6824 19th West, #282, Tacoma WA 98466, 206-788-0162.

Puget Sound Enduro Riders, 116 E 21st Avenue, Olympia WA 98501, 943-9575.

RidgeRunners, Inc., PO Box 2403, Yakima WA 98907.

Darrell Harting, **Snohomish County Property Rights Alliance,** 121 Glen Ave., #5, Snohomish WA 98290, 206-568-1955.

Cliff Courtney, **Stehekin Heritage,** Box 1, Stehekin WA 98852.

Tom Jesmer, **Stumpjumpers Motorcycle Club**, 27616 Florence Acres Road, Monroe WA 98272, FAX 206-258-1929.

Marilyn Sheard, **Tacoma Motorcycle Club,** 13120 Bingham Avenue East, Tacoma WA 98446.

Ted LaDoux, **The Umbrella Group,** PO Box U, Highway 7, Morton WA 98356, 206-564-0452, FAX 206-565-7265.

Barbara Lindsay, **United Property Owners of Washington,** PO Box 3336, Redmond WA 98073

Dale E. Knowlton, **Washington ATV Association,** PO Box 6060, Kent WA 98031, 206-228-9959.

Kent Lebsack, **Washington Cattlemen's Association,** 1720 Canyon Road, PO Box 96, Ellensburg WA 98926, 509-925-9871, FAX 509-925-3004.

Betsy Robertson, **Washington Citizens for World Trade - Washington Agricultural Export Alliance,** 1501 S. Capitol Way, Suite 103, Olympia WA 98501, 206-786-1770, FAX 206-786-0138.

Larry Mason, Washington Commercial Forest Action Committee, PO Box 1159, Forks WA 98331, 206-374-6699, FAX 206-374-9498.

Bill Pickell, **Washington Contract Loggers Association,** PO Box 2168, Olympia WA 98507, 206-352-5033, FAX 206-943-8544.

Greg Pattillo, **Washington Farm Forestry Association,** 2029 E. Bay Drive, Olympia WA 98506, 206-357-3072.

Earl Dedman, **Washington Floraculture Association,** 16925 NE 190th, Woodinville WA 98072.

Duncan Wurm, **Washington Friends of Farms & Forests,** PO Box 7644, Olympia WA 98507, 206-754-1622, FAX 206-357-9939.

Sherrie Bond, **Washington Lands Coalition,** PO Box 578, Chehalis WA 98532, 206-748-7030, FAX 206-748-0244.

Phil Kawdoll, **Washington Log Truckers Conference - Lower Columbia Chapter,** 227 Louise Street, Kelso WA 98626.

John Swartz, **Washington Log Truckers Conference,** 4101 4th Avenue South, Seattle WA 98134, 206-682-0250, FAX 206-622-0565.

Michael Achen, **Washington Private Property Coalition,** 21604 NE Allworth Rd., Vancouver WA 98604, 206-687-2058, FAX 206-687-2058.

Jim Klauser, **Washington Property Rights Network,** 8000 212 Ave. SW, Suite B, Edmonds WA 98026, 206-670-2448, FAX 206-775-1877.

Merrill English, **Washington Property Owners Coalition,** Rt. 2, Box 186, Dayton WA 99328, 509-382-2329.

Washington Public Forest Institute, 6824 19th St. W. #320, Tacoma WA 98466.

Karen Anderson, **Washington Rivers Coalition,** 12338 Bretz Road, Leavenworth WA 98826, 509-763-3313.

Dedi Hitchens, **Washington State Dairy Federation,** 711 South Capitol Way, Olympia WA 98501.

Bill Roberts, **Washington State Farm Bureau,** PO Box 2009, Olympia WA 98507, 206-357-9975, FAX 206-357-9939.

Mike Leibold, **Washington State Motorcycle Dealers Association,** 215 SW Everett Mall Way, Everett WA 98204-2781, 206-343-7980.

Alan L. Matson, **Washington State Snowmobile Association,** 55 West Washington #191, Yakima WA 98903, 206-452-1506.

Karien Collins, **Washington Women In Timber,** 229 E. Main, Con-
crete WA 98237, 206-853-8769.
Judy Marr, **Washington Women In Timber,** PO Box 617, Everson
WA 98247, 206-966-7312.
Sandra Godfrey, **Washington Women In Timber - Cowlitz Chap-
ter,** Box 296, Glenoma WA 98336, 206-498-5351.
Barb E. Mossman, **Wild Rivers Conservancy Federation,** PO Box
1294, Forks WA 98331, 206-374-5582, FAX 206-327-3887.
Winter Knight Snowmobile Association, PO Box 4292, Spokane
WA 99202, 509-535-7699.
Kellee Haynes, **Women In Timber,** PO Box 779, Kettle Falls WA 99141,
509-738-2525, FAX 509-738-2117.
Pat Zimmerman, **Women Involved in Farm Economics,** Box 6,
Almira WA 99103, 509-639-2257, FAX 509-639-0164.
Sandi Petersen, **Wood Industry Seeks Equality,** PO Box U, Morton
WA 98356, 206-496-5995, FAX 206-496-6040.
Dick Haas, **Yakima Ski Benders,** PO Box 9682, Yakima WA 98909-
9682.
Steve Silvestri, **Yakima Valley Dust Dodgers Motorcycle Club,** PO
Box 716, Selah WA 98942, 509-453-4161.

West Virginia (2)
F. Scott Rotruck, **Association of Natural Resource Workers of West
Virginia,** Rte. 12, Box 143, Suite M13, Morgantown WV 26505, 304-
594-2662, FAX 304-594-2811.
R. Killingsworth, **Tri State ATV Club,** PO Box 123, Mill Creek, WV,
26280.

Wisconsin (31)
Gene Luebker, **Alliance for America,** 15930 Shady Hollow, Woodman
WI 53827, 608-533-3677.
Sister Thomas More Bertels, American Agri-Women, 2406 S.
Alverno Rd., Manitowoc WI 54220, 414-684-6691.
Dennis Sorensen, **Association of Wisconsin Snowmobile Clubs,**
PO Box 1029, Neenah WI 54957, 414-725-9133, FAX 414-725-9101.
Bo-Boen Snowmobile Club, PO Box 192, St. Germain WI 54558.
Boulder Junction Snowmobile Club, Box 461, Boulder Junction
WI 54512, 715-385-2978.
Marilyn F. Hayman, **Citizens for Responsible Zoning & Landowner
Rights,** PO Box 16, Maiden Rock WI 54750, 715-448-3213.
Douglas County Association of Snowmobile Clubs, PO Box 172,
Poplar WI 54864-0172.
Drifters Snowmobile Club, 3670 Vinland Center Rd., Neenah WI
54956, 414-836-2413.
Kiel Snowmobile Club, Inc., PO Box 212, Kiel WI 53042, 414-894-
2353.
Lakeshore ATV Club, Inc., PO Box 1183, Sheboygan WI 53082-1183.
Larry Zernach, **Lake State Resource Alliance Inc.,** PO Box 483,
Hayward WI 54843, 715-634-3065, FAX 715-634-5755.

Joe Timmerman, **Lake States Resource Alliance,** 100 Wisconsin River Dr., Port Edwards WI 54469.

Mercer Sno-Goers, Inc., PO Box 484, Mercer WI 54547, 715-476-2175.

Maxine King, Treasurer, **Polonia Sno-Bos Snowmobile Club,** 810 Brilowski Road, Stevens Point WI 54481, 715-344-8482.

Gene Luebker, **Private Landowners of Wisconsin,** 15930 Shady Hollow Lane, Woodman WI 53827, 608-533-3677.

Larry Peterson, **Protect Americans Rights and Resources,** HCR 2, Box 171, Park Falls WI 54552.

Redstone Riders, 300 Union, Lavalle WI 53941, 608-985-8543.

Riverton Sno-Goers, PO Box 305, Riverton WY 82501-0305.

Bob Dreher Jr., **Roberts Knight Riders, Inc.,** 306 W Maple St., Roberts WI 54023, 715-749-3965.

Rocky Run Riders Snowmobile Club, N6309 Hillcrest Rd., Pardeeville WI 53954, 608-742-2712.

Sam Pritzl, **Sno Gypsies,** Rt. 1, Box 53A, Park Falls WI 54552, 715-762-4614.

Southern Wisconsin Experienced Area Riders, PO Box 14512, Madison WI 53714-0512.

Vista Cruisers Snowmobile Club, Rt. #5, Box 57, Menomonie WI 54751, 715-235-5208.

Washburn Valhellers Snowmobile Club, PO Box 731, Washburn WI 54891, 715-373-2715.

Waukesha County Snowmobile Club, 730 E Harvard St., Oconomowoc WI 53066.

Weyerhaeuser Snowmobile Club, N3055 County Rd W, Weyerhaeuser WI 54895, 715-353-2431.

Randy Harden, **Wisconsin ATV Association,** PO Box 1183, Sheboygan WI 53082-1183, 414-458-3000.

Harold Hoernke, **Wisconsin Four Wheel Drive Association,** 203 Gruenwald Avenue, Neenah WI 54956, 414-722-3777.

Robert J. Engelhard, **Wisconsin Woodland Owners Association,** PO Box 285, Stevens Point WI 54481, 715-341-4798, FAX 715-346-3624.

Cathy Nordine, **Women In Timber - Lake States,** PO Box 89, Land O'Lakes WI 54540.

Wyoming (22)

Troy Mader, Abundant Wildlife Society, 12665 Hwy. 59 N., Gillette WY 82717, 307-682-2626, FAX 307-682-3016.

Big Horn Mountain Snomads, PO Box 397, Sheridan WY 82801.

Karen Budd-Falen, Attorney At Law, **Budd-Falen Law Offices,** 204 East 22nd, Cheyenne WY 82001, 307-632-5105.

Ann S. Strand, **Colorado River Water Users Association,** 2632 Foothill Blvd., Suite 106, Rock Springs WY 82901.

R.D. Black, **Dubois ATV Association,** PO Box 965, Dubois WY 82513, 307-455-2624.

Dubois Sno-Kat-ers, PO Box 1064, Dubois WY 82513.

Fremont County ATV Association, PO Box 574, Riverton WY 82501-0574.

Jackson Snow Devils Club, PO Box 3440, Jackson WY 83001.

Cheri McKinney, **Lander SnowDrifters**, PO Box 281, Lander WY 82520-0281, 307-332-3472.

Arlene Hanson, **No-Wolf Option Committee**, P.O. Box 104, Wapiti WY 82450, 307-587-5796.

Patrick O'Toole, Box 26, Savery WY 82332, 307-383-2418, FAX 307-383-2419.

Marlene Simons, **Outdoors Unlimited**, Beulah WY 82450, 307-283-2664 or 307-638-3301.

Richard T. Robitaille, **Petroleum Association of Wyoming**, 951 Werner Court, Suite 100, Casper WY 82601, 307-234-5333, FAX 307-266-2189.

South Lincoln County Snow Bears, Box 322, Kemmerer WY 83101.

Francis Brown, **Star Valley Snowskippers**, PO Box 621, Afton WY 83110, 307-886-3353.

Alice Gustin, **Wind River Multiple Use Advocates,** PO Box 468, Riverton WY 82501, 307-856-3699.

Larry Bourret, **Wyoming Farm Bureau**, 406 So. 21st St., Laramie WY 82070, 307-745-4835, FAX 307-721-7738.

William Schilling, **Wyoming Heritage Society,** 139 West 2nd Street, Suite 3E, Casper WY 82601.

Marion E. Loomis, **Wyoming Mining Association,** PO Box 866, Cheyenne WY 82003, 307-635-0331, FAX 307-778-6240.

Carolyn Paseneaux, **Wyoming Public Lands Council,** PO Box 115, Casper WY 82602, 307-365-5250.

Steve Adams, **Wyoming Public Lands Council,** Box 177, Baggs WY 82321.

Bev Floretta, **Wyoming State Snowmobile Association**, PO Box 7235, Sheridan WY 82801.

Bob Budd, **Wyoming Stock Growers Association,** PO Box 206, Cheyenne WY 82003.

INDEX

If you have enjoyed **It Takes A Hero**, you'll want to own these other exciting titles from The Free Enterprise Press.

Trashing the Economy: How Runaway Environmentalism is Wrecking America, by Ron Arnold and Alan Gottlieb. 672 pages, paperback, $19.95.

The Asbestos Racket: An Environmental Parable, by Michael J. Bennett 256 pages, paperback, $9.95.

Storm Over Rangelands: Private Rights in Federal Lands, by Wayne Hage, 288 pages, paperback, $14.95.

Stealing the National Parks: The Destruction of Concessions and Public Access, by Don Hummel, 428 pages, hardcover, $19.95.

Ecology Wars: Environmentalism As If People Mattered, by Ron Arnold, 182 pages, paperback, $14.95.

The Wise Use Agenda, edited by Alan Gottlieb, 168 pages, paperback, $9.95.